Revolution by Law

Revolution by Law

THE FEDERAL GOVERNMENT AND THE DESEGREGATION OF ALABAMA SCHOOLS

Brian K. Landsberg

University Press of Kansas

Published by the University Press of Kansas (Lawrence, Kansas 66045), which was organized by the Kansas Board of Regents and is operated and funded by Emporia State University, Fort Hays State University, Kansas State University, Pittsburg State University, the University of Kansas, and Wichita State University.

Library of Congress Cataloging-in-Publication Data

Names: Landsberg, Brian K., author.
Title: Revolution by law : the federal government and the desegregation of Alabama schools / Brian K. Landsberg.
Description: Lawrence, Kansas : University Press of Kansas, 2022. | Includes bibliographical references and index.
Identifiers: LCCN 2021043873
ISBN 9780700633203 (cloth)
ISBN 9780700633210 (ebook)
Subjects: LCSH: Lee, Anthony T.,—Trials, litigation, etc. | Macon County (Ala.). Board of Education—Trials, litigation, etc. | School integration—Law and legislation—Alabama—Cases. | United States. Department of Justice. Civil Rights Division—History—20th century.
Classification: LCC KF228.L443 L36 2022 | DDC 344.761/0798—dc23/eng/20220131
LC record available at https://lccn.loc.gov/2021043873.

British Library Cataloguing-in-Publication Data is available.

Printed in the United States of America

10 9 8 7 6 5 4 3 2 1

The paper used in this publication meets the minimum requirements of the American National Standard for Permanence of Paper for Printed Library Materials Z39.48-1992.

Contents

Preface, *vii*

Introduction: Tuskegee, Alabama, September 9, 1963, *1*

1 The Ratchet Principle: Truman Sets Federal Civil Rights Policy for His Successors in Office, *9*

2 Macon County and Alabama's Racial Caste System, *39*

3 The School Desegregation Case Begins, *57*

4 New Year, New Schools, New Law, *77*

5 The Case Goes Statewide, *100*

6 Aftermath: Response to the Statewide Decree, *125*

7 "Watch What We Do," *148*

Conclusion, *184*

Notes, *189*

Bibliographic Essay, *231*

Index, *233*

Preface

Over the door of the limestone entrance to the Department of Justice in Washington, DC, a visitor sees these words: "Justice in the life and conduct of the state is possible only as first it resides in the hearts and souls of the citizens."[1] That was a troublesome message in the 1960s to lawyers assigned to the Civil Rights Division (CRD) who were challenging the racial caste system of the South embedded in the hearts and souls of white Southerners. When I walked through that entrance in November 1963 as a newly minted lawyer from California, one day after President Kennedy's assassination, I had little idea of what I was getting into.

In the 1960s and 1970s, I worked on various aspects of the groundbreaking case *Lee v. Macon County Board of Education*. Initially about a small rural school district in Tuskegee, Alabama, the case morphed into an effort to desegregate most public-school systems in the state, becoming the model for other statewide school desegregation cases and for cases challenging conditions in prisons and institutions for mentally ill people. It attracted the notice of scholars such as Robert Cover, who invited me to speak about the case at a seminar at Columbia Law School. Professor Owen Fiss celebrated the case in his eponymously titled casebook on injunctions, and journalist Jack Bass devoted to it a chapter of his biography of US district court judge Frank M. Johnson. Finally, legal scholar Larry W. Yackle's book about Judge Johnson's decisions ordering structural changes in the Alabama prison system acknowledges the influence of *Lee*, while historian Joseph Bagley explores the case in more detail.[2]

This book is the first focused solely on *Lee* and, in particular, on the federal government's role in the case. As *Lee* played a central role in dismantling Alabama's official racial caste system, examining it closely helps us better understand the methods that the federal government used to desegregate the schools of the Deep South. It also helps us understand how the actions of the courts and of the executive branch in this instance profoundly affected the options open to later administrations. Finally, studying *Lee* points the way toward the renewal of federal actions to secure equal educational opportunity, without regard to race.

I confess I do not approach this subject as a disinterested third party. I worked on the case in several capacities for many years—as a trial attorney in 1966, as the coordinator of the Civil Rights Division's preparation of the statewide case, as chief of the education section of the division from 1969–1974, and as chief of its appellate section from 1974–1986. Years later, I was touched when Jack Greenberg, who headed the NAACP's Legal Defense Fund (LDF) in those years, inscribed on my copy of his book, "To Brian Landsberg, comrade in arms . . ." Even more meaningful to me was a silk-screen print created by Ross Connealy of the education section and given to me by the section staff when I stepped down as its chief in 1974. The print contains the names of cases the education section had litigated, including *Lee v. Macon County Board of Education*, arranged around a picture of a run-down school that had housed Black students prior to desegregation.

Since that time, though, my scholarly effort has been to approach issues neutrally to the extent humanly possible. I can promise the reader that the facts presented here are accurate. They come primarily from court decisions, pleadings, briefs, and memoranda of the CRD, the Department of Health, Education and Welfare, and the White House. Other sources include news articles, speeches made by the players in this drama, and interviews. You may safely assess my conclusions based on those facts.

The book is written primarily in the third person. However, I use the first person when referring to my own actions. Despite occasional reference to my personal experiences, though, this is not a memoir. The *Lee* case began in 1963, before I began work in the CRD, was ongoing when I left the division in 1986, and portions of it continue to reverberate to this day.

I am indebted to Rob Gunnison for help in organizing this book and for his contributions to the discussion of the political background. Joseph Bagley, Stephen Wasby, Stephen J. Pollak, and Dorothy Landsberg generously contributed ideas and editing suggestions. I also benefited from comments by Ira Strauber, Thomas Keck, Margot Schlanger, and participants at the Duke Law School Conference on the Present and Future of Civil Rights Movements: Race and Reform in 21st Century America. Dedicated research assistants helped: Jade Wolansky, Robert Mayville, Keith Banks, Michael Heumann, Jocelyn Blinn, Jacqueline Hassell, Abby Maurer, Aman Grewal, Michelle Aharonowitz, and Ryan Matthews. Thanks also to archivists at Tuskegee University, the Library of Congress, the National Archives and Records Administration College Park, the Kennedy, Johnson, and Nixon Presidential Libraries, the Alabama State Archives, and the Princeton Library Archives.

When I joined the CRD, garnering the support of the public—those hearts and souls of Plato's citizens—seemed almost impossible. Or so it appeared in early 1964 when I watched from a window in the federal courthouse in Selma as Sheriff Jim Clark, wearing his "NEVER" button, harassed African Americans lined up outside the Dallas County Courthouse to register to vote. Nor did it seem any more achievable on Bloody Sunday in March 1965, as I stood near the Edmund Pettus Bridge and watched hundreds of marchers flee back to Selma to escape tear-gas, police dogs, and batons. But revolution by law was on the way, a revolution that would end the official racial caste system of the South.

Introduction: Tuskegee, Alabama, September 9, 1963

> The problem of the twentieth century is the problem of the color-line.
>
> —*W. E. B. Du Bois,* The Souls of Black Folk

> The Negro needs neither segregated schools nor mixed schools. What he needs is Education.
>
> —*W. E. B. Du Bois,* Does the Negro Need Separate Schools?

The lawyers of the US Department of Justice (DOJ) have seldom—maybe never—been called revolutionaries. Yet in the 1960s, we participated in a "Revolution by Law," later so described by Burke Marshall, an assistant attorney general for the Civil Rights Division (CRD). He observed that *Brown v. Board of Education*—the 1954 Supreme Court ruling that state-imposed racial segregation of schools was unconstitutional—had "required radical change, specifically the eradication of the Jim Crow system."[1] Still, as the CRD responded to this imperative and employed federal law to radically transform the Deep South's official structure of race relations, *Brown* identified no road map, just a destination. Before *Lee v. Macon County Board of Education*, desegregation required litigation one recalcitrant school system at a time. Before *Lee*, the federal government did not play a prominent role in litigating how school systems were to desegregate. Before *Lee*, the schools of the South were the nation's most segregated. All that would change, as the country experienced a revolution by law.

The DOJ faced a dual question: what should the role of the federal government be and, along with private plaintiffs, how to reach the destination, desegregation of the public schools. The federal government supported African American citizens when it became clear that they lacked the power to change the system on their own. In the end, though the residue of racial discrimination remains, during the relatively brief civil rights revolution civil rights activists and litigators ended the official racial caste system, with the aid of federal coercive force—federal court orders, the threat of withholding federal funds, and the use of federal troops to support compliance with court orders. In Alabama, which had been completely segregated in January 1963, most Black students attended integrated schools by the mid-1970s, despite white flight.[2] Racially segregated schools had played a central role in maintaining the caste system, because unequal education was tied to deprivation of the vote and of economic opportunity. The end of state-imposed school segregation signaled that the discriminatory system would end, even if its effects might linger.

The torrent of words written about school desegregation describes the development of legal doctrine, the travails of individual African American parents and children, the work of their private sector lawyers, and the intensity of white Southern resistance. Except for occasional mentions in those writings, however, the role of the political branches of the federal government has elicited much less analysis.[3] Yet, the executive and legislative branches played important roles, both positive and negative. This book explores those roles and the interaction of the political branches with the courts and private plaintiffs in school desegregation cases. The vehicle of exploration, *Lee v. Macon County Board of Education*, engaged more federal resources and desegregated more school districts than any other case.

Some studies of *Brown* describe the arc of the case law and compliance. An outstanding example is J. Harvey Wilkinson's *From Brown to Bakke.* Also in that category is the more recent book by James T. Patterson, *Brown v. Board of Education: A Civil Rights Milestone and Its Troubled Legacy*, which argues that whether *Brown* is a success depends on the goals one has set. *With All Deliberate Speed: Implementing Brown v. Board of Education*, edited by Brian J. Daugherty and Charles C. Bolton, explores the success of *Brown* in chapters devoted to individual school systems.

One may study *Brown* from an institutional perspective. For example, the point of view presented in *Revolution by Law* stands in contrast to the leading critique by Gerald Rosenberg, *The Hollow Hope: Can Courts Bring About Social Change?* The title of that book poses a straw question. As *Lee* demonstrates, school desegregation was the result of a multipronged attack in which the courts were an essential element, in litigation brought by private plaintiffs and supported by the DOJ.[4] Although the Nixon administration wished to go slow on school desegregation, Supreme Court rulings forced it to take actions that transformed the South's public schools from the most to the least segregated in the nation. Addressing the issues through the lens of a concrete case provides a perspective missing in Rosenberg's analysis. It also helps us evaluate Michael Klarman's suggestion that the schools of the South might have desegregated faster if the Supreme Court had not decided *Brown v. Board of Education.*[5]

In contrast to Rosenberg, Bruce Ackerman in *The Civil Rights Revolution* treats the enforcement of *Brown* in the 1960s and '70s as a "triumph of judicial leadership." Ackerman contrasts school desegregation, where "the Supreme Court's leadership remained absolutely crucial," with other areas of racial discrimination, where "it was the president and Congress that pushed the law and its enforcement."[6] Discussion of *Lee* fills out the details of that judicial leadership and its impact on executive and legislative action.

Leading institutional studies include Gary Orfield's contemporaneous examination of the roles of the DOJ and the Department of Health, Education, and Welfare (HEW) and Stephen Wasby and Anthony D'Amato's study of the work of the NAACP Legal Defense Fund (NAACP LDF, or LDF). Orfield's view of the federal role—especially his claim that desegregation was largely completed when Nixon took office—conflicts with mine, as developed in later chapters of this book.[7] For their part, Wasby and D'Amato illuminate the challenges faced by private litigation in desegregating the schools; our works are complementary.

Normative studies ask whether *Brown* and its progeny appropriately advanced equal educational opportunity. Towering above other critics is Derrick Bell, the only author to have worked on school desegregation for the DOJ, HEW, and the NAACP LDF. Bell argues that *Brown* "has proved of greater value to whites than blacks." It gave credibility to the United States in the struggle with the Soviet Union; it reassured African Americans; and it helped the South transition to a stronger economic model. Bell places the caselaw under *Brown* within what he calls the racial interest convergence principles. He concludes that if whites and civil rights advocates agree on "integration as a component in and not the sine qua non of an effective education," then their interests might converge and make progress possible.[8] Bell's work inspired others; for example, *Making the Unequal Metropolis: School Desegregation and Its Limits* by Ansley T. Erickson uses Bell's analytical method to show how desegregation in Nashville prioritized the interests of white students.

Today, school desegregation is embattled and revisionism regarding *Brown* is rampant. From one side, critics say that it has accomplished little; they point to the large number of children of color who attend schools that enroll very few white students. Other critics challenge the very premise of desegregation, which, they claim, has destroyed a valuable institution in the African American community, the all-Black school. Criticism of *Brown*, once an iconic decision, has ranged from arguing that it is poorly reasoned to claiming that it unrealistically sought more change than society would tolerate. Indeed, since *Brown*, the Supreme Court has placed major obstacles to race-based efforts to desegregate school systems and has adopted rules that allow school systems that had desegregated under court orders to resegregate their schools.

Lee offers partial answers to the critics. The case followed a trajectory that, in one sense, paralleled desegregation cases throughout the South: from segregation to allowing individual Black students to transfer to white schools; subsequently allowing all students free choice of schools; and finally, systemwide desegregation. What makes *Lee* distinctive is its pioneering methods for enforcing *Brown*: statewide desegregation orders; shifting of the burden of proof to the school authorities; collaboration of two branches of the federal government, the courts and, within the executive, the DOJ and HEW; and the active involvement of the president and a cabinet-level committee. This experience suggests why integration was and is worth pursuing. It gives us a road map for future federal efforts to overcome racial disparities if and when the country reawakens to the need for educational equity. It is a map for completing the revolution by law, which began in Macon County with the clash between Governor George Wallace and African American parents.

On September 9, 1963, Anthony Lee and twelve other African American students boarded a bus for a short ride to Tuskegee High School. A few days earlier, Judge Frank M. Johnson had ordered that the students be admitted to the school, which for decades had allowed only white pupils. The Tuskegee school board and superintendent C. A. "Hardboy" Pruitt promised to comply with the judge's order. The sheriff and business leaders worked to ensure a peaceful and successful opening of school.

Other signs were less hopeful. Pete Johnson, a white senior from the nearby Macon County community of Hardaway, was a member of the Tuskegee High School football team. After the desegregation order, he missed practice because of illness. The next day he went to practice and found no players on the field. Instead he found the coach in his office, sobbing. The coach told him that the day before, the team had voted to disband rather than have Black teammates.[9]

As the bus neared the high school, it was halted by Alabama state troopers. They boarded and read an order from Governor Wallace, who had declared in his first inaugural address eight months earlier that he stood for "segregation now, segregation tomorrow, segregation forever."[10] The order read:

"There now exists [*sic*] in the State of Alabama conditions calculated to result in the disruption of the peace and tranquility of this state, and to occasion peril to the lives and property of the citizens thereof, this situation resulting from the threat of forced and unwarranted integration of the public schools of this state." A week earlier, the governor had ordered that the opening of the school be delayed a week "to preserve the peace and the domestic tranquility and to protect the lives and property of all citizens of the State of Alabama."[11] After reading the proclamation and giving each student a copy, the troopers ordered the bus driver to turn around and would not let the Black students off the bus.[12] These events began the four-year road to what *Time* magazine called "perhaps the most important school order since the Supreme Court's decision of 1954."[13]

Wallace was part of a remarkable cast of characters involved in the *Lee* case. The two-time Golden Gloves bantamweight champion had burnished his segregationist reputation as a state court judge. After losing his first race for governor of Alabama in 1958 to segregationist John Patterson, Wallace vowed he would never be "outsegged" again and won the office on his next try. In law school at the University of Alabama, Wallace had been a friend of Frank Johnson. However, as a federal district court judge, Johnson had required Wallace to produce for the US Commission on Civil Rights voter records that state court judge Wallace had refused to turn over. Thus began a battle in which the *Lee* case—filed just two weeks after Wallace's inauguration—was central.[14]

Johnson, appointed to the bench by President Dwight Eisenhower in 1955, became one of the "unlikely heroes" who presided over the dismantling of the racial caste system in his home state.[15] Representing Anthony Lee and the other plaintiffs was Fred Gray, one of the few African American lawyers in Alabama. He had already represented Rosa Parks and Martin Luther King Jr. when he agreed to represent Black parents in Macon County who sought a better education for their children. Joining the case was John Doar, of the DOJ, who helped transform the CRD into a lean and effective law enforcement agency, doggedly challenging racial discrimination in voting. At Johnson's request, Doar joined in the Macon County school desegregation case even though Congress had not yet authorized the DOJ to take part in enforcing the ban on racial segregation of public schools. The interactions of these four—Wallace, Johnson, Grey, and Doar—would lead to the desegregation of the schools of the Deep South.

Ten years earlier, the public schools throughout the region were completely segregated, as required by state laws. The federal government had been complicit in the maintenance of racial segregation. In 1952, however, the US government took its first step in support of school desegregation, when the administration of President Harry Truman filed a brief as amicus curiae, or friend of the court, in the Supreme Court, in *Brown v. Board of Education.* The federal government argued that state-imposed racial segregation of the public schools violated the equal protection clause of the Fourteenth Amendment to the US Constitution and that the court should not follow *Plessy v. Ferguson,* its 1896 ruling upholding a Jim Crow law that required "separate but equal" facilities. In 1953 the Eisenhower administration, faced with the question of whether to step back from the Truman administration's position, acquiesced, despite the new president's apparent reluctance. Eisenhower found himself, as Nixon would later, bound by what I call the ratchet phenomenon: it is legally and politically difficult for the executive branch to roll back rights secured by the actions of a previous administration.

Truman could not have predicted how his civil rights policies would affect government policy under future presidents. With the *Brown* brief he began a process that would bind future administrations to progressively specific and strong actions until school desegregation in the South had been largely completed. The next four presidents found their freedom of action limited by the ratchet principle, which at least for a time allowed no backsliding. In Nixon's second term the progress gradually ended. A later Supreme Court oversaw regression, but there could be no return to *Plessy.*

The Eisenhower administration enforced court decisions applying *Brown* but rested there and made no effort to develop the still formless law of school desegregation. The administrations of Presidents John Kennedy and Lyndon Johnson, by comparison, filed Supreme Court briefs arguing for more desegregation, and the Johnson administration began to participate in court cases and administrative actions that expanded school desegregation requirements. Exercising new responsibilities under the Civil Rights Act of 1964, the Johnson administration began by simply supporting the right of every child to choose a school, but experience with what was known as "freedom of choice" led to asking the courts to require the complete dismantling of the racially dual school system.

When President Richard Nixon took office in 1969, he faced Supreme Court decisions holding that the school systems of the South must transition from Black schools and white schools to "just schools." He, too, quickly discovered the ratchet principle. Once the Supreme Court announced the law, he was bound to enforce it and did so successfully. However, like Eisenhower, as a policy matter, he did not wish to further enlarge the right to school desegregation beyond existing case law. After unsuccessfully opposing court orders to bus students in large urban school districts, he eventually succeeded in blocking the expansion of desegregation into neighboring school districts in large metropolitan areas such as Detroit and its suburbs.[16]

Presidents Truman, Eisenhower, Kennedy, Johnson, and Nixon were all acting under article II, section 3 of the Constitution, which commands that the president "shall take Care that the Laws be faithfully executed." However, from Truman's initial decision to urge the Supreme Court in *Brown* to revise its interpretation of the Fourteenth Amendment to Nixon's decision to complete the task of desegregating the schools of the Deep South, the DOJ was called upon to apply a mixture of law and policy. Policy influenced positions on legal principles. Law constrained policy.

The history of the Macon County case generally parallels the history of school desegregation after *Brown*. First came the breaking of the segregation barrier in 1963 by a handful of Black students, despite interference by the governor. Next, the dam of resistance to desegregation in Alabama was broken, and in 1967 a flood of school systems began the transition to racial integration. A series of court decisions followed, developing standards for desegregation and culminating in the declaration in 1968 that all schools, not just the formerly white schools, must be desegregated. By 1973 the public schools of the South were the least segregated in the country, although later Supreme Court decisions eroded that progress. Macon County—80 percent African American in a state that was two-thirds white—became both a center of white resistance to *Brown* and the vehicle for desegregating the entire state school system.

This book recounts the story of a unique hybrid case in the United States District Court for the Middle District of Alabama. The first aspect of the case, initiated by parents of Anthony Lee and other African American students, ended the state's imposition of racial separation in the public schools of Macon County. The second—an outgrowth of the first—desegregated ninety-nine school systems in Alabama.

The US government played a key role in both the local and statewide stages of the case. The DOJ was a key party even before 1964 when the Congress reluctantly and belatedly authorized the executive branch to enforce *Brown*. After Congress acted, HEW worked with the DOJ to help shape the desegregation process. The *Lee* case can be seen as a classic confrontation between federal and state government, in which eventually national values triumphed. Or it can be understood as a brief break from the political paralysis that continues to impede efforts to bring equal educational opportunity to the United States. In either event, it reflects how federal agencies employed hard work, attention to facts, legal ingenuity, and the weight of the federal government to help bring about revolutionary change.

1. The Ratchet Principle: Truman Sets Federal Civil Rights Policy for His Successors in Office

> Asked why he was breaking with the Democratic Party now, when Roosevelt made similar promises as Truman on civil rights, Strom Thurmond responded, "But Truman means it."
>
> —*David McCullough,* Truman, *citing Alfred Steinberg, "How Harry Truman Does His Job,"* Saturday Evening Post, *March 3, 1951*

> The very basis of our individual rights and freedoms rests upon the certainty that the President and the Executive Branch of Government will support and insure the carrying out of the decisions of the Federal Courts, even, when necessary with all the means at the President's command.
>
> —*Dwight D. Eisenhower, "Mob Rule Cannot Be Allowed to Override the Decisions of Our Courts," September 24, 1957*

The full force of the government's role in the revolution by law represented by *Lee v. Macon County Board of Education* came to bear under Presidents Lyndon Johnson and Richard Nixon. But the actions of Presidents Harry Truman, Dwight Eisenhower, and John Kennedy laid the foundation for the government's policy of desegregating all school systems in the South. Truman enlisted the DOJ to participate as amicus curiae arguing for the end of state-imposed racial segregation of public schools and commissioned a study urging the creation of a civil rights division within the department. Eisenhower supported legislation to create the CRD and the DOJ participated as a litigating amicus curiae to enforce school desegregation orders in Little Rock and elsewhere. Under Kennedy the CRD litigated voting rights cases in Macon County and entered the *Lee* case as a litigating amicus to not only enforce court orders but also to participate in shaping the content of desegregation orders. Finally, Kennedy proposed the legislation that gave the DOJ authority to bring some school desegregation cases and that denied federal financial assistance to segregated schools.

TRUMAN

With the death of Franklin Delano Roosevelt on April 12, 1945, Harry Truman became president of a racially segregated nation. Historically, the federal government had promoted the racial caste system. It had imposed segregation on federal facilities, military forces, and the federal civilian workforce and promoted segregated housing. It had run segregated schools in the District of Columbia and had provided financial assistance to segregated schools elsewhere. It had helped states to create segregated land grant universities.[1]

Although Roosevelt began combatting some forms of discrimination against African Americans, as legal historian Risa Goluboff has observed, "neither Roosevelt nor his Justice Department was prepared, politically or doctrinally, to take on the entire system of racial segregation." Goluboff quotes a 1943 DOJ memorandum worrying that "so long as the South feels the Federal government means to regulate its intimate relations with the Negro, the South will fight any Federal intervention. This flame can easily be fanned into a terrible conflagration."[2] In his State of the Union speech on January 11, 1944, Roosevelt presented a "second Bill of Rights," which he prefaced by saying, "We have accepted, so to speak, a second Bill of Rights under which a new basis of security and prosperity can be established for all regardless of station, race, or creed." The eighth and last right was the right "to a good education."[3] Roosevelt, however, did not link racial segregation of public schools to this proclamation. Although no legislation to create the new rights was ultimately introduced, Roosevelt used the proposal as a platform for his easy reelection to a fourth term eleven months later.[4]

However modest Roosevelt's efforts, they were a first step toward reversing the freeze on civil rights legislation that marked the end of Reconstruction. The Reconstruction Congress had taken the lead in protecting the civil rights of the newly freed slaves, enacting the Civil Rights Act of 1866 and then, concerned about the act's constitutionality, the Fourteenth Amendment and the Civil Rights Act of 1870. Section 5 of the Fourteenth Amendment authorized Congress to enact legislation to enforce the substantive provisions: due process, equal protection, privileges and immunities, and citizenship. Congress enacted a series of civil rights laws but then fell silent after the Hayes-Tilden Compromise of 1877 began to unwind Reconstruction and leave African Americans once more vulnerable to violent suppression of their rights. Gone, too, was the Freedman's Bureau, which had opened 4,000 small schools in the South attended by 250,000 people in five years, in what Richard Kluger called "the most extraordinary governmental effort at mass uplift in the nation's history."[5]

Disfranchisement of Black voters contributed to the election of Southern members of Congress who opposed civil rights legislation. The seniority system and the filibuster combined to make it nigh impossible to pass laws against race discrimination. Despite repeated attempts to convince Congress to enforce the Reconstruction Amendments, its only legislative response was to repeal some protections in the 1890s, refusing even to ban the growing practice of lynching.[6]

While Congress was stalled, in the two decades following the end of Reconstruction the Supreme Court defanged the Fourteenth and Fifteenth Amendments, eviscerating protections for African American voters, nearly guaranteeing that all-white juries would prevail, and limiting cases in which due process would apply. In 1896 the Supreme Court, in *Plessy v. Ferguson*, left the decision of whether to maintain segregation to the states. Although *Plessy* was about a Louisiana law that required African Americans to ride in segregated railroad cars, the court cited the practice of school segregation as a rationale for the sweeping legalization of the "separate but equal" doctrine that turned its back on the Fourteenth Amendment while insisting it did not treat African Americans as an inferior race:

> The object of the (Fourteenth) amendment was undoubtedly to enforce the absolute equality of the two races before the law, but, in the nature of things, it could not have been intended to abolish distinctions based upon color, or to enforce social, as distinguished from political, equality, or a commingling of the two races upon terms unsatisfactory to either. Laws permitting, and even requiring, their separation in places where they are liable to be brought into contact do not necessarily imply the inferiority of either race to the other, and have been generally, if not universally, recognized as within the competency of the state legislatures in the exercise of their police power.
>
> The most common instance of this is connected with the establishment of separate schools for white and colored children, which has been held to be a valid exercise of the legislative power even by courts of States where the political rights of the colored race have been longest and most earnestly enforced.[7]

African Americans, while not again placed in the iron chains of slavery, were locked in political and economic chains for decades. Southern states largely annulled their right to vote and their access to adequate and equal education and the amenities of everyday life, from water fountains, to libraries, parking places, and cemetery plots.[8] Among the disparities in Macon County, discussed in a later chapter, Alabama's version of separate but equal provided per capita expenditures in the white schools 14.75 times the expenditures in Black schools.

Justice Elena Kagan has written, "The history of the American administrative state is the history of competition among different entities for control of its policies."[9] This seems hardly the case with school desegregation policies of the federal government. Congress, the branch of government most responsive to grass-roots sentiment, was paralyzed when it came to school segregation. It could not agree on a provision relating to schools in the Civil Rights Act of 1875 or on desegregating the schools of the District of Columbia.[10] In short, when Truman took office in 1945, the federal government was not only acquiescing to state segregation rules, it was also imposing racial segregation.

"We Cannot Wait Any Longer"

Truman had both political and ideological reasons for wishing not only to end racial discrimination by the federal government but also to enlist the government in ending state-level discrimination against African Americans. To win the 1948 election he would need to keep African Americans in the Democratic Party.[11] He also believed that "the main difficulty with the South is that they are living eighty years behind the time and the sooner they come out it the better it will be for the country and themselves." Adding, "I am not asking for social equality because no such thing exists, but I am asking for equality of opportunity for all human beings, and, as long as I stay here, I am going to continue that fight." The blinding of an African American veteran by a South Carolina police chief pointed to the need for federal action, and Truman instructed Attorney General Tom Clark to look into the case.[12] He acknowledged, though, that he thought "it is going to take something more than the handling each individual case after it happens—it is going to require the inauguration of some sort of policy to prevent such happenings."

Truman, descended from families who lived in slave-holding Missouri, may seem an improbable candidate to meet this challenge. But his actions ultimately set the terms of debate over civil rights for decades, affecting hundreds of thousands of African American citizens, including those in Macon

County. Acquittals in federal prosecutions in the South Carolina case and of individuals accused of perpetrating lynchings in Georgia and Louisiana underscored the need for stronger federal tools to combat race discrimination.[13] Concerned African American leaders met with Truman in the White House and called on him to protect civil rights. Outside the gates, picketers demanded action. In response, Truman, faced with a Congress inclined to block civil rights legislation and a Supreme Court that had reinforced segregation for decades, brandished the only political tools at his disposal: a public campaign. He began making speeches and issuing executive orders reversing the federal government's complicity in the racial caste system. The first step, announced exactly one month after the acquittal in the South Carolina case, was the creation of the President's Committee on Civil Rights. As Truman explained, "The Constitutional guarantees of individual liberties and of equal protection under the laws clearly place on the Federal Government the duty to act when state or local authorities abridge or fail to protect these Constitutional rights." He continued:

> Yet in its discharge of the obligations placed on it by the Constitution, the Federal Government is hampered by inadequate civil rights statutes. The protection of our democratic institutions and the enjoyment by the people of their rights under the Constitution require that these weak and inadequate statutes should be expanded and improved. We must provide the Department of Justice with the tools to do the job.[14]

In January 1947 Truman underscored his commitment to civil rights in his State of the Union speech to Congress, noting that the United States had witnessed "numerous attacks upon the constitutional rights of individual citizens as a result of racial and religious bigotry." In calling for change, Truman exhorted, "the will to fight these crimes should be in the hearts of every one of us." Turning to the federal role, he concluded:

> For the Federal Government that fight is now being carried on by the Department of Justice to the full extent of the powers that have been conferred upon it. While the Constitution withholds from the Federal Government the major task of preserving peace in the several States, I am not convinced that the present legislation reached the limit of Federal power to protect the civil rights of its citizens.[15]

Six months later, Truman became the first president to address the NAACP. Speaking to ten thousand people assembled at the Lincoln Memorial and via a national radio broadcast, he delivered the strongest presidential statement on civil rights since Abraham Lincoln: "Many of our people still suffer the indignity of insult, the narrowing fear of intimidation, and, I regret to say, the threat of physical injury and mob violence. Prejudice and intolerance in which these evils are rooted still exist. The conscience of our Nation, and the legal machinery which enforces it, have not yet secured to each citizen full freedom from fear." Because "we cannot, any longer, await the growth of a will to action in the slowest state or the most backward community," Truman concluded, "National Government must show the way."[16]

In October 1947 Truman's Committee on Civil Rights issued a lengthy report detailing the many ways in which people of color faced racial discrimination in the United States and recommending action. Most relevant to the *Lee* case, the committee recommended that the Civil Rights Section of the DOJ's Criminal Division be strengthened and elevated to full division status. Although this recommendation would take a decade to fulfill, it would have enormous benefits for African Americans seeking to desegregate their schools and vote in elections in Macon County and throughout the South.

When it came to segregation in the public schools, the report was cautious. While stating that "the gap between white and Negro schools can never be completely eliminated by means of state funds alone," the report refrained from explicitly recommending desegregation. Instead it suggested that federal financial assistance would be needed and added, "Whether the federal grant-in-aid should be used to support the maintenance of separate schools is an issue that the country must soon face."[17]

Truman, typically clear and emphatic, answered that question when, several years later, he vetoed a bill that would have provided extra federal funds to public schools burdened by federal defense activities. His veto message noted that the bill would require that even schools operating on federal facilities in the Deep South be segregated "to the maximum extent practicable." Thus, he said, the measure "would require a group of schools on Federal property which are now operating successfully on an integrated basis to be segregated." This, he emphasized, "would constitute a backward step in the efforts of the Federal Government to extend equal rights and opportunities to all our people."[18] Truman's veto reflected the beginning of a divergence between the executive and legislative branches of government on the issue of school desegregation.

The veto also demonstrated a growing divide within the executive branch itself. The Office of Education resisted Truman's commitment to civil rights and continued to grant funding to segregated public schools located on military bases. NAACP's Clarence Mitchell Jr. commented on the Office of Education's "stubborn resistance by local officials and sabotage by some Federal officials." Education officials endorsed states' rights on education and emphasized the agency's traditional policy of "non-interference" on segregation, granting eleven Southern states $63 million for segregated schools as late as 1960.[19]

Adopting many of the recommendations of his Committee on Civil Rights, Truman sent his civil rights program to Congress in early 1948, noting that "the Federal Government has a clear duty to see that Constitutional guarantees of individual liberties and of equal protection under the laws are not denied or abridged anywhere in our Union." He asked Congress to enact legislation against lynching, poll taxes, and discrimination in interstate travel. The legislation would protect voter rights and establish a Fair Employment Practices Commission. However, the proposal was mute on the issue of school segregation.[20] But this was not enough to placate the legislature: in the end, Congress failed to pass any civil rights legislation during Truman's presidency.

Stymied by Congress, Truman turned to two executive tools, the executive order and amicus curiae briefs. In 1948 he issued Executive Order 9981, ordering an end to racial discrimination in the armed forces. The United States' first venture into participation as an amicus curiae in a racial discrimination case took place in the Supreme Court that same year, when the court was considering whether the Constitution allows the state to enforce racially restrictive housing covenants.[21] The amicus process would evolve into a critical tool for the DOJ and the federal courts in civil rights cases, including *Lee*.

Truman and the Court

In the covenant cases, *Shelley v. Kraemer* and *Hurd v. Hodge*, the solicitor general filed a brief arguing that the state could not enforce the covenant. In doing so, he gave two reasons why the United States had an interest that warranted filing an amicus brief. "First, the Federal Government has a special responsibility for the protection of the fundamental civil rights guaranteed to the people by the Constitution and laws of the United States. The President of the United States recently stated: 'We must make the Federal Government a friendly vigilant defender of the rights and equalities of all Americans. Our National Government must show the way.'" Coupled with this extremely expansive statement of government interest was a more practical one: state enforcement of the covenants had "become a source of serious embarrassment to agencies of the Federal Government in the performance of many essential functions, including the programs relating to housing and home finance, to public health, to the protection of dependent native racial minorities in the United States and its territories, to the conduct of foreign affairs, and to the protection of civil rights."[22]

The court unanimously (with three justices recused) outlawed judicial enforcement of the restrictive housing covenants that discriminated against African Americans, Jews, and other minorities. Chief Justice Vinson's opinion for the court signaled a change from the *Plessy* regime:

> We have noted that freedom from discrimination by the States in the enjoyment of property rights was among the basic objectives sought to be effectuated by the framers of the Fourteenth Amendment. That such discrimination has occurred in these cases is clear. Because of the race or color of these petitioners, they have been denied rights of ownership or occupancy enjoyed as a matter of course by other citizens of different race or color.[23]

In 1950 Truman's administration continued its legal attack on racial discrimination, filing amicus briefs attacking segregated railroad dining cars and segregated graduate education. "Segregation as enforced by regulation imports the inferiority of the Negro race," the administration argued in the dining car case. "Enforced racial segregation in itself constitutes a denial of the right to equal treatment. Equal treatment means the same treatment."[24] On June 5, 1950, the court ruled 8–0 that racial discrimination violated the Interstate Commerce Act. The same day, the court ruled unanimously against racial segregation in state-sponsored graduate education.[25]

The court and the Truman administration had created momentum for change. The following year the president extended the push for change to public school segregation, when the set of five cases we know as *Brown v. Board of Education* reached the Supreme Court. In these cases, the stakes were higher—could nearly two dozen states and the District of Columbia require or allow separation of the races in public elementary and secondary education? Truman's solicitor general filed a brief supporting the right to be free from state-imposed racial separation in the public schools. The brief identified two reasons for the government to file. First:

> The Federal Government has a clear duty to see that constitutional guaranties of individual liberties and of equal protection under the laws are not denied or abridged anywhere in our Union. . . . Few Americans believe that government should pursue a *laissez-faire* policy in the field of civil rights, or that it adequately discharges its duty to the people so long as it does not itself intrude on their civil liberties. Instead, there is general acceptance of an affirmative government obligation to insure respect for fundamental human rights.

Second, racial segregation was a foreign relations embarrassment, especially as African nations were winning their independence. Referring implicitly to the Cold War efforts to gain influence in newly independent states, the brief argued, "It is in the context of the present world struggle between freedom and tyranny that the problem of racial discrimination must be viewed."[26]

The case was argued in December 1952, but the badly divided court was unable to come to a quick decision. To buy time, the justices devised a series of questions for the parties and invited the Attorney General to file another brief and participate in a reargument. By this time, Truman had left office, succeeded by Dwight D. Eisenhower. Then, on September 8, 1953, the legal landscape changed abruptly when Chief Justice Vinson suffered a fatal heart attack.

EISENHOWER

Dwight D. Eisenhower, the last American president born in the nineteenth century, often struggled in the middle of the twentieth with the emerging effort to resolve the racist legacy of post-Reconstruction America. The quick growth of television news in the 1950s brought the ferocity of the resistance to desegregation into the homes of millions of Americans. The depth and extent of the racial caste system were no longer hidden. The battle was now cast for the nation in personal, political, and moral terms.

The new president grew up in Abilene, Kansas, about ninety miles west of Topeka, where the lead case in *Brown v. Board of Education* originated. Abilene was an almost all-white town, where "segregation existed . . . but was not as rigid as in the Deep South." Eisenhower graduated from the US Military Academy at West Point, which had had only a sprinkling of Black cadets through the years. Serving in a racially segregated army, he rose to be commanding general, European Theatre of Operations during World War II. There, he pushed for equal opportunity for Black soldiers, including the opportunity to serve in combat, albeit in racially segregated units. After the war, he became army chief of staff and told the head of the NAACP that he opposed racial segregation in the military. However, in testimony before a Senate committee, he argued that Blacks would have more opportunity in segregated units because "if we attempt merely by passing a lot of laws to force someone to like someone else, we are just going to get into trouble." His ambivalence on civil rights carried into his presidential campaign in 1952, when he sought Southern votes with states' rights rhetoric but also said, "We should eliminate every vestige of segregation in the District of Columbia."[27]

After his landslide victory in 1952, Eisenhower took steps to support desegregation of public accommodations in the District of Columbia and, in an early application of the ratchet principle, to carry out Truman's executive order desegregating the armed forces.[28] He had been in the White House about eight months when Chief Justice Vinson's death created an opportunity to appoint a new chief justice. Vinson's replacement, Earl Warren, was able to break the stalemate over *Brown* and alter forever the nation's civil rights direction.

Since the Truman administration had staked out a position of the United States as amicus in *Brown*, the Eisenhower administration could hardly refuse the Supreme Court's request that the government participate in the reargument of the case. At the same time, pressure was brought to bear on the other side, as Texas's governor urged Eisenhower to defer to local law.[29] As a result, the DOJ filed a brief that took no position on the merits of the case. Still, though NAACP lawyer Thurgood Marshall feared that the government "might well undermine his legal strategy in making his case," that did not happen.[30] Instead, at the 1953 reargument, Assistant Attorney General J. Lee Rankin, when pressed by Justice William O. Douglas, supported the plaintiffs: "It is the position of the Department of Justice that segregation in public schools cannot be maintained under the Fourteenth Amendment."[31] Rankin's answer ratifying the Truman administration's position implicitly placed the force of the federal government behind any Supreme Court ruling requiring desegregation.

With the backing now of both Democratic and Republican administrations, the court ruled on May 17, 1954, that the doctrine of separate but equal public education violated the Fourteenth Amendment.[32] In the companion case from the District of Columbia, the court held that the federal enclave's official racial segregation of its public schools violated the due process clause of the Fifth Amendment.[33] Although not explicitly overruled, *Plessy v. Ferguson* was finally dead, as a matter of law, but would segregated schools in fact become a thing of the past? The Supreme Court scheduled the case for yet another set of arguments, this time limited to what relief was appropriate.

Eisenhower did not speak publicly of the decision until two days after it was handed down, and then with a singular lack of enthusiasm: "The Supreme Court has spoken, and I am sworn to uphold the constitutional process in this country; and I will obey."[34] Never did he utter a positive word about *Brown.* Eight years later, Warren—who felt that the president's enthusiastic support would have helped build public support for the decision—complained "that no word of support for the (*Brown*) decision emanated from the White House."[35]

During the April 1955 arguments on relief, the court heard a wide range of ideas about how to end the system of separate schools for whites and African Americans. The arguments previewed issues that would occupy the courts for more than twenty years. Lawyers described geographic zoning, student transfers, freedom of choice, student reassignments, grade-a-year desegregation, teacher assignments, funding, and transportation. Lawyers for the school districts expressed doubt that any desegregation could succeed. For example, the attorney general of Virginia said, "White parents will keep their children out of school."[36] At one point, Justice Felix Frankfurter, anticipating issues that would confront the trial court in *Lee v. Macon County Board of Education* a dozen years later, asked whether the court could "go into particularities" about "what would or would not operate not as a fair opportunity for a fair choice but some kind of a 'huggamugger,' some kind of a manipulation whereby what is deemed to be a fair choice is not really a fair choice." The attorney for North Carolina suggested that the "jobs of 8,500 Negro teachers are hanging in the balance" because almost all school superintendents thought it would not be possible to use them in mixed schools.[37]

Solicitor General Simon E. Sobeloff, arguing for the United States, offered "the counsel of moderation, but with a degree of firmness," a position, he said, that rejected the extremes presented by the two sides. He argued that the variety of conditions in the school districts before the court meant that "no single formula can be devised by the ingenuity of man that will fit aptly all cases." He suggested that the court leave the details up to the district courts, subject to general guidelines, with some discretion as to timing of desegregation, but "not for the purpose of paralyzing action or of emasculating" *Brown.*[38] The justices remanded the cases to the lower courts to "enter such orders and decrees consistent with this opinion as are necessary and proper to admit to public schools on a racially nondiscriminatory basis with all deliberate speed the parties to these cases."[39] The Supreme Court gave no substantial additional guidance to the lower federal courts until 1968. The Fifth Circuit Court of Appeals, which then extended from Texas to Florida and Georgia, became a leader in developing the law on how to desegregate.

With the decision in *Brown,* the judicial and executive branches had taken a stand against state-imposed racial segregation of the public schools. Meanwhile, Congress remained silent. And the future role of the federal government in school desegregation was uncertain.

In the first State of the Union speech of his second term, Eisenhower informed Congress that he planned to reintroduce his civil rights legislation that had failed to win passage the prior year. While "we are moving closer to the goal of fair and equal treatment of citizens without regard to race or color," the president declared, "unhappily much remains to be done."[40] The president outlined the four main provisions of the proposed bill—creation of a civil rights commission, creation of a civil rights division in the DOJ, strengthening laws to protect voting rights, and allowing the federal government to seek relief in civil courts in civil rights cases.

The states of the Deep South girded for a battle to maintain racial segregation in the public schools and other public venues. Every Southern school system would remain racially segregated unless a federal court or agency ordered the system to desegregate. Courts, however, could act only when a plaintiff brought a case to them, and Congress had not empowered any federal agency to require desegregation. Private plaintiffs supported by the NAACP continued the long and expensive effort to bring about desegregation through case-by-case litigation. In the segregated states the "full burden of forcing compliance, of presiding over this major social revolution, [fell] on forty-eight [*sic*] United States district judges."[41]

Congress acquiesced in the desegregation of the District of Columbia schools but enacted no legislation to enforce *Brown* until the passage of the

Civil Rights Act of 1964. After *Brown II*, all three branches largely failed to take steps to bring about compliance with *Brown*, with one exception: while the executive branch took the position that it could do nothing to facilitate desegregation, it would enforce court orders when politicians or private citizens interfered with the school authorities who were trying to comply.[42]

Eisenhower stressed, both privately and publicly, the desirability of moderate progress in desegregating the schools.[43] His administration, however, was consistent in following principles (found in an undated and unsigned document in Press Secretary James Hagerty's files) that while the executive branch would not "participate in the formulation of plans affecting desegregation" or in proposing the timetable for desegregation, it would enforce federal court orders.[44]

When white leaders of the Deep South decided to resist enforcement of *Brown*, African Americans alone could not muster the needed legal resources. They could bring a few dozen cases every year, but that would relegate to one-race schools most of the eleven million school children in the states that were segregated by law, including almost three million African American children.

Civil Rights Act of 1957

Southern members of Congress opposed part III of the civil rights bill, which would have authorized the attorney general to sue for injunctive relief against state officials who violated constitutional rights. They feared that part III would allow the DOJ to bring or participate in school desegregation cases. For their part, Eisenhower and Attorney General Brownell took a more limited view of part III as a tool to enforce court rulings rather than to initiate desegregation cases.[45] Brownell testified before the House Judiciary Committee that part III would be potentially useful in the area of school segregation. Using a case from Hoxie, Arkansas, as an illustration, the attorney general described a situation where school board members, complying with *Brown*, were threatened with private violence when they moved to desegregate a school. In response, the superintendent and the school board filed a suit in federal court seeking to restrain the defendants from interfering with the operations of the school. Part III would have allowed the DOJ to bring the suit. Brownell argued that where the local communities fail to respect federal law and federal rights, the federal government must have the right and power to effectively act to remedy the situation.[46]

Ultimately, despite objections from Southern members that "this legislation will be widely used against the State boards of education, county and city boards of education, and against the school systems of the various municipalities," the House passed the bill.[47] It now headed to the Senate, where it found a leading opponent in Senator Richard Russell of Georgia, who had earlier drafted the Southern Manifesto asserting that states need not comply with *Brown.* Russell complained that the measure would allow the attorney general to "compel the intermingling of the races in the public schools and in all places of public entertainment in the Southern states." Part III, Russell complained, "was cunningly designed to use the whole power of the Federal Government to destroy the separation of the races in the South on which our way of life is based."[48] He feared that approving part III would "approve the race-mixing decision of the Supreme Court of May 1954."[49] Russell charged that passage of such a bill would create "unspeakable confusion, bitterness and bloodshed in a great section of our common country." If the federal government were to move into the South to enforce civil rights, as this bill proposed, "the concentration camps may as well be prepared because there will not be enough jails to hold the people of the South who will oppose the use of raw federal power forcibly to comingle white and Negro children in the same schools."[50] In the end, the Senate rejected part III by a vote of 52–38 before overwhelmingly voting to pass the Civil Rights Act of 1957 as amended.

Southern senators and representatives also succeeded in watering down enforcement of federal court civil rights orders by requiring contempt of court charges in civil rights cases to be presented to a jury. Thus, not only did the 1957 act not authorize the DOJ to bring school desegregation cases, it made it more difficult for private plaintiffs to enforce such orders. Still, law professor Robert McKay predicted, "if the situation should deteriorate to a point of actual resistance to specific judicial decrees, the President could exercise additional powers" and use the militia or armed forces to enforce school desegregation decrees. Moreover, the support of the public and the other branches "adds immeasurably, though intangibly, to the prospect of eventual success."[51]

Eisenhower signed the bill on September 10 but made no public statement.[52] Instead, he was consumed with the emerging crisis in Little Rock and two weeks later issued the order he had said in July he could not imagine.[53] On September 23, 1957, he sent a brigade of the 101st Airborne Division to enforce a federal court order to desegregate Central High School in Little Rock.

Little Rock

In the build-up to the desegregation of Central High School in Little Rock in 1957, the DOJ learned that segregationists would try to interfere when the African American children attempted to enroll. Fanning the flames was Governor Orville Faubus, eager to burnish his anti-desegregation credentials. "I'm going to run for a third term and if I don't do this (segregationists) will tear me to shreds," the governor declared.[54]

The trial judge in a suit filed by the NAACP LDF wanted the United States to enter the case to seek an injunction against Faubus. He "requested and authorized [the DOJ] to appear in these proceedings as *amici curiae* and to accord the Court the benefit of their views and recommendations with the right to submit to the Court pleadings, evidence, arguments and briefs, and for the further purpose, under the direction of this Court, to initiate such further proceedings as may be appropriate."[55] The DOJ had already entered two Arkansas cases to enforce federal desegregation orders despite its position that it lacked authority to bring school desegregation cases.[56] This work-around became a pattern that culminated in the statewide desegregation suits beginning with *Lee v. Macon County Board of Education.* Still, while Brownell advised the president "that the court had the power to make this request,"[57] the department confined its amicus activities to protecting against interference with the federal court order.[58]

Meanwhile, the situation deteriorated further, as the court ordered Faubus to stop using the National Guard to keep African American children out of Central High School. Having riled up the white population, Faubus then withdrew the National Guard completely, leaving the children at the mercy of a mob. Only then did the president take forceful action, ordering 1,200 paratroopers of the 101st Airborne Division to maintain order. Eisenhower explained that he had a constitutional obligation to "use whatever means may be required" to stop mob obstruction of justice.[59] He told the nation, "Our personal opinions about the [*Brown*] decision have no bearing on the matter of enforcement." He argued, "The very basis of our individual rights and freedom is the certainty that the President and the Executive Branch of Government will support and insure the carrying out of the decisions of the Federal Courts. . . . Mob rule cannot be allowed to override the decisions of the courts."[60] The revolution came to Arkansas, not through violent mob action but through disciplined federal military force forcing the state to comply with the court's order. And Little Rock was on television for the world to see. Journalist David Halberstam observed:

> The President, uneasy with the course of events, had failed to give any kind of moral leadership, and he had deliberately refused to define the issue in moral terms; now, almost unconsciously, the media was doing it instead, for the ugliness and cruelty of it all, the white mob encouraged by a local governor tormenting young children, carried its own indictment. The nation watched, hypnotized, from its living rooms every night.[61]

The Little Rock episode awakened the Eisenhower administration to the need to know what was happening with school desegregation in the South. Presidential aide Sherman Adams asked Solicitor General J. Lee Rankin for a list of court orders and school desegregation plans, which Rankin sent to him in October. Notably, the only indication of US government involvement was the entry about Little Rock. The list also reflected that the court in the Delaware case that had been part of *Brown*, *Evans v. Buchanan* had ordered the Delaware State Board of Education to submit a plan for statewide desegregation.[62]

The following year the Supreme Court convened a special session and entered a ruling, individually signed by each of the nine justices, that Little Rock could not use the fear of further disruption as a reason to suspend desegregation. In doing so the court sent a strong signal that defiance of *Brown* must end.[63] However, a DOJ staff proposal for legislation allowing the attorney general to sue for school desegregation went nowhere.[64]

In November 1960, Judge J. Skelly Wright of the Eastern District of Louisiana, confronted with recalcitrant Louisiana officialdom, asked the United States government to participate in the New Orleans school desegregation case as a friend of the court. Unlike many in the South, M. Hepburn Many, the US attorney in New Orleans, believed in equal rights for African Americans. While there are conflicting stories as to whether Eisenhower or the DOJ in Washington were willing to help Wright, Many did appear as Wright had requested. Traditionally an amicus curiae provides legal briefing for the court, but Wright's order followed the Little Rock model of creating a new kind of participant, a litigating amicus with rights of a party.[65] Wright requested and authorized the United States not only to provide "its views and recommendations" but also "to submit to the court pleadings, evidence, arguments and briefs, and to initiate such further proceedings as may be appropriate." Slightly modifying the language the court in Little Rock had used, Wright said that the purpose of this invitation was "in order to maintain and preserve the due administration of justice and the integrity of the judicial processes of the United States."[66] Little Rock and New Orleans messaged the need for early involvement by the DOJ in school desegregation cases facing political hostility, laying the foundation for federal action in *Lee v. Macon County Board of Education.*

A Man Named Doar

While a modest accomplishment, the 1957 Civil Rights Act, the first such act since 1875, created the Civil Rights Division within the DOJ. The division would inexorably grow into an effective law enforcement machine, with ever-expanding responsibilities. The act authorized the attorney general to bring suits to remedy racially discriminatory election practices but went no further. It also created the Commission on Civil Rights, which had no enforcement authority but was empowered to investigate denials of equal protection of laws and report to the president and Congress. The reports could include recommendations for action. In 1961 the commission recommended legislation requiring segregated school systems to adopt desegregation plans and directing the attorney general to enforce this obligation. The 1963 report made a similar recommendation.[67]

At first, the CRD was a sleepy, small unit, bringing only a few cases to enforce voting rights while handling numerous non–civil rights cases.[68] Foreshadowing the *Lee* litigation, the first department voting rights case in Alabama was filed against Macon County voter registrars. The division also brought contempt proceedings against George Wallace for his refusal to comply with a Civil Rights Commission subpoena for voting records.[69] For all that, the division sprang to life in the waning months of the Eisenhower administration, when the energetic Harold Tyler, a former assistant US attorney, became assistant attorney general for civil rights and brought in a small-town lawyer from Wisconsin, John Doar, as his top assistant. Tyler and Doar, both in their late thirties, brought vitality to the division, transforming its lawyers from desk-bound bureaucrats to active enforcers. Doar would shape the CRD's policies and methods of enforcement in ways that lasted for decades.

The son of a lawyer in New Richmond, Wisconsin (population 3,316 in 1960), Doar met Tyler when the two were students at Princeton University. After serving in the army during World War II, Doar studied law at Boalt Hall, the law school of the University of California, Berkeley. In Doar's tenth year of practice, Tyler offered him the job of first assistant in the last year of the Eisenhower Administration. Doar accepted despite advice that "it's reckless to move to Washington six months before an election because you're liable to be out on your ear sooner than you'd like."[70] His six months stretched to seven eventful years, in which "he showed the nation in vivid detail how radical change can be achieved through law and what should be expected of an attorney . . . representing the United States: an unqualified and absolute devotion to justice."[71] President Obama awarded him the Presidential Medal of Freedom, and New Richmond has recognized Doar's impact on our history by creating the John Doar History Trail at the millpond on the banks of the Willow River, near the offices of the Doar law firm.

During the final months of the Eisenhower administration, Doar developed an understanding of the pervasiveness and insidiousness of the racial caste system in the Deep South: "Everywhere I found a complex legal and social network designed to protect and preserve the caste system. The means used were official corruption, discrimination, and official and unofficial intimidation."[72] He also began to apply the lessons from his law practice. He was fond of saying, "When I got to the Justice Department, I was a small town [*sic*] lawyer. Small town lawyers investigate their own cases."[73] His method would drive the federal government's contribution to the revolution that overthrew the official caste system. After the 1960 presidential election Doar would find himself challenging racial discrimination in voter registration in Macon County, Alabama, and then litigating the Macon County school desegregation case.

KENNEDY, THE RELUCTANT ACTIVIST

In 1960 John F. Kennedy defeated Richard Nixon by the narrowest of margins.[74] Support from the African American community, fueled by Kennedy's call to Coretta King when her husband was jailed in Georgia and by his views on African independence, played a significant role in Kennedy's victory.[75] Still, he took office with little understanding of civil rights issues. In his book, *Profiles in Courage*, which won the Pulitzer Prize for Biography in 1957, Kennedy deeply embraced the canard that Reconstruction had been a disaster. He wrote, "No state suffered more from carpetbag rule than Mississippi." He complained that Governor Adelbert Ames, a former Union soldier, had been elected "by a majority composed of freed slaves and radical Republicans, sustained and nourished by Federal bayonets."[76] In discussing the Hayes-Tilden election of 1876, Kennedy was sympathetic to the South: "Four more years of Republican rule meant four more years of Southern bondage and exploitation, four more years before the South could regain her dignity and her rightful place in the nation." He praised Lucius Quintus Cincinnatus Lamar, Mississippi governor, congressional representative, senator, and Supreme Court justice, for his skill in getting "Hayes committed to concessions for the South, including the withdrawal of military occupation forces and a return to Home Rule in key states."[77]

African Americans could rightly be concerned that Kennedy at best did not understand the racial caste system. His vice president, Lyndon Johnson, came from a Southern state, Texas, and had voted reliably against early civil rights legislation. At the same time, Johnson had played a key role in the passage of the 1957 and 1960 civil rights acts. Clarence Mitchell, legislative director of the Leadership Conference for Civil Rights, thought Kennedy's New Frontier looked "suspiciously like a dude ranch with [Mississippi] Senator James O. Eastland as the general manager and [Virginia Representative] Howard Smith as the Foreman."[78] Kennedy's inaugural address, though, inspired many to public service:

> Let the word go forth from this time and place, to friend and foe alike, that the torch has been passed to a new generation of Americans—born in this century, tempered by war, disciplined by a hard and bitter peace, proud of our ancient heritage—and unwilling to witness or permit the slow undoing of those human rights to which this nation has always been committed, and to which we are committed today at home and around the world. . . .
>
> The energy, the faith, the devotion which we bring to this endeavor will light our country and all who serve it—and the glow from that fire can truly light the world.
>
> And so, my fellow Americans: ask not what your country can do for you—ask what you can do for your country.[79]

Nowhere did those words resonate more than in the three-year-old CRD, whose lawyers and staff were experiencing for the first time a change in presidential leadership. Ten days later, President Kennedy reinforced the message. In his first State of the Union address he singled out the civil service, finding it "full of honest and useful public servants." Like a football coach exhorting his team, Kennedy added, "Let the public service be a proud and lively career.

And let every man and woman who works in any area of our national government, in any branch, at any level, be able to say with pride and with honor in future years: 'I served the United States government in that hour of our nation's need.'"[80]

While critics have argued that President Kennedy did too little for civil rights and did it too late, the staff of the CRD found his brother supportive from the beginning.[81] On his first day as attorney general, Robert F. Kennedy came to the division's offices and told John Doar he wanted to bring a school desegregation case in New Orleans. Doar explained that the attorney general lacked the power to bring such a suit and that, in any event, the United States was already an amicus curiae in the case. Kennedy later pressed Assistant Attorney General Burke Marshall to sue segregated school districts receiving federal funds to educate children of federal employees or military personnel. As we will see, the courts held the DOJ had no authority to bring such suits.

Kennedy chose to deliver one of his earliest speeches as attorney general at the University of Georgia, an intellectual center of the Deep South where Senator Richard Russell had attended law school.[82] The attorney general selected this occasion to state his position regarding *Brown*: "I happen to believe that the 1954 decision was right. But my belief does not matter. It is now the law. Some of you may believe the decision was wrong. That does not matter. It is the law."[83] The following month the *Montgomery Advertiser* reported from Tuskegee: "A Negro special assistant [Frank D. Reeves, one of the lawyers for plaintiffs in *Brown v. Board of Education*] to President John F. Kennedy said here Tuesday night that equal voting, court decisions, direct community action such as sit-ins, and equal job opportunities will improve life 'for all Southerners'—white as well as Negro."[84] In the summer of 1961, Burke Marshall quietly visited ten or so Southern cities, talking with the "mayor, police chief, the school board, businessmen, church people," to offer help and tell them "that it was good for business and good for their city if they got this thing over with in a peaceful manner."[85]

The Kennedy administration brought a dramatic change of attitude, spurred on by the rising tide of civil rights activism and the accompanying violence against activists. President Kennedy installed a strong team to lead the CRD, appointing Marshall and keeping Doar on as Marshall's top assistant. The cerebral Marshall and the experienced litigator Doar, both committed to eradicating the racial caste system, were the right law enforcement team for the tumultuous years that followed, 1961–1965. Neither of the army veterans had a civil rights background. The Kennedys apparently chose Marshall, an antitrust lawyer with a large Washington firm, partly because he had no ties with civil rights organizations and would be easily confirmed by the Senate as a neutral enforcer of the law.[86] Doar and Marshall, as described by a special assistant to Doar, "were two incredible people who each had complementary talents, and each thought the other was the finest lawyer in the world. And they worked together in a complementary way that just couldn't, you couldn't reestablish."[87]

We have no clear explanation as to why the Kennedy administration decided to retain Doar, a Republican holdover. Doar himself liked to tell the story that he had served as a water boy for the Pittsburgh Pirates (now the Steelers) in 1939, when Byron White was one of their star players. As Doar told the story, on his first visit to Attorney General Kennedy's office White, then the deputy attorney general (and later to become Supreme Court Justice), came in and said, "General, this is John Doar. He's a cousin of Johnny Blood, he played for Green Bay." Doar related that Kennedy responded, "Johnny Blood, that's a household name in our family, have him come to the White House and meet Jack." Doar concluded, "I don't think that hurt me."[88]

Marshall, a modest man who resisted any fanfare, quietly worked behind the scenes, while Doar spent most of his time in the Deep South, forging close ties with African American leaders, building factual cases, and mediating racially explosive situations. Marshall argued groundbreaking cases in the appellate courts, successfully stopping a state prosecution of an African American voter-education advocate.[89] In the wake of the police violence against African American demonstrators in Birmingham in the spring of 1963, Marshall "forged an agreement with the city's business and civic leaders that began the process of desegregation and ended the demonstrations."[90] Doar escorted James Meredith as he registered for class at the University of Mississippi in 1962, brought and tried voting rights cases, enforced the right of civil rights supporters to march from Selma to Montgomery, and successfully prosecuted the "Mississippi Burning" conspirators who killed three civil rights workers in Philadelphia, Mississippi. He developed a close relationship with Marshall, even naming his fourth child Burke. Marshall and Doar's record followed the admonition of Attorney General Robert H. Jackson (later Supreme Court Justice) to United States attorneys in 1940: "A sensitiveness to fair play and sportsmanship is perhaps the best protection against the abuse of power, and the citizen's safety lies in the prosecutor who tempers zeal with human kindness, who seeks truth and not victims, who serves the law and not factional purposes, and who approaches his task with humility."[91] Even "those who disagreed, especially those who fiercely resisted the changes afoot and sought to preserve the Jim Crow system . . . in time, came to admire" Marshall.[92]

Doar's work ethic was legendary and infectious. As one United States attorney observed, "Doar makes high demands of his associates but sets high standards for himself as well and does not ask more of others than he is willing to do himself."[93] His focus on the highest standards of preparation earned him the enmity of FBI director J. Edgar Hoover. Hoover complained that Doar "unjustly accused the Bureau of unnecessary delays and unnecessarily requested extremely expeditious handling of matters where such urgency was not indicated."[94] The assistant attorney general for administration, S. A. Andretta, while viewing Doar as an outstanding attorney who had "accomplished much in the civil rights field," described him as "demanding and intolerant, and . . . considered a 'slave driver' as he drives his subordinates with extreme zeal."[95] Doar would have agreed that he was demanding. As he said, "I like to see the attorneys have a full day's work."[96] A job in the CRD was no sinecure, and many of the raw, young lawyers in the division benefited from Doar's demanding expectations, as should be apparent from this description in the *New York Times*:

> Mr. Doar has frequently expressed impatience with vague briefs filed by young lawyers and sent them back with instructions for more "facts, facts, facts." To illustrate his point he sent to every lawyer in his division a copy of the Rolls Royce advertisement saying the only noise one can hear in the automobile is the ticking of the clock. This, Mr. Doar pointed out, is much better than saying the auto is quiet.[97]

Andretta also viewed Doar as lacking administrative ability, citing the high expense of long-distance phone calls, some lasting ninety minutes, in the CRD.[98] In the 1960s, of course, there were no cell phones, and long-distance calls were generally used sparingly. But Doar insisted that lawyers who were on travel in the Deep South check in with him by phone daily. I once got a frantic call from my supervisor saying that Doar was about to make me return to Washington because I had failed to call in that day from Alabama.

The phone check-in reflected Doar's personal approach, which became more difficult as the division grew from 15 lawyers in 1957 to 105 in 1965.[99] Doar also cemented relations with division lawyers by meeting with them to discuss litigation, by trying cases himself with support from attorneys, and by helping lawyers prepare for trial. Litigation decisions were both top down and bottom up. Doar or his section chiefs would send lawyers to investigate possible cases, and he closely controlled deployment of resources. But litigation recommendations came from below; attorneys drafted proposed complaints accompanied by memoranda (called justification memoranda) explaining why they recommended filing suit. Doar reviewed the memoranda, often sending them back for more information but ultimately deciding whether to file the complaint. This system led to close relationships between Doar and his attorneys, relationships that often lasted a lifetime.

The incoming Kennedy administration almost immediately had to decide its posture in the New Orleans school desegregation case. When desegregation was at last to occur, the attorney general embraced US attorney Many's wish to help Judge J. Skelly Wright. Marshall, during the hearing before the Senate Judiciary Committee on his nomination to be the assistant attorney general for civil rights, told a hostile Senator James Eastland of Mississippi that the DOJ had a legal duty to enter the case "to protect . . . the integrity of the orders of the court and the administration of justice in the area."[100] The state legislature and governor sought to interfere with the desegregation process, and the DOJ did not wait for the private plaintiffs to act but instead took the initiative and filed a motion asking the court to block the interference. The Louisiana officials objected that the United States had no authority to file such a motion and that the defeat of part III of the 1957 act showed that Congress wanted the DOJ to stay out of school desegregation cases. Wright rejected Louisiana's argument and distinguished between the DOJ initiating a suit for desegregation and the department initiating a motion to protect the authority of the court: "Nothing in the history of the recent civil rights legislation indicates that Congress sought to withdraw the right of the United States to intervene under these circumstances."[101] He cited statements of Louisiana's Senator Allen Ellender and Mississippi's Senator John Stennis supporting the right of the government to prevent obstruction of federal court orders.[102] He added that, from the point of view of federal courts, they must be able to "call on the Justice Department to enforce their decrees by resort to arms if necessary." It followed, therefore, that the department's more moderate approach of filing a motion was permissible.[103] Wright's formulation served as a model in 1962, when the United States Court of Appeals for the Fifth Circuit appointed the United States as an amicus curiae in the litigation to admit James Meredith as the first African American student at the University of Mississippi. The order gave the United States the right to initiate proceedings and present evidence "as may be appropriate in order to maintain and preserve the due administration of justice and the integrity of the judicial processes of the United States."[104]

"The Execution of the Laws of the United States"

This law enforcement phase required the government to protect African American children from the violence that threatened those who asserted their right to a nonsegregated education. In Little Rock in 1957, that meant federal troops. In New Orleans in 1960, federal marshals accompanied six-year-old Ruby Bridges as she made her way through a mob of white women, a moment captured in an iconic Norman Rockwell painting. At the University of Mississippi in 1962, Doar and Chief US Marshal James J. P. McShane accompanied James Meredith, but there were not enough US marshals to avert a white riot in which one reporter was murdered and other reporters and even marshals were wounded. As in the previous school desegregation cases, the United States took no position on desegregation, with President Kennedy instead invoking his inescapable responsibility to enforce the court's orders.[105]

The law enforcement phase continued into 1963, when Attorney General Kennedy visited Governor Wallace and urged him not to interfere with desegregation of the University of Alabama. The attorney general told the governor, "I have a responsibility that goes beyond integration or segregation to enforce the law of the land, and to insure that court orders are obeyed."[106] This justification for federal action was repeated in President Kennedy's proclamation of June 11, 1963, regarding the desegregation of the University of Alabama, which referred to an unlawful combination of the governor and others "against the authority of the United States" and concluded, "whereas this unlawful combination opposes the execution of the laws of the United States and threatens to impede the course of justice under those laws [the President commands them to cease and desist]."[107]

By the time *Lee* was filed in January 1963, the DOJ had amassed experience and expertise with the law enforcement aspect of civil rights but had only recently attempted to define the contours of the obligation to desegregate schools. The reaction of Southern politicians to the early desegregation cases required the federal authorities to display not only commitment but also skill in navigating the intersection of politics, federalism, and complex logistics. One can see a clear learning curve in the way the federal government responded to the repeated crises. For example, in Little Rock and the University of Mississippi, false signals, poor relations with local law enforcement, and lack of strong federal presence had contributed to the inability to control mob violence.[108]

In an effort—not always successful—to avoid another Little Rock, Burke Marshall took proactive steps to anticipate and minimize interference with desegregation. During the presidential election campaign, Kennedy had been "critical . . . of President Eisenhower just sitting back and letting Little Rock turn into a crisis, and he wanted to avoid that as much as possible." So Marshall and Kennedy aide John Seigenthaler traveled "in the summer of '61 [to] the school districts that might have a problem in the fall."[109] In July 1961, Marshall advised Deputy Attorney General White that he would go to New Orleans to arrange meetings to ensure that scheduled desegregation was successful.[110] By contrast, the prior year, when Judge Wright had asked the DOJ for help in New Orleans, Attorney General William Rogers advised Wright "that he should just postpone the whole thing."[111] By November 1961 a DOJ press release stated that "in school intergration [*sic*] there has been a basic change in policy—in implementing the U.S. Supreme Court's desegregation decision from abstention by the Federal Government, except during crisis or disaster—to affirmative and anticipatory action." The release cited the increase in desegregation in some large Southern cities, noting that department officials had "worked informally with officials in these cities throughout the summer to help bring about peaceful school desegregation."[112]

In 1962 Burke Marshall began speaking publicly about the DOJ's need for congressional authority to bring school desegregation cases. He repeatedly pointed out Congress's failure to grant such authority. In March, he lamented that school desegregation "is one area in which the Department has in the past sought authority from Congress, and it has been refused."[113] By May, he spoke with greater urgency: "Congress has not seen fit to enact any legislation to implement the Constitutional decision of the Supreme Court in the school cases of 1954, but we cannot avoid our responsibility to the Constitution and the law for that reason."[114] While HEW arguably could have suspended federal aid to segregated schools, or at least those schools receiving federal impact aid money, it declined to do so.[115] Testifying before a congressional committee, Marshall suggested that "Congressional action giving effect to the *Brown* ruling would be most helpful if there is to be significant progress in guaranteeing hundreds of thousands of children their constitutional rights." He preferred "the positive, direct approach of a desegregation suit to a withdrawal of funds" from segregated school systems and argued that fund termination would interfere with the objectives of federal funds for education programs.[116] Marshall's preference for court orders rather than fund termination foreshadowed the Nixon administration's controversial policy.

Even without congressional authority for the DOJ to bring school desegregation suits, Marshall needed to proactively monitor compliance with the growing number of desegregation orders in private cases. He noted that thirty-three school systems would begin implementing desegregation plans in fall 1962 and another twenty-four would expand desegregation "in some significant degree." Marshall envisioned his role as monitoring for potential problems.

Marshall and Doar believed that the division lacked authority to bring suits to desegregate ordinary school districts, except for suits to desegregate school districts receiving federal "impact aid" because of the large number of children of federal employees enrolled. At the beginning of the Kennedy administration, Attorney General Kennedy had asked Marshall what action was planned "with respect to segregated schools supported primarily for military bases."[117] Subsequently, Marshall began to plan for suits on behalf of children of federal employees in school districts receiving impact aid money because of the large federal presence, such as military bases, in their district. The division filed a case in September 1962 against the school system in Prince George County, Virginia, home of Fort Lee. While it won the case the following June, the victory would prove to be fleeting. Still fresh off this triumph, Marshall pressed US attorneys in Texas to negotiate with twenty-two impact districts and in January 1963 filed impact cases in five school districts.[118] If he won those suits, Marshall said, "It follows that within the limits of staff and time we are going to desegregate all impacted schools. Civil rights groups objected that this "piecemeal approach. . . . sounds good, but it doesn't really deliver anything."[119]

Initially, the Kennedy administration said it had little other authority over school desegregation. As Doar explained, "We didn't have any jurisdiction to bring school cases at that time, and we only entered school cases as friends of the court, or if there was a violation of a federal court order."[120] But the new administration soon returned to the Truman administration's model of filing amicus briefs to enforce not only court orders but also constitutional rights.

President Kennedy, however, continued to regard desegregation as an educational and not a legal problem.[121]

In January 1963, the DOJ filed a brief as amicus curiae in the only school desegregation case decided by the Supreme Court during the Kennedy administration.[122] Marshall argued the case, involving Knoxville, Tennessee, schools, in the Supreme Court. The issue was the validity of a desegregation order that allowed students whose race was in the minority in the school to which they were assigned to transfer to a school in which their race was in the majority. The brief asserted that the nature of the issues presented made it "again incumbent upon the United States to express its views." It pointed out that enforcement of *Brown* "is of extreme importance to millions of American citizens, and the attainment of a nation-wide system of non-discriminatory-public education with the least disturbance or other interference with public education is of vital interest to the country as a whole." The department argued that the plan was unconstitutional, and the court agreed. The DOJ also pointed out the snail's pace of school desegregation in the South and argued that Brown required "the elimination of segregation as soon as possible" and that the school boards had a heavy burden to justify any delays. The brief argued, "A prerequisite of every acceptable plan of desegregation is that it move definitely and expeditiously away from the old regime of racial discrimination."[123] The move to the desegregation phase reflected in part the values of the law enforcement phase: as Marshall wrote, to the extent that court decisions limiting the power of the police are ignored by the police "as the school decisions of 1954 have been ignored by most school boards in eleven states, cynicism, distrust of government, and disbelief in any kind of law will increase."[124]

Marshall had met with leaders in Huntsville, Alabama, in early 1962 and had concluded that voluntary desegregation was unlikely, that Alabama governor John Patterson would likely interfere if the Huntsville schools desegregated that fall, and that if desegregation were to occur the following year, the new governor, George Wallace, likely "will have to make a lot of noise but will give in at the end." He thought that for desegregation to occur in the fall of 1963 in Huntsville, "we will have to file suit.[125] The DOJ did sue Huntsville's surrounding school district in 1963, but the courts held the department had no authority to bring a school desegregation suit. A year earlier, the courts had allowed the department to sue to stop racial segregation in bus terminals governed by the Interstate Commerce Act. The court declined to extend that ruling to Huntsville, which was benefiting from federal impact aid owing to the large number of federal employees at the Redstone Arsenal.[126]

Marshall expressed pragmatic concerns about desegregation, in a letter in early 1963 to the executive director of the Southern Regional Council, an organization promoting better race relations in the South. Marshall straightforwardly warned that "it is not possible to get school desegregation legislation through Congress this year," though he acknowledged "next year may be a different question." Instead, Marshall thought that it might be possible to get Congress to pass legislation authorizing federal assistance to school districts undergoing desegregation. He thought that requiring all school districts to start desegregation was a bad idea because "obviously they would not," and this would lead to disrespect for the law. For their part, Martin Luther King Jr. and Student Nonviolent Coordinating Committee leader Robert Moses thought that the ballot was the key to Black civil rights. King had argued in 1957, "Give us the ballot and we will no longer have to worry the federal government about our basic rights." Agreeing, Marshall said that when African Americans had the vote and therefore could exert political influence in the South it would be easier to deal with desegregation.[127] Marshall did, nonetheless, actively and with a few successes seek desegregation of school systems serving students from US military families.

By contrast, as late as 1963, HEW persisted in its view that it could not withhold funds from racially discriminatory programs. Its secretary, Abraham Ribicoff, did agree, in March 1962, that impact aid should not be extended to segregated schools any longer. However, HEW staff opposed integrated schools on military bases and tried to delay implementing Ribicoff's decision. Finally, in July 1963, the DOJ told HEW that it could no longer fund racial discrimination.[128]

The peaceful integration of the University of Alabama in June 1963, by contrast with earlier events, reflected careful planning by the president, Attorney General Kennedy, Marshall, armed forces, and federal marshals. The lack of violence most likely also indicated a desire of Governor Wallace to treat his stand in the schoolhouse door as a symbol of his position rather than as a spark to riot as at the University of Mississippi a year earlier. The subsequent police riot at the Edmund Pettus Bridge in Selma in 1965 reflected his more aggressive side.[129] In any event, the plaintiffs in *Lee* could hope that the peaceful desegregation of the University of Alabama would be repeated when Tuskegee High School opened in September. And the DOJ could legitimately believe that it could ensure a peaceful opening of school in Tuskegee as well as the big cities in Alabama that were to be desegregated in September. The CRD already had established strong relations with the Macon County African American community, by bringing a voter discrimination suit against the county registrar. Doar spoke at the annual meeting of the Tuskegee Civic Association a month after desegregation of the University of Alabama and a month before Judge Johnson made the United States a litigating amicus and party in the *Lee* case.[130]

A DECADE AFTER THE BROWN ARGUMENT

In April 1963 Dr. Martin Luther King Jr. led the Good Friday peaceful demonstration in Birmingham. King's arrest for violating an injunction against the parade landed him in solitary confinement with no mattress or linens. There King wrote his famous "Letter from the Birmingham Jail." The letter's message, that African Americans would no longer wait for equal treatment and that white moderates had been part of the problem rather than the solution, slowly made its way into the country's consciousness. Not until June did it reach Attorney General Kennedy.[131] Meanwhile, Birmingham's treatment of the "children's" marchers in early May galvanized the country. This time Birmingham Commissioner of Public Safety Eugene "Bull" Connor's police broke up peaceful marches. The police used police dogs and "monitor guns" that combined water from two fire hoses into one nozzle to attack the children. They then arrested hundreds of African American youths. Photographs of the attacks shocked the nation.

A decade after *Brown v. Board of Education*, almost all the public schools of the Deep South remained segregated. As Marshall pointed out in a speech at the law school of historically African American Howard University, "It must be recognized that for the most part the period of compliance with the constitutional command is at an end. What more is to be accomplished must be accomplished by compulsion."[132] But what would be the source of that compulsion?

Civil rights had become a multipronged movement, with the activist organizations focusing their efforts on access to voting, employment, and public accommodations. Few lawyers in the region were willing to bring school desegregation cases. Instead, Marshall added, Southern lawyers "have counseled defiance, rather than compliance." And the federal government had been stymied in its efforts. Lacking statutory authority to sue for school desegregation, the DOJ had participated as an amicus curiae in a few cases, had tried to bring desegregation suits against school systems receiving federal aid for their students who were children of federal military or civilian families, and had initially but unsuccessfully backed part III of the Civil Rights Act of 1957, which would have allowed such DOJ suits.[133]

2. Macon County and Alabama's Racial Caste System

> I can only say that segregation is wrong today, it was wrong yesterday. Segregation was never right. But it is one of the most lamentable frailties of mankind that when one's wrong is most grievous, his self-justification is most passionate, perhaps in the pitiful hope that the fervor of his self-defense will somehow prove him right. But this doesn't make it so. And he doesn't fool himself.
>
> —*Former Virginia member of Congress, Richard Poff, quoted in an obituary by Paul Vitello, "Richard H. Poff, Who Withdrew Court Bid, Dies at 87,"* New York Times, *July 1, 2011*

> The caste interest is not merely economic. The whites have told themselves that education will make the Negro conscious of "rights" which he should not know about.
>
> —*Gunnar Myrdal,* An American Dilemma

Alabama's racial caste system was deeply embedded in Macon County's social fabric. It was within this context that *Lee v. Macon County Board of Education* became a central element of the African American resistance to Alabama's laws relegating them to secondary caste status. This chapter describes the soil from which the case grew: Alabama's caste system, the state's efforts to preserve the status quo after *Brown v. Board of Education*, the particulars of caste in Macon County, and the evolution of African American efforts to achieve equal treatment.

Under Presidents Kennedy and Johnson, the DOJ viewed its task as no less than dismantling the official caste system that had kept African Americans down for centuries, first through slavery and then through Jim Crow.[1] The Civil War had been over for a century, but the legacy of slavery was still very much with us. African American slaves in Alabama had been forbidden to learn how to read and write. Alabama's whites fought a bloody war seeking to maintain their mastery. Having lost the war, Southern whites sought to win the peace and to assert their superiority over the newly freed slaves. Once freed, African Americans could read and write without criminal penalty, but Alabama was slow to provide public schooling for Black students. As social scientists have explained, "The belief that education spoiled the slave carried over with but little modification for many years into the belief that education spoils a field hand."[2]

Segregated public schools were indispensable to the continuation of the racial caste system. Segregation was embedded in the 1901 Alabama constitution, which insisted that "separate schools shall be provided for white and colored children, and no child of either race shall be permitted to attend a school of the other race."[3] Those words remain in today's Alabama constitution, despite efforts to repeal it.[4] Even after *Brown*, the force of tradition and politics continued to govern and to exclude African Americans from attending school with white students. Segregation was, and remains, deep in the hearts and souls of white Alabamians.

ALABAMA AND THE POST-RECONSTRUCTION STATUS QUO

It is hard today to comprehend the completeness of the racial caste system. As Isabel Wilkerson notes, "caste and race are interwoven in America." Caste establishes a hierarchy, and racism places African Americans below the dominant whites in that hierarchy.[5] Alabama historian Wayne Flynt explains:

> The 1901 constitution not only stripped the ballot from black men but also prohibited interracial marriages and required separate schools for blacks and whites. Local custom as well as ordinances insisted that mental institutions, TB sanatoriums, prison, reform schools, public transportation, and hospitals also be racially segregated . . . Industries and unions sometimes excluded them, and when they were allowed, generally separated them from whites.[6]

Flynt could have added that restaurants, hotels, parks, water fountains, restrooms, and theaters were also racially segregated. White institutions such as churches and private clubs remained segregated. A white student at Tuskegee High School related, fifty years later, her experience as a church choir member: she watched as the church greeter locked the church doors to stop Black worshippers from entering; above her she looked at a stain glass window illustrating Jesus saying, "Knock and you shall enter."[7] Hobart Grooms, the conservative federal judge from Birmingham who served on the three-judge court that heard the statewide desegregation motion in *Lee*, resigned from his church of forty years when it refused to allow Black people to worship there.[8]

Macon County played a mixed role in Alabama's caste system, as home both to influential white plantation owners and to highly educated African Americans who worked at the Tuskegee Institute (now Tuskegee University) and the Tuskegee veterans' hospital. Macon is one of some eighteen counties that comprise Alabama's Black Belt, named for the richness of its cotton-producing soil and representative of its majority Black population, largely descended from the enslaved people who tilled that soil before the Civil War. In 1860 the population of Macon included more than 18,000 slaves and just 8,600 whites.[9] Today, the total population is about eighteen thousand—and 81 percent African American, one of the highest percentages in the nation. Tuskegee, the county seat, is about thirty-five miles east of Montgomery, the state capital and the first capital of the Confederacy. *Tuskegee*, in the language of the Creek, the region's original inhabitants, means warrior.

Macon County, like much of the South, experienced social upheaval following the Civil War. White residents of Alabama feared the destruction of their way of life, anticipating interference by the federal government in empowering the state's newly free Black citizens, who far outnumbered the whites in Black Belt counties. Indeed, after the Civil War more than 70 percent of Blacks in Alabama voted, resulting in a period of political equality, in which both whites and Blacks held office.[10]

Yet, that period would be brief. In 1870 James Alston, the leader of the local Black Republicans, was elected as a state representative. Local whites attacked his house, wounding him and his pregnant wife and leaving more than three hundred buckshot holes. Although several hundred armed Blacks came to protect Alston, most of them departed when their opponents promised no further violence. Alston's house was fired upon the following night, and whites warned that Blacks holding office could expect to be killed. Alston left Macon County shortly afterwards, and Macon County whites continued to dismantle Black and progressive political power, jailing several Blacks who had protected Alston and burning churches used for Republican meetings. In Macon County, as in Alabama and the rest of the Deep South, a violent revolution against the Reconstruction governmental order cemented the racial caste system as the new order. Although this new situation contradicted basic protections of the Reconstruction constitutional amendments, the federal government largely abandoned its enforcement responsibilities and left African Americans without effective recourse. By 1876 Blacks had been politically marginalized and would remain so for at least another nine decades. With Black political power removed, Macon County whites began solidifying the racial caste system. Yet they also viewed retention of the Black population as critical to success of the region's economy.[11]

Economic factors would prevent those Blacks who stayed from effectively asserting their equality. Most African Americans in Macon County remained dependent upon white landlords or storeowners for credit. A sociologist surveying Black farmers in the early 1930s found that nearly 90 percent were tenants.[12] This indebtedness to local whites meant any assertion of their rights risked crushing economic retaliation. As legal historian Risa Goluboff notes, "For black agricultural workers in the 1940s South, racial barriers were only one part of a full-blown white assault. Their complaints depict a world of white economic domination and black economic dependence; of white political power and black disfranchisement; of the ubiquitous potential for legally unrestrained white violence and the almost certain swift retribution against black violence, real or imagined."[13]

Even in the 1960s, some Black farmers still could afford only mules to plow their land. In 1932, some six hundred uneducated, poor, rural African Americans in Macon County—399 of then infected with syphilis—became the subjects of a study, conducted by the federal Public Health Service and Tuskegee Institute, which offered them free medical care but, unbeknown to the subjects, withheld syphilis treatment. A 1944 study of Tuskegee and the Black Belt noted that "in most particulars, the Supreme Court of the United States has given the States a free hand in dealing with the rights of the Negro. . . . The unquestionably unequal opportunities for public education have all become just as much a part of the social system of the United States as was slavery at the time of the Civil War."[14]

Macon County might have been an ordinary rural Black Belt county but for its cultivation of an African American community of middle-class professionals associated with Tuskegee Institute, the premier African American private college in Alabama, and the Tuskegee veterans' hospital. The Hospital for Sick and Injured Colored World War Veterans opened on February 12, 1923. While Macon County whites insisted that the hospital staff be all white, the president of Tuskegee Institute "used his influence with national Republican officials to ensure an all-black staff."[15]

Tuskegee Institute was founded by Booker T. Washington, its first principal, in 1881.[16] As the prominent Congregational minister Lyman Abbott put it in his introduction to Washington's autobiography, "In 1881 the Legislature of Alabama had appropriated two thousand dollars for starting a school for colored people in Tuskegee, which had been previously an educational center for the whites."[17] When the Hampton-educated Washington arrived from Virginia, he found "hundreds of hungry, earnest souls who wanted to secure knowledge." Yet Washington was surprised to find no teachers, no buildings, and no signs of a school. Washington understood that Tuskegee Institute was dependent upon white approval and ensured the school did not contest white dominance. He was convinced that Blacks must achieve educational and economic success to demonstrate their equality to whites. This position was controversial, and nationwide African Americans heatedly debated whether equality would come through education and hard work, as Washington urged, or through voting and litigation, as W. E. B. Dubois and other founders of the NAACP believed. Washington privately supported voting rights for African Americans, however, by helping to finance an unsuccessful challenge to Alabama's restrictive voting laws in 1903.[18]

Washington's experiences in Macon County illustrated concerns the Tuskegee Civic Association would face nearly sixty years later. The end of slavery freed people who had been denied the opportunity to learn how to make a budget, live within their means, and progress economically. Washington expressed frustration that some Blacks prioritized items associated with "higher" classes over the basics. He recounted one experience visiting a rural family: "I noticed that, while there were five of us at the table, there was but one fork for the five of us to use. In the opposite corner of that same cabin was an organ for which the people told me they were paying sixty dollars in monthly installments. One fork, and a sixty-dollar organ!" Washington also noted that most of the Black farmers he encountered were in debt. He found a similar focus on appearance over utility in education. "The students who came first seemed to be fond of memorizing long and complicated 'rules' in grammar and mathematics, but had little thought or knowledge of applying these rules to the everyday affairs of their life." Yet Washington was encouraged that "they were all willing to learn the right thing as soon as it was shown to them what was right." The Tuskegee Institute found itself not only teaching the higher subjects in education but also creating a "solid and thorough foundation" so that what students learned would benefit them economically and socially.[19]

Washington's hope that whites would voluntarily accept Blacks as equals did not come to pass. Instead, the white community came to view Tuskegee as a "model community," proof to the world that segregation and white domination were ideal for both races. White domination was cemented by ratification of Alabama's new constitution in 1901, which barred Blacks from registering to vote as a practical matter and imposed a cumulative poll tax as an additional barrier to voting.[20] Indeed, in 1900 "one hundred thousand black men had been enrolled as voters in Alabama. Ten years later all but 3,752 had been 'cleansed' from the voting rolls.'"[21] At the same time, although no change in political power occurred, Black economic power grew substantially. The Tuskegee Institute provided a substantial source of high-paying jobs and higher education to Black residents, and a middle-class community developed around it, comprising more than a thousand Black professionals by 1940. The addition of the Black Veterans Administration hospital in 1923 and the Tuskegee Army Airfield, designed for a training program for Black pilots, assisted in the creation of this community.[22] When Blacks began to assert their rights once again, this educated and independent community would be invaluable in defeating economic coercion.

The noted African American sociologist Charles Johnson wrote of Macon County in 1934, "It has been impossible to escape the force of tradition, as represented in the customs established under the institution of slavery, and adhered to by the white population in their relation to the Negroes, and by the Negroes in relation to themselves."[23] In the midst of World War II, the governor of Alabama attended Tuskegee Institute's Founder's Day celebration and suggested that perhaps things might change. "Do you want educational training, helpful aid, and a moving, step by step, to higher planes of achievement," he asked. "You are entitled to this and it should be granted more abundantly." The governor made it clear, however, that equality was to be achieved by "absolute racial segregation [and] independent racial development."[24] Foreshadowing the position that state officials would take in the 1960s, he insisted, "The two races are distinct. They occupy spheres in life that began in different origins, have continued in diverging channels and should remain separate, as they have always been since the creation."[25] The governor's speech cloaked inequality in the language of equality, reflecting the Booker T. Washington approach as most white people understood it. A little over a decade later, *Brown* punctured that illusion of separate but equal. By that time, African Americans, dissatisfied with the quality of their children's education, would be ready to abandon the tradition of segregation, even if most whites were not.

State Representative (later state senator) Samuel Martin Engelhardt Jr., elected in 1950, quickly became the leading opponent of Black equality in Macon County and a leader for racial segregation in Alabama. Engelhardt was a talented politician who used his wry sense of humor and public events such as dove hunts to appeal to voters. His family had deep ties to Macon County, and he owned a sixty-five-hundred-acre plantation near Shorter.[26] Arguing that increasing Black rights would lead to Black domination, he campaigned on a six-word platform: "I stand for white supremacy, segregation."[27] Engelhardt worked tirelessly to diminish and slow Black voter registration in Macon County.[28]

Engelhardt was also concerned by the potential for school desegregation. In 1952 the Alabama Legislative Reference Service prepared a memorandum for Engelhardt regarding options for maintaining the existing system. The memo was deeply pessimistic about the ability of the state to continue segregating schools and suggested that the only effective measure would be to use state funds to operate private schools. The following year, foreshadowing the complexities of *Lee*, the legislature explained, "The employment, seniority and tenure of teachers, the location and design of schools, the number and routing of school busses, the content and arrangement of the curriculum in every school, the standards of instructions and practically every other aspect of the educational system of the State are based upon the present separation and would have to be drastically revised if the principle of separation should be invalidated."[29] A further study of approaches taken by other Southern states was sent to Engelhardt in 1954.[30] Engelhardt—by then a state senator—threatened after *Brown*, "We will have segregation in the public schools or there will be no public schools."[31]

Like most Southern states, Alabama had sought ways around the abolition of slavery—a series of laws that effectively kept many African Americans in thrall to their former masters. White politicians could choose between two approaches to the racial caste system: they could either explicitly advocate for racial discrimination or engage in subterfuge. A prominent Southern columnist noted, "Subterfuge is something [white Southerners] have had to go in for all our lives, because of this race question."[32] In the wake of *Brown*, the Deep South opted for a mixed approach. Much of the rhetoric was couched in nonracial terms—judicial tyranny, states' rights, federal interference with education, and freedom of choice.[33] But other rhetoric was overtly racial—segregation, inferior Blacks, white supremacy, harking back to an earlier age when lynching was justified as necessary to protect chaste white women from brutish Black men.[34] Whatever the rhetoric, after the decision in *Brown*, Southern legislatures sought ways to circumvent the ruling instead of seeking to comply with the least possible disruption. Massive resistance became the call of the white politician.

Alabama whites assigned many reasons for their opposition to school desegregation. Some believed that racial segregation was divinely inspired, embracing a recurring misinterpretation of a biblical text describing a curse on Canaan, son of Ham, as referring to African Americans.[35] A legislative report stated, "The overwhelming majority of white citizens of Alabama are unalterably opposed to the idea of permitting the use of the public school system to coerce integration."[36] Opponents of desegregation expressed concern about sexual relations and marriage between whites and Blacks. They chanted "Integration means intermarriage," as if it followed that intermarriage must be bad, characterizing the result of intermarriage as "a mongrel race." The descendants of slave owners retained the antebellum knowledge that interracial sex was inevitable and could undermine the privileged status of whites. The Alabama constitution still prohibits "any law to authorize or legalize any marriage between any white person and a negro, or descendant of a negro." [37]

The racial caste system rested on three legs: political, economic, and social. Education was closely linked to all three. Educated Blacks were more likely to vote and even run for political office. Lack of education consigned Blacks to rely on whites economically, as sharecroppers and servants. Segregated schools reinforced social separation, a cornerstone of the racial caste system seen to benefit whites.[38] As Reinhold Niebuhr has observed, "The individual or the group which organizes any society, however social its intentions or pretensions, arrogates an inordinate portion of social privilege to itself."[39] The threat of desegregation drew out deep expressions of hostility, often directed at the federal courts. One letter to Judge Frank M. Johnson, the judge in *Lee* and other desegregation cases, argued, "If God had intended us to be equal he would never have had two races."[40] Other themes were disease, morals, and communism. A writer from Notasulga in Macon County wrote, "With the social diseases so prominent among our negro race, our innocent children will suffer from using the same facilities." The writer added that "desegregation will be the end of our white race" and "a mixed race will be a weak race."[41]

These sentiments were not confined to Alabama or the South. One letter to Johnson from New Hampshire threatened, "The day is approaching when our traitorous communist federal judges will face the wrath of the white people in America. . . . Your name is high on the list."[42]

In this political climate, officials and lawyers from four Southern states met in Birmingham in mid-1956 to discuss strategy to combat public school desegregation. John Patterson, the attorney general of Alabama, attended along with his assistant, Gordon Madison. The attendees realized that integration was inevitable but thought they had an obligation to Southern whites to delay it. As explained by Patterson's biographer Gene L. Howard,

> One of the delaying tactics proposed by the lawyers was to decentralize the power of school boards so that each system would be autonomous. The shift of power would require a multiplicity of suits to integrate individual schools or local school systems rather than having the entire state legally overwhelmed by the Justice Department in a single court order.[43]

Alabama writer John Hayman concluded, "The belief was that delays would be very expensive to the NAACP and other civil rights organizations and would finally deplete their treasuries."[44]

The strategy depended on Patterson and other Alabama officials resisting the temptation to deploy white supremacist rhetoric or action. It also assumed that local school authorities would fight for continued school segregation on their own, with no need for state interference. This proved problematic in places like Little Rock, where the local school boards decided to comply with *Brown* and state officials were compelled to use state power to enforce segregation. Segregationists there were inspired by lawmakers like Senator Eastland, who, unlike Patterson, argued that, in the words of historian Elizabeth Jacoway, "the only way to protect segregation was to use the power of the states." The Capital Citizens Council in Little Rock, citing Eastland, suggested that relying on resistance from individual districts would mean that "we are sitting ducks and will be picked off one by one."[45]

The Arkansas strategy had not been needed in Alabama in 1956, because no local school boards would comply with *Brown* without a court order. But the strategy of localizing the issue of school desegregation assumed that African American parents who wanted their children to attend desegregated schools lacked the resources to challenge the state or local authorities in court. While this was perhaps true in the short run, and while local officials remained faithful to segregation and state officials managed to tread carefully, it all began to fall apart within a few years. By 1963 the temptation of political gain from asserting state power over the schools led Wallace to interfere with school desegregation. And the NAACP LDF had found a new ally, in the Civil Rights Division of the United States Department of Justice.

For the first several years after *Brown*, no Alabama school system voluntarily complied with the decision. The Macon County school system ignored requests from African American parents to desegregate. Alabama repealed compulsory attendance laws and authorized the closing of schools and the public funding of private schools. While the Alabama legislature adopted a resolution declaring the *Brown* decision invalid, that resolution had no legal force. A court characterized it as "an escape valve through which the legislators blew off steam."[46] Alabama, like other Southern states, also adopted a pupil placement law creating a facially neutral procedure for pupil assignment and placing responsibility for assignments in the hands of the local school boards. This law replaced overt racial classifications with "more neutral classifications that could be used as substitutes for race, such as academic performance and moral background."[47] When Patterson left the Alabama governor's office in January 1963, the policy he had embraced as attorney general and continued as governor enabled him to say, "There was no integration in the schools when I took office and there is none today."[48]

"SEGREGATION FOREVER"–1963

In January 1963 Wallace delivered his now-infamous promise of "segregation forever." Given the adamant opposition of most white Alabamians to desegregation of any kind, civil rights advocates faced a difficult road. The solid-South congressional delegation blocked meaningful federal legislation and the small number of African American lawyers in the Deep South could not bring all the lawsuits that would be needed to bring about desegregation. The leading lawyer for desegregation, Thurgood Marshall, had predicted in 1952 that even if the *Brown* case were won, "We will have to go from county to county and from state to state even after we get it. . . . Bear in mind in Georgia you have two hundred and some counties. So . . . there is no short-cut to it."[49]

The organization that had spearheaded *Brown*, the NAACP LDF, like the NAACP proper, had limited resources. And, as the US Civil Rights Commission observed, "The only way for black families . . . to send their children to a white-attended public school was for one of their number to step forward, find a lawyer willing to take the case, and sue the local school officials."[50] Even where lawyers were available, fear prevented African American parents from seeking desegregation. Violence, loss of jobs, eviction from farms, refusal to mill their cotton—all these consequences had plagued Southern African Americans who had sought to assert their rights.

Despite those obstacles, 1963 proved to be a pivotal year for school desegregation in Alabama, as Black families retained local attorneys, who partnered with the LDF and sued local school boards for the admission of their children to white schools. The year began with Wallace's inaugural address, which set the tone for a decade of confrontation between the state and the federal government. Before the year ended, Wallace would have staged his unsuccessful "showdown" to block the desegregation of the University of Alabama and used state troopers to block the desegregation of K–12 public schools in four districts, including Macon County, where the *Lee* case was filed. The April demonstrations in Birmingham that year captivated the nation and were followed by the murder of four Black girls in the Sixteenth Street Church bombing in September. While the Kennedy administration initiated some enforcement efforts, not until passage of the 1964 Civil Rights Act did the federal executive have statutory authority to enforce *Brown*. It then became instrumental in bringing about substantial desegregation over the next ten years.

By the time *Lee v. Macon* landed on Judge Johnson's docket in 1963, school desegregation law had progressed little. Since *Brown II* and the Little Rock case, the Supreme Court had been remarkably quiet. The issue of what "all deliberate speed" actually meant had been left to the lower courts. The Supreme Court had upheld pupil placement laws on their face, while not addressing how they were implemented.[51] District and appellate judges reluctant to move on segregated education had fallen in line behind Judge John Parker of the Fourth Circuit Court of Appeals. Parker had ruled that the Fourteenth Amendment did not require integration; it simply forbade state enforced segregation.[52] Yet, at the same time, Black plaintiffs and their attorneys were beginning to find judges willing to consider their claims. In this period of volatility parents in Macon County, Alabama, set the stage for revolutionary change.

THE RISE OF THE TUSKEGEE CIVIC ASSOCIATION

In 1940 the racial population of Macon County remained much as it was before the Civil War. Despite the substantial Black majority, whites had successfully denied Black people political power. Only seventy-seven African Americans in the county were registered to vote in 1940.

Education was similarly unequal. White schools stayed open longer, 173 to 146 days, and featured half the students per teacher. In the 1938–1939 year the school system spent 14.75 times more on white students than on Black students. In that same year, the district spent no money at all on improving or creating new Black schools or on maintenance personnel, supplies, or even fuel or water for Black schools.[54]

Further, more white students were economically able to attend school. In the 1938–1939 school year only 73 percent of Black children were enrolled in school, and only 57 percent of those enrolled attended class daily. That number declined sharply in high school, to 8 percent of enrolled Black students attending class on a daily basis, compared 44 percent of enrolled whites. The disparity in both learning environment and the ability of Black children to attend school led to significant differences in education. While only 2 percent of whites were illiterate, 23 percent of Blacks were illiterate.[55]

The organization that represented African American teachers in Alabama observed in 1939,

> Maintenance of separate schools makes it easy for [the Southern] states to deprive Negroes of an equitable share of public school [*sic*] funds. . . . Thus, through disfranchisement and the separate

GEORGE WALLACE'S INAUGURAL SPEECH

George Wallace gave an inaugural speech written by a member of the Ku Klux Klan. The governor declared on January 14, 1963, that the nation looked to the "South for their hope to win this fight to win and preserve our freedoms and liberties."[53]

> Today I have stood, where Jefferson Davis stood, and took an oath to my people. It is very appropriate then that from this Cradle of the Confederacy, this very Heart of the Great Anglo-Saxon Southland, that today we sound the drum of freedom as have our generations of forebears before us done, time and again through history. Let us rise to the call of freedom-loving blood that is in us and send our answer to the tyranny that clanks its chains upon the South. In the name of the greatest people that heave ever trod this earth, I draw the line in the dust and toss the gauntlet before the feet of tyranny . . . and I say . . . segregation today . . . segregation tomorrow . . . segregation forever.

Those words by Klansman Asa Carter formed the foundation of Wallace's rise to national prominence and three campaigns for president—a rise only halted by an assassination attempt in 1972.

school system, the South has excluded the Negro from consideration in the equitable distribution of (state) funds to all citizens of school age.[56]

By 1950 the state NAACP had disavowed the "separate but equal doctrine" and asserted "vigorous opposition to any and all forms of compulsory segregation on the basis of race."[57] At the Alabama NAACP convention in Anniston that year, the principal speaker was national NAACP executive secretary Walter White. Decrying the "Negro-white caste system," White called for an end to discrimination in the public schools, noting, "The most direct educational discrimination against the Negro can be found in the South's segregated school system."[58] The following year White spoke again to the Alabama NAACP convention, stressing the cost of segregation and its role in weakening the United States in its fight against Communism. He urged the "enlightened South" to "persuade churches, trade unions, parent-teachers association and others to oppose the philosophy and propaganda of fear of the [segregationist politicians] Byrneses, Byrds, Talmadges, and Fielding Wrights that horrible things will occur if segregation is broken down."[59]

Charles Gomillion had come to Tuskegee Institute as a sociology professor in 1928 and immediately found himself at odds with whites after he was insulted by a local merchant. As he settled into Tuskegee, he became concerned about the inequality in money spent on education.[60] Gomillion combined Booker T. Washington's focus on education with W. E. B. Du Bois's focus on voting and came to believe that greater political participation was necessary to right this and other inequalities. Over time, he emerged as the clear leader of

Two weeks after Wallace's 1963 inauguration, *Lee v. Macon County Board of Education* was filed in federal court in the Middle District of Alabama, setting up years of confrontation between Judge Frank Johnson and Wallace. In Johnson, Wallace found the perfect target as he desperately tried to prevent desegregation of Alabama schools.

Wallace spared no rhetorical quarter for Johnson, calling the latter's decisions products of a "judicial tantrum" and asserting that he was "unstable and erratic" in addition to being "rash, headstrong and vindictive." Johnson responded with his court orders and did his best to not to make Wallace a political martyr. They later tangled over the state's treatment of prisoners and patients in state mental hospitals. After a 1976 decision by Johnson against the state, Wallace, again running for president, said that a vote for him "might give a barbed wire enema to some federal judges." And there was no mistaking who he meant.[61]

the movement for Black equality in Tuskegee. Growing up in South Carolina, Gomillion became intimately familiar with discrimination. During his education in Georgia, he read the *Crisis* magazine, edited by Du Bois, and grew skeptical of Washington's accommodationist stance. However, his studies at Tuskegee and Fisk University softened this position. Gomillion returned from Nashville to Tuskegee inclined to advocate for equality in a measured and orderly manner.[62] Tuskegee civil rights activists adhered to Gomillion's leadership for many years.

Substantial Black efforts to achieve political equality accelerated in the late 1930s. The Tuskegee Men's Club, formed in 1910, pushed greater Black political participation, focused on voter registration. It later became the Tuskegee Civic Association (TCA), to reflect the efforts made by women, who had earned the right to vote in 1920.[63] White people felt threatened by its activities. By 1939 Probate Judge William Varner, a leading local conservative, described the Black vote as "getting to be a serious menace." The TCA worked on a number of fronts "to achieve a type of society in which all citizens [had] the opportunity to participate in societal affairs, and to benefit from and enjoy public services in keeping with their interests, abilities, and needs, without limitations or restrictions based on race, color, creed or national origin."[64]

The TCA was grounded in the beliefs of Booker T. Washington and devoted substantial resources to Black education, promotion of Black economic knowledge and businesses, and maintenance of a healthy Black community. However, the TCA became impatient with discrimination, perhaps because the members realized they held a stronger position than earlier, as a result of their economic independence, and indeed white economic dependence upon them. They began to take a more aggressive stance, persistently asserting their political rights and filing lawsuits. Yet they retained elements of moderation, accepting liberal whites as members, and asserting their rights in a way that would convert rather than alienate whites.[65]

The TCA frequently petitioned local government to improve the infrastructure in the Black sections of town. Some petitions were successful, as when traffic lights were requested and installed in 1949.[66] Other requests were less so, as when the city council delayed fifteen years before responding to a request for a sewer system, or refused to improve the roads in Black neighborhoods, citing a lack of funds. The TCA also worked to facilitate mail service by ensuring that streets were named and maintained, houses numbered, and mailboxes properly located.

Fighting alongside the TCA was the Tuskegee branch of the NAACP, formed in 1944. Alabama attorney general John Patterson briefly put the branch out of business in 1956 by requiring it to reveal its membership lists, but it played a vital role in the struggle in Tuskegee before and after the Supreme Court in 1958 overturned Patterson's effort to shut the organization down. The branch answered to the state NAACP, which initially sought equalization of Black and white teacher salaries, school facilities, buses, and curricula.[67] The president of the Tuskegee branch, though, argued in 1951, "There can be no real elevation or equality in politics, in education, in housing, in transportation, or in the courts, until segregation is eliminated from our system and our thinking. That is our goal."[68] After the decision in *Brown*, one Tuskegee branch newsletter urged that new members join so that the NAACP could "put to full use, the instruments fashioned by our highest judiciary, and work incessantly toward a true emancipation of the Negro."[69]

MOBILIZING FOR THE RIGHT TO VOTE

A number of obstacles impeded registration of Black voters in Alabama. The first was the requirement that white voters vouch for would-be Black voters. The economic independence and wealth of middle-class Black people were crucial in overcoming this obstacle. Black buyers could make large purchases conditional on merchants vouching for them before the registration committee. Gomillion secured his right to vote in return for agreeing to have a white contractor build his house, for example.[70]

In addition to the strictly legal barriers, the Board of Registrars also misread the law. When T. Rupert Broady in 1941 secured local merchants to vouch for him, he was told that registration required both land ownership and literacy, although the law clearly stated that only one was required. After Broady threatened a lawsuit the registration board caved and permitted his registration.[71] VA hospital worker William P. Mitchell went twice to the court of appeals with his challenge to the voucher requirement before the board registered him.[72]

State officials responded to these challenges by intensifying their resistance. The registrars simply stopped meeting, and when they did meet, they often concealed the meeting location in order to avoid and discourage applications from rural Black registrants. It became difficult to find willing members to serve on the board, further compounding registration difficulties.[73]

African Americans briefly enjoyed access to registration after populist governor Jim Folsom appointed Herman Bentley to the board of registrars at the end of 1948. Bentley registered hundreds of Black voters before the other members of the registration board stopped attending meetings, causing the board once again to fall into inaction. But too many Black citizens were now registered for politicians to safely ignore them. In 1950 a notoriously racist sheriff, Pat Evans, was replaced by a moderate white, Preston Hornsby, in what was the first Black political victory in eighty years.[74] On the eve of the decision in *Brown*, the NAACP drafted questions for candidates in the May 1954 Democratic primary, including, "Will you be willing to abide by the decision of the United States Supreme Court and sponsor legislation designed to carry out the spirit of this decision in the pending school cases?"[75] Jim Folsom won the primary, and the NAACP drew up for presentation to the incoming administration, "a simple statement as to what the Negro in Alabama expects" from it. The expectations included "spend no public funds for the erection of segregated public schools" but said nothing about abolishing racially segregated public schools.[76]

As a result of Black voting power, the degree of racism politicians were able to exhibit while remaining electable decreased. Yet whites strongly resisted the idea of a Black person holding office, as demonstrated when the highly qualified Jessie Parkhurst Guzman ran for the school board and lost on a strictly racial vote in 1954.[77]

In 1957 State Senator Engelhardt successfully sponsored legislation to gerrymander the city of Tuskegee into a twenty-eight-sided figure that excluded 410 of the 420 Black voters from the city limits. In addition, Engelhardt attempted to dissolve Macon County and incorporate it into the surrounding counties to dilute the power of the Black vote. However, this effort was unsuccessful because the Tuskegee Institute and the VA hospital were centers of Black power that no other county was willing to absorb.[78]

In response to the gerrymander, the African American population of Macon County mobilized to a degree not seen since Reconstruction, boycotting white businesses in 1957. The boycott persisted for three years until Gomillion successfully challenged the gerrymander in the Supreme Court case of *Gomillion v. Lightfoot.*[79] As a result, two African Americans, the Reverend K. L. Buford and Dr. Stanley Hugh Smith, were elected to the city council—the first

Blacks elected since Reconstruction ended. The council adopted a statement, acknowledging, "today may well mark the end of one era and the beginning of another in the life of our community." The council statement promised to base policies on "justice and fairness to all concerned."[80]

LITIGATING THE RIGHT TO REGISTER TO VOTE

The Civil Rights Act of 1957 established the United States Commission on Civil Rights and authorized it to investigate complaints of racial discrimination. The first complaint the new commission received came from William P. Mitchell of the TCA in September 1958. He sent fourteen affidavits from African Americans in Macon County whom the county registrars had refused to register. The complainants included "teachers, house-wives, students, farmers, and U.S. civil service employees."[81] The commission's investigations and hearings met resistance from Patterson, the Macon County registrars, and Judge Wallace, who impounded registration records from nearby Barbour County. Macon County African Americans testified to their experiences and their desire to become registered voters, and the DOJ sued in federal court to compel the state and local officials to cooperate with the hearings. Judge Johnson ordered them to appear and testify and produce the records. The commission concluded that the records reflected racial discrimination.

In February 1959, the United States sued Alabama and the Macon County Board of Registrars, alleging racial discrimination in voter registration in Macon County. This was the DOJ's first Alabama voting rights lawsuit under the 1957 act. The registrars resigned from office, but the Supreme Court held that the suit could go forward against the State of Alabama. Department attorneys became intimately familiar with Macon County, the TCA, and local officials. Seventy witnesses testified at the trial. In March 1961 Judge Johnson found that the registrars had discriminated against African American applicants for registration. Less than 10 percent of the approximately 11,900 eligible black citizens of voting age in Macon County were registered, as compared with almost all the approximately 2,800 whites of voting age. The court identified six activities of the board that discriminated against Black aspiring voters, ranging from helping whites but not Blacks to complete their applications to registering whites but rejecting Blacks with errors on their applications.[82]

Given the board's history of discrimination and creativity the court determined that prohibiting the discriminatory practices was insufficient. Instead, the court entered a positive decree mandating practices by the board. The decree first ordered the immediate registration of sixty-four Black applicants who had been rejected. The court further required the board to meet for two full days each month, limited the length of any writing samples, allowed Blacks to act as vouchers for applicants, established procedures for notifying applicants, and required monthly reports on the board's activities.[83]

Six months later, the court found that the board had briefly complied before reverting to earlier practices, reducing the average applicants heard each day from forty-four to eighteen.[84] The court ordered an additional eighty-four applicants registered and reiterated its earlier order prohibiting the rejection of applicants for technical errors.

The matter effectively ended there. The court retained jurisdiction over the matter in order to ensure compliance, finding further violations in 1965, but the tide had turned. By the end of 1963 Black voters outnumbered whites, 4,040 to 2,800.[85] The DOJ's voting case destroyed one leg of the official racial caste system in Macon County. What the CRD and the court had learned would help them navigate the next challenge, education.

3. The School Desegregation Case Begins

> "Separate but equal" has had its day. And what has it netted us? Nothing more than a two-standard existence.
>
> —*Della D. Sullins, speech to Tuskegee Civic Association, October 6, 1959, printed in* Women and the Civil Rights Movement, 1954–1965, *eds. Davis W. Houck and David E. Dixon*

> A great change is at hand, and our task, our obligation, is to make that revolution, that change, peaceful and constructive for all.
>
> —*John F. Kennedy, televised address to the nation on civil rights, June 11, 1963*

The Tuskegee Civic Association then turned its attention to the schools. For years, Macon County Blacks had appealed to state and local officials to end school segregation.[1] In 1955 D. I. Beasley, president of the Tuskegee chapter of the NAACP, wrote to the Macon County School Board on behalf of thirty-two African American parents to ask what steps the board was taking to comply with *Brown v. Board of Education.* When the board brushed off Beasley's request, the president of the state NAACP forwarded the correspondence to Thurgood Marshall, asking his "approval and guidance" for litigation.[2] The TCA sent telegrams to Governor Jim Folsom protesting state legislation intended to prevent *Brown* from going into effect. In 1956 the TCA published a letter in a local newspaper asking the school board to consider desegregation, and other appeals followed in the intervening years.[3] Della Sullins, one of the petitioners, argued that "only where there is equal opportunity for a minority group may a society begin to achieve a toleration for it."[4]

White resistance to desegregation was especially vehement in the Black Belt, where white students were both heavily outnumbered and tended to receive highly favored access to educational resources. For example, Macon County's schools enrolled 5,317 African American students and only 970 white students.[5] Two of the three white schools each covered grades 1–12, and only one of them had enough students to meet Alabama's minimum size standard.[6] The pupil-teacher ratio in the white schools was half that of the Black schools.[7]

The buildings for white schools were valued at more than five times per pupil than the schools for African Americans, and there were three times as many books per white child than per Black child.[8] Despite these obvious disparities, the all-white school board failed to respond to the petition to desegregate.

At this point, it would have been reasonable to expect that the United States government would step in to insist that the school board comply with the United States Constitution. The US criminal code made it a crime for state and local officials to willfully deny constitutional rights, and the Macon County officials were doing exactly that. However, it was well known that a criminal prosecution, tried before a predominantly white Alabama jury, would never result in a conviction for such an offense. As Robert Carr has explained, while some barriers to obtaining such a conviction might be fixed, the core barriers would remain, to wit, "local prejudice against the victim, and antagonism caused by federal interference."[9] And although there had been efforts to authorize the US attorney general to bring civil suits to remedy denials of constitutional rights, Congress had rejected the idea. Perhaps the attorney general could have tried to sue on behalf of the children of the federal employees at the Veterans Administration hospital in Tuskegee, but an Alabama federal court rejected this approach in a May 1963 decision involving children of employees at the Redstone Arsenal in Huntsville, saying the suit "represents an attempt by the executive arm of the Government to use the judicial arm to bypass the legislative arm in contravention of the principle of separation of powers. Except in the field of voting rights, the Congress has granted the Government no authority to bring such a suit as this. In fact, it has refused to grant such permission."[10]

Meanwhile, the secretary of defense also wrote to school superintendents to tell them that the military would help dependents apply to white schools; that letter seems to have had no effect. For their part, members of the House of Representatives pointed out that the federal government was not shouldering its responsibility to secure constitutional rights "when the U.S. Government is only free to enter a desegregation suit as *amicus curiae*."[11] Still, this is how the DOJ would soon become involved in the *Lee* case.

Initially, however, it fell to the African American parents to undertake the litigation in Macon County and elsewhere. In the 1962–1963 school year, all the school districts in Alabama remained segregated.[12] In September 1962 the TCA petitioned the Macon County School Board to develop a desegregation plan. The board did not respond.[13] In December the TCA revealed that it was "working with certain persons interested in the immediate availability of improved educational opportunities for their children. . . . [on] certain plans."[14] The association hired a young Black lawyer, Fred Gray, along with his colleague, Solomon Seay, and lawyers from the NAACP LDF, headquartered in New York, to file their case. Gray had graduated from law school in 1954 and rapidly took on major civil rights cases, including the cases to desegregate city buses in Montgomery, the University of Alabama, and the *Gomillion v. Lightfoot* challenge to the racial gerrymander that excluded African Americans from voting in Tuskegee.

In early January 1963, Charles Gomillion wrote to Gray that the TCA would pay him $500 immediately, another $500 when Gray filed the school desegregation case, another $500 after district court argument, and $500 each for appeals in the Court of Appeals and Supreme Court. The letter added, "If the Macon County schools are desegregated before the case reaches the U.S. Circuit Court of Appeals or the U.S. Supreme Court, the TCA will pay you the difference between the $2,500 agreed upon and what it will have paid you on account."[15] That same day he wrote as well to parents who had attended a conference with Gray "last Saturday" and another letter to the parents who did not attend, setting a meeting with Gray with their children for Saturday, January 12.[16]

On January 28, 1963—two weeks after Wallace's "segregation forever" inauguration speech—parents representing sixteen school-age children from eight families living in Tuskegee filed their suit. A photograph of some of the plaintiffs shows a grimly determined Detroit Lee, slender and balding, while his wife, Hattie Lee, looked at the camera quizzically.[17] They brought the case in Montgomery, seat of the US District Court for the Middle District of Alabama, which meant that the case would be heard by the only federal judge in that district, Frank M. Johnson.

Two years before the *Lee* case landed on Johnson's desk, J. W. Peltason's study of the demands on Southern federal judges assigned to school desegregation cases contrasted the situations of Johnson and Wallace, his former law school classmate, and, at the time, a state court judge. Peltason described the case in which Wallace had defied Johnson's order to turn over voter registration records to the US Civil Rights Commission. The commission had asked that Johnson enforce the order. "As a white Southerner, he . . . would endanger his stature within Alabama if he actively supported the Civil Rights Commission." According to Peltason, Johnson's dilemma was "characteristic of the difficult position of Southern district judges. These judges will do what they must; they can hardly be expected on their own initiative to move against the local power structure."[18] Johnson, though, was one of a group of Eisenhower judicial appointees who were not beholden to the white supremacist Southern branch of the Democratic Party. Growing up in Winston County, Alabama, which had declined to secede from the Union during the Civil War and was sometimes known as the Free State of Winston, Johnson was surrounded by people with "a fiercely independent attitude and personality." As he put it, "They believe in a person's dignity, and they believe each person is possessed of and is entitled to integrity. They believe that without regard to race."[19] As a United States attorney, Johnson in 1954 successfully prosecuted an Alabama plantation owner who had treated an African American employee as a virtual slave, beating him to death when he tried to run away.

Johnson had already heard two voting rights cases involving Macon County, which made him even more familiar with the operation of the racial caste system there. The United States had been the plaintiff in one of those cases and had litigated others before Johnson. At the beginning of the Kennedy administration, he had told John Doar that he planned to ask the United States to enter any school desegregation case filed in his district.[20] *Lee* was the first school desegregation case to come before Johnson, and his initial actions reflected some concern on his part. Specifically, Johnson immediately visited the chambers of Judge Richard Rives of the US Court of Appeals for the Fifth Circuit to ask him whether the case required a three-judge district court, as it might lead to the court finding Alabama's "pupil placement statute" unconstitutional. Rives, in turn, asked Chief Judge Tuttle, who responded that prior cases had held that a three-judge court was not required.[21] Johnson had developed great respect for the CRD, and within days of the filing, he made good on his promise and contacted the division to say he planned to ask the United States to participate as amicus curiae.[22]

Rules of the Supreme Court and US courts of appeals allow the United States to participate in cases in those courts as amicus curiae, as the government had done in *Brown v. Board of Education.* In early 1961 the DOJ was invited to file an amicus brief in a school desegregation case in the Southern District of New York, which it did, also filing one on the appeal of the trial court decision to the court of appeals during the summer of 1961. The department had also filed such a brief in the *Goss* case in the Supreme Court in January 1963, and Assistant Attorney General Burke Marshall argued the case in the Supreme Court in March.[23]

Johnson believed that the power to call on amici was a traditional judicial tool for getting help "not only in the decree's formulation, but also in its implementation and, if necessary, its monitoring."[24] He had developed trust that Doar and the CRD would ably discharge the role of amicus. In this he was not alone. Legal scholar and former Doar assistant Owen Fiss explained, "Federal judges attached great weight to whatever the attorneys of the Department of Justice said, partly because of the traditional relationship between the federal judiciary and the department, and partly because the department was speaking not only for the alleged victims, but also for the United States."[25] One court explained:

> Unlike the situations in which we fear that a party may be attempting to profit at the expense of unrepresented individuals, e.g., class actions and shareholder derivative suits, we here have as plaintiff the government department charged with seeing that the laws are enforced. We therefore need not fear that the pecuniary interests of the plaintiff and defendant will tempt them to agree to a settlement unfair to unrepresented persons, but can safely assume that the interests of all affected have been considered.[26]

Johnson's relationship with the CRD was complicated. Whether based on the mutual respect between Doar and Johnson or on the judge's felt need for backup in what had become a battle with Wallace, Johnson often called upon Doar to investigate, provide advice, and enforce his orders. The

FRED GRAY, CIVIL RIGHTS ATTORNEY

If Fred Gray had been white, his name on the official stenographic court transcript in Alabama would have been "Mr. Gray." Instead, it read "Lawyer Gray," one of the hundreds of ways the racial caste system made African Americans smaller and less human.[27]

When he graduated from Alabama State College for Negroes, there was no law school in his home state that he could legally attend. Instead, Alabama had what were called "out-of-state arrangements," which reimbursed African Americans to attend graduate schools in states that did not discriminate based on race. Gray was accepted at Case Western Reserve Law School in Cleveland and began his studies in September 1951, taking a segregated train to Ohio.[28] Ironically, payment for his legal education had been approved by Austin Meadows, the state superintendent of education, with whom Gray was soon to battle in the courts.[29]

While his name may not be as well known nationally as those of the prominent civil rights leaders of the '50s and '60s, Gray was involved at important moments in ways both big and small, and, as a lawyer, tried landmark cases. On December 1, 1955, he had lunch in Montgomery with his friend Rosa Parks, who later that day

(continued on the next page)

refused to move from the whites-only seats to the back of a city bus and was arrested. A few days later, Gray represented Parks in her first court appearance in a case that ignited a year-plus-long boycott that ended segregation on city buses.

In 1962 Gray represented four prominent clergymen in *New York Times Co. v. Sullivan*, in which the US Supreme Court eventually established the right of news organizations to write critically about public figures without fear of being found guilty of libel. The case stemmed from a newspaper ad exposing the brutal police response to civil rights demonstrations in Montgomery.

In 1965 Gray successfully litigated an action, *Hosea Williams v. George C. Wallace*, which forced the governor to protect protesters marching from Selma seeking the right to vote. The case was filed after Wallace's state police and local deputies viciously beat and teargassed marchers at the Edmund Pettus Bridge in Selma. Television footage of this event helped galvanize public opinion that pressured Congress to pass the Voting Rights Act of 1965.

requests ranged from asking for analysis of school district reports to the court or for investigation of reports of state assistance to segregated private schools, to asking that the government tape a speech that Lurleen Wallace was planning to make regarding the anticipated statewide order in *Lee*.[30] When Doar did provide analysis of school district reports to the court, Johnson carefully reviewed the analyses and sometimes commented on errors in them.

Johnson's request for the United States to enter the Tuskegee case came at a time of intense activity in the CRD. In January 1963, for example, the division had filed appeals in two voting rights cases, filed a motion for contempt in one such case, had worked with the solicitor general to file a school desegregation amicus brief in the Supreme Court, and had filed the suits seeking to desegregate school systems in federally impacted areas. In July 1963, when the CRD formally entered *Lee* as a litigating amicus, the division was trying four voting rights cases and filing four more voting rights cases and a records inspection case while also preparing Attorney General Kennedy for his testimony that month on the proposed civil rights act. When the department entered *Lee*, it had not yet adopted a goal to pursue other than allowing those Black children who wished to attend white schools to do so. Nor had it developed a plan for implementing desegregation throughout Alabama or the Deep South.[31]

Although the defendants filed a perfunctory motion asking the court to dismiss the case, the law was clear, and the facts of segregation were indisputable: no public school in Alabama enrolled both white and Black students. Wallace had promised at his inauguration in January: to fight the federal government and the courts: "That from this day, from this hour . . . from this minute . . . we give the word of a race of honor that we will tolerate their boot in our face no longer. . . . and let those certain judges put that in their opium pipes of power and smoke it for what it is worth."[32]

While Wallace's words fed on the biases of most white Alabamians, some white citizens spoke out in favor of compliance with federal desegregation orders. The newly elected attorney general, Richmond Flowers, while promising to fight for segregation, warned against taking actions that "can only bring disgrace to our state, military law upon our people." A group of religious leaders issued "An Appeal for Law and Order and Commonsense," predicting that "rebellion against desegregation will bring 'violence, discord, confusion, and disgrace' to Alabama." However, the Episcopal Diocese convention tabled a motion to endorse the clergy resolution.[33]

Wallace followed up with a dangerous charade designed to give the impression that he was preventing the desegregation of the University of Alabama, announcing that he would defy the order to do so. On June 11, 1963, he made his famous stand in the schoolhouse door, confronting Deputy Attorney General Nicholas Katzenbach. President Kennedy and Attorney General Kennedy treated Wallace's defiance as a law enforcement issue. The next day the African American students, Vivian Malone and James Hood, quietly enrolled in the university, with federalized National Guard troops ready to protect them. This became the catalyst for President Kennedy's speech the next night proposing that Congress adopt a new civil rights act that would allow the federal government to bring school desegregation cases. "It ought to be possible

FRANK M. JOHNSON AND JOHN DOAR

On May 17, 1954, as Frank M. Johnson was persuading the federal court jury to convict a plantation owner of holding a Black man as a slave, and as a country lawyer in New Richmond, Wisconsin, named John Doar was growing bored with his practice, the Supreme Court of the United States decided in *Brown v. Board of Education* that state-imposed racial segregation in the public schools was unconstitutional. These two veterans of World War II would become central figures in the desegregation of Alabama's public schools.

When Assistant Attorney General for Civil Rights Harold Tyler asked his Princeton classmate John Doar to become his top assistant during the last months of the Eisenhower administration, Doar jumped at the offer. He had little knowledge of the Deep South and later admitted that he had not seen how bad the corruption was when he was stationed in Clarksdale, Mississippi, when he was in the Army Air Forces in 1943. "Maybe I was just blind to seeing it," he thought. However, he found it unfair that the racial caste system had allowed the Deep South to dominate the Congress through the seniority system.[34]

Frank Johnson had returned to his home in Winston County, Alabama—the only reliably Re-

(continued on the next page)

publican county in the state—after his army service. He left his private practice in nearby Jasper when Eisenhower appointed him to be United States attorney in Birmingham. He moved to Montgomery in 1955 as Eisenhower elevated him to become the sole United States District judge in Alabama's capital, a post that would later bring him into conflict with his former classmate at the University of Alabama Law School, George Wallace.

Johnson and Doar grew to respect one another as Doar brought voting rights cases in Johnson's court. While they were not social friends, Doar had many conversations with Johnson in the 1960s. According to Owen Fiss, "They relied upon each other because they had this total respect, and they respected their differences."[35] But when Doar, who had never before tried a criminal case, prosecuted in Johnson's court the men who killed Viola Liuzzo in 1965 as she drove from Selma to Montgomery, Johnson did not let his regard for Doar interfere with his conduct of the trial, reprimanding Doar when he asked leading questions. The jury found the defendants guilty.[36]

The two Republicans had much in common besides practice as country lawyers and their common uniform of blue suit and white shirt. Tall, ramrod straight, with penetrating eyes and a commanding presence, they were stern and demanding and held lawyers

. . . for American students of any color to attend any public institution they select without having to be backed up by troops," the president declared. "We are confronted primarily with a moral issue. It is as old as the Scriptures and is as clear as the American Constitution." He rested the need for US government action to desegregate schools on a two-pronged argument: "The orderly implementation of the Supreme Court decision, therefore, cannot be left solely to those who may not have the economic resources to carry the legal action or who may be subject to harassment."[37] In other words, we needed "orderly" implementation of *Brown*, and private plaintiffs faced difficult barriers in completing the task.

SCHOOL OPENING, FALL 1963

Six months after *Lee* was filed, the pace in Johnson's court suddenly quickened. In July 1963, a month after President Kennedy's civil rights speech, Fred Gray filed a motion for immediate relief for his clients in Tuskegee. A few days later, the Fifth US Circuit Court of Appeals ordered immediate relief in desegregation cases in Birmingham and Mobile. Thus, the court in *Lee* knew it was required to act and also knew Wallace was likely to make trouble. So the following week, some six months after first indicating he wanted the United States to enter the case as a friend of the court, Johnson not only joined the United States in that capacity, as the courts in Little Rock, New Orleans, and Mississippi had done, but he took the important additional step of appointing the United States of America as a party. He justified this unusual order by expressing "the opinion that the public interest in the administration of justice, of law and order, and of protecting the authority and integrity of the lawfully constituted courts of the United States should be represented in these proceedings."[38] This formulation altered the language Judge Skelly Wright had used in bringing the United States into the New Orleans case and the Fifth Circuit had used in the University of Mississippi case: "in order to maintain and preserve the due administration of justice and the integrity of the judicial processes of the United States." The addition of the words "law and order" transformed the role of the United States from protector of court orders to protector of law, which in the context of school desegregation cases meant protector of constitutional rights, the very role that Congress had twice denied the DOJ. From then on, the case would be called "Anthony T. Lee, et al., Plaintiffs and United States of America, Plaintiff and Amicus Curiae v. Macon County Board of Education." Burke Marshall immediately requested the Federal Bureau of Investigation to use "such sources as may be available" to monitor plans or activities that might interfere "with the carrying out of the court's order."[39] The government's agreement to enter the case signaled that the administration was prepared to support a revolution by law—a radical change in Alabama society imposed by the superior force of the federal government.

St. John Barrett, Burke Marshall's second assistant, characterized the government's role as "twofold." First, the DOJ should "advise and assist with respect to enforcement" of the court's orders. Second, it should "prevent obstruction to the carrying out of the order." However, the advise-and-assist function that Barrett envisioned included views of what relief the court should order: "If the Judge

to high standards. Doar liked to paraphrase an opinion of Justice Holmes: CRD lawyers must turn square corners.[40] Above all else, they shared a deep commitment to fairness and enforcing the law. Finally, they shared a bête noir in Johnson's law school classmate and one-time friend Wallace. Beginning with the case challenging Wallace's refusal to provide voter records to the United States Commission on Civil Rights, to the desegregation of schools, to the right of civil rights advocates to march from Selma to Montgomery, the CRD repeatedly found itself in Johnson's court with Wallace on the other side. Wallace was equally contemptuous of Frank Johnson and the government attorneys. Government lawyers were "pointy-headed bureaucrats with thin briefcases full of guidelines."[41]

Faced with Wallace's repeated resistance and grandstanding, Johnson needed trusted assistance in handling the race discrimination cases. Doar had found a courageous federal district judge willing to go where the law and facts took him.

orders a large number of Negroes assigned to formerly white schools he should so frame his decree as to require that initial assignments be made without regard to race."[42]

Less than a month later, the court held the first of many hearings in Montgomery, with Gray representing the plaintiffs. Gray was a corresponding attorney for the NAACP LDF Fund, and the LDF assigned Constance Baker Motley, later a distinguished federal district judge in New York, as the lead co-counsel. Looking at all of Gray's activities during this time, one can see why he might welcome the presence of the United States, particularly in light of the enforcement issues that emerged.

Alabama assistant attorney general Gordon Madison represented the defendants. He had a record of defending racial segregation in Alabama in scores of cases and had participated in a 1956 meeting about how to stave off desegregation. A career lawyer in the Alabama attorney general's office, Madison now had a new boss, Richmond Flowers, whose inaugural speech had promised to fight for segregation but not to defy federal decrees. Flowers created a new federal section in the attorney general' and named Madison, "an experienced and brilliant lawyer," as its chief.[43] In another case, Madison compared defending desegregation suits to playing bridge: "You play each hand so that you lose as few hands as possible." He added, "As an individual, I would say (the reform schools) are still better the way they are (segregated), but as a lawyer I can't say that."[44] Although he believed in segregation, he got along with his opponents in race cases and acted the role of a gentleman lawyer. CRD attorney David L. Norman represented the United States. The LDF lawyers and the DOJ lawyers worked cooperatively.[45] Norman was a lawyer's lawyer upon whom Doar relied for legal strategy. He would later become the first career lawyer to receive a presidential appointment as assistant attorney general for civil rights.

At a hearing on August 13, 1963, less than three weeks before the scheduled start of school in Tuskegee, the evidence showed that the school district was maintaining a racially segregated school system and had done nothing to bring about desegregation. However, unlike most other Deep South school districts, the defendants offered to prepare a desegregation plan by December 1963 and testified that they were "at the present time ready and willing to start immediately in the desegregation of the schools of Macon County, Alabama, by putting into effect for the school year commencing in September 1963, the Alabama School Placement Law, without any racial discrimination."[46] The court ruled from the bench in favor of the plaintiffs, enjoining segregation of the schools, requiring nonracial assignments under the pupil placement law, and requiring a plan for desegregation to be filed by December.

Norman asked the court to add a requirement that the defendants report to the court on their actions on applications for assignment under the pupil placement law, and the court accepted this important modification, which would help the court and the parties to ensure compliance.[47] The court stressed the good faith of the school board, indicating that continued good faith would lead to minimal court involvement. This decision, nine years after *Brown*, promised very modest relief—not the demise of the dual school system but the ability of some African Americans in a few grades to transfer from a Black school to a white school.

Meanwhile, the nation, including the president and attorney general, had been preoccupied with concern over the March on Washington. As Taylor Branch graphically explains, Washington, DC, "banned liquor sales for the first time since Prohibition. President Kennedy and his military chiefs were poised with pre-drafted proclamations that would trigger suppression by 4,000 troops assembled in the suburbs, backed by 15,000 paratroopers on alert in North Carolina." Even the Washington Senators postponed their baseball games until the march was over.[48] On August 28, 1963, some two hundred thousand peaceful marchers converged on the mall to hear songs and speeches, most notably Martin Luther King Jr.'s "I Have a Dream" speech.[49]

While the march may have marked a turning point in public consciousness of the civil rights movement, the Department Justice lawyers were too busy to spend much time contemplating its meaning, as they were preparing for integration to come to a record number of Deep South school districts in the fall. The assistant attorney general for the Lands Division, a Texan named Ramsey Clark who later became attorney general, had been sent to assess conditions in desegregating districts in South Carolina, Georgia, and Louisiana. As the marchers assembled on the mall, Clark, in the nearby DOJ building, was busy writing a memorandum to Burke Marshall summarizing his conclusions. He was disturbed by the inconsistency he saw—some districts under suit, others not; some beginning with high school desegregation, some with elementary. He argued, "The national interest must be represented in the school desegregation cases." He believed "private prosecution of school desegregation cases is ineffective, unfair and capricious."[50]

Doar developed a plan for using the scant resources of the CRD to prepare for school opening in four Alabama districts, including Macon County, as well as districts in South Carolina, Georgia, and Louisiana. When school opened in 1963, Mississippi would be the only state with no African American students attending elementary or secondary school with white children. In Alabama, Doar planned to send three lawyers, himself included, to Macon County and one each to Huntsville, Birmingham, and Mobile, with still another splitting his time among those three districts. He must have thought that the small, rural, and predominantly Black county would pose greater problems than the large, urban majority white school districts.[51] In addition, Macon County schools would open a week before the other school systems.

After Johnson entered the desegregation order, Doar, two days before the March on Washington, wrote a detailed memorandum about plans for school opening in Macon County. His memo reflects a sea change in the role of the United States. He proposed to return to Tuskegee the next morning "to go over the list of applicants to determine that the Board has been fair with respect to acceptance and rejection." He acknowledged that "this puts the Department of Justice deep into the supervision of the school system prior to any objections by the Negroes" and noted that this "takes the burden of policing the school board off the back of the Negroes' attorney." Another reason for taking on this role was that "this is what Judge Johnson wants." He deemed the deep involvement of the DOJ as necessary, because the plaintiffs, court, and school board "face tremendous problems in working out a satisfactory school system in Macon County (5 Negro school children for every one white child)." Finally, he argued, "The experience that we gain here will be useful in counseling with the Board and the Court on a feasible school desegregation plan."[52]

This remarkable memo reflects optimism, hard-nosed analysis of the situation, and a view that DOJ participation in this case had to go beyond enforcing court orders and must reach into shaping the relief in the case. It evinced the close relationship between Doar and the judge, probably including ex parte conversations. The rest of the memorandum, devoted to security issues and community relations, showed that Doar was creating close ties with both the Black and white leadership, including local law enforcement. He had a high opinion of the school superintendent and chairman of the school board. He noted that Johnson was also "thinking overtime about this case" and using court employees to reach out to the community "to lend support to the school Board and to the Court." Johnson also met with Attorney General Flowers and his assistant, Gordon Madison, "and urged them to support the school board." What must have been on everyone's minds remained unsaid: What would George Wallace do?[53]

Before the court had even entered its order, twenty-seven African Americans applied under the pupil placement law to attend white schools, the *Tuskegee News* reported. The story noted that observers believed the law could not be used to maintain segregation.[54] The school board, after consulting with the Tuskegee mayor and some city council members, unanimously voted to comply with the order. The day after the March on Washington, the board approved the enrollment of 13 of the 48 African American students who had by then applied to attend Tuskegee High School, where 550 white students were enrolled. The superintendent of schools, C. A. Pruitt, did "not anticipate any trouble." In any event, Pruitt added, local police could take care of any problems that might occur.[55] The *News* reported that many white students were expected to transfer from Tuskegee High School to the white schools in Shorter (about fifteen miles west of Tuskegee) and Notasulga (about ten miles north) or even to Union Springs High School (twenty-three miles south) in neighboring Bullock County.

After the school board selected the thirteen African American students to attend Tuskegee High School, the students met regularly with Fred Gray and community leaders to prepare themselves for integration. Everyone was aware of what had happened in Little Rock six years earlier, and according to one of the students, Willie Wyatt, the adults at the meeting "would tell us things like you can expect to be hollered at, you can expect to maybe even be spit upon. But you are to take no action." Then, Wyatt recounted, in a 2012 interview:

> In the back, a guy's raising his hand, and it's John Doar. And he gets up and introduces himself. He wants to assure us that the Justice Department is there for our benefit, to look out for us, for our security, "don't do anything that's going to be overt that makes people think you're going to do something," you know, "that you're not going to do; we're following you," that kind of thing. And he normally had another attorney with him and a couple of US marshals at those meetings. And they would basically just reinforce what we were told: "this is a non-violent thing; you have a right to do this; the government is behind you; and that kind of thing." [how did that make you feel?] To me it was just "all of this for me?!" It made you feel like you were, you know, really something special. But at the same time you couldn't understand, you know, why do I need all of this, just to go and do what a kid of another color can do. [you need the federal government to

> protect you from what the local government or the state government won't allow you to do].[56]

The DOJ thus viewed its role in the case as going beyond giving advice or presenting evidence in court. While the students were not in an attorney-client relationship with the department, its lawyers had a responsibility to ensure that the students' rights were protected. They could only do this by establishing personal relations with the students. Marshall and Doar had recognized this when James Meredith desegregated the University of Mississippi the year before and again when Vivian Malone and James Hood desegregated the University of Alabama. Doar and the chief US marshal, James McShane, had accompanied Meredith to register, and a department attorney stayed with Meredith in his dorm room. Doar had briefed Vivian Malone and James Hood before they enrolled at the University of Alabama, and Deputy Attorney General Nicholas Katzenbach had accompanied them to the confrontation with Governor Wallace and then to register. The following year, Doar's ability to form a bond while enforcing the law led a fourteen-year-old African American girl to write him a letter expressing her thanks "for bearing with us during" the desegregation of Sidney Lanier High School in Montgomery. "Because of your kindness to us, you will be long remembered as one of those who stood by." She noted that, after six weeks, "We started walking to school today, and no one said or tried to do anything to us." And she enclosed test papers, to show she was doing well in school.[57] She did not mention the harassment and ostracism she had faced but said she had made "real nice" friends.[58]

GOVERNOR WALLACE'S QUANDARY

The governor had promised "segregation forever." And the elementary and secondary schools of Alabama all remained segregated during the 1962–1963 school year. But the delay strategy of Wallace's predecessor, John Patterson, had begun to run its course. Not only had Johnson ordered desegregation of the Macon County schools, but judges in Alabama's other two federal judicial districts had complied with appellate court directives to order a start to desegregation by fall 1963 in Birmingham and Mobile, all under the pupil placement law. In addition to the thirteen African American children who were to begin classes at the formerly all-white Tuskegee High School, seven African

American children had been admitted to white schools in the two urban centers and in Huntsville.

But segregation still reigned supreme in more than one hundred school districts in Alabama. The strategy of leaving school segregation as a local matter might at least preserve segregation in those other districts for a while longer. Wallace, however, had achieved national notoriety and the approval of most Alabama whites when he had stood in the schoolhouse door at the University of Alabama, and he once again chose to take the politically popular route, this time using brute force to keep Black children out of white schools. This was the first of many legal missteps that would expand *Lee v. Macon County Board of Education* from a case about sixty-three hundred students into a statewide case that would eventually desegregate hundreds of thousands of students. Surely Wallace—a lawyer himself—knew from his experience at the University of Alabama and Governor Orval Faubus's failed attempt to block desegregation in Little Rock that his ploy was doomed legally. However, Wallace undoubtedly calculated that his bravado would enhance his notoriety and his popularity with the Alabama electorate, which still included very few Black voters.

It appeared that the Tuskegee school system was ready for desegregation, that many whites were ready, and that law enforcement was ready. Overseeing the effort to integrate was Superintendent Pruitt, who gathered the PTA on August 29 to discuss integration. During the meeting, many attendees opposed integration. However, instead of urging the school board to defy Johnson's order or otherwise resist at a local level, they focused their efforts on appealing to the state government, as Wallace was more aligned with their views. Although the school board proceeded with plans to integrate, the state intervened on September 2 with Wallace's order to delay the opening for one week. On September 9, as the Tuskegee School opened, it was surrounded by approximately 216 state troopers, who prevented all schoolchildren from entering the school.[59]

As Willie Wyatt put it, "I thought well, okay, there's going to be three to four hundred other kids in the school. How am I going to make friends? How am I going to be accepted? Is there anything that's going to happen that's going to cause me to react and respond? So that was a thought running through my head."[60] Similarly, Anthony Lee recalled. "The events that had happened that day just caught us by surprise because we thought we had prepared for everything and everything was supposed to be a very smooth transition until the closing and things like that happened."[61] A white student described her mother's reaction on opening day: "At one point, she [the student's mother] turned around and asked all of us 'do you students want to go to school?' And we all said, 'Yes ma'am.' And so she walked up to the nearest trooper who was standing stone-faced and said, 'Please give a message to Governor Wallace that these students want to attend school.' And of course, he said nothing."[62]

The mother was reacting to a surprise move by Wallace. He first issued an executive order requiring Macon County to delay the opening of Tuskegee High School from September 2 to September 9. This first order was based on "conditions calculated to result in a disruption of the peace and tranquility of this State . . . resulting from the threat of forced and unwarranted integration."[63] Attorney General Flowers, a political rival to Wallace, advised the school board that it should ignore the governor's order.[64] The school superintendent announced that school would open as scheduled, but the governor ordered his all-white state troopers and members of Sheriff Jim Clark's infamous all-white Dallas County special deputies to surround Tuskegee High School and prevent students from entering. These were the same forces who two years later would mount the attack on marchers at the Edmund Pettus Bridge in Selma.

Although there were some calls for court action against the governor, neither the plaintiffs, the United States, nor the school board filed any papers at this point. The delay was only for a week, and the closing affected students of both races, so the interference with desegregation was minimal. However, another development would gravely endanger desegregation: a group set about organizing a white private school in Macon County, with full support from Wallace, including the promise of tuition grants from the state.[65] Sam Engelhardt, Macon County's state senator, had successfully laid the foundation for state support for this private school, to which parents could send their children if and when the inevitable desegregation finally took place. Engelhardt also supported the adoption of a policy to fire "any Negro teacher who assists desegregation efforts."[66]

The following week, schools throughout Alabama were scheduled to open. In endeavoring to fulfill his promise to stop integration, Wallace could turn to two models. Faubus had justified blocking Black children from entering the all-white Central High School in Little Rock by arguing he was simply maintaining the safety of the children in the face of threats of violence. Governor Ross Barnett had issued an order of interposition to stop the enrollment of

James Meredith in the University of Mississippi. He squarely based his order on the right of states to govern their schools and the "direct usurpation of this power by the Federal Government through the illegal use of the judicial decree."[67] Wallace did not issue an interposition order but relied primarily on the public safety rationale. The governor issued three more executive orders, "each directing that 'No student shall be permitted to integrate the public schools' of each of the cities of Mobile, Tuskegee and Birmingham, respectively." Joseph Bagley notes, "Wallace had conceded Huntsville, where white moderate sentiment was strongest."[68] In a remarkable rhetorical turn, the executive orders stated that the court-ordered integration would not only "totally disrupt and effectively destroy the educational process" but would abridge "the civil rights of other children attending the schools," apparently based on a freedom of nonassociation theory positing that white pupils had a right not to have Black classmates.

On September 9, the Black students who had been admitted to Tuskegee High School met once more at the office of Superintendent Pruitt, who was "as cordial as he could be." A Black driver then drove them in a school bus the block or two to the school, where they were met by state troopers. A trooper boarded the bus and read the governor's proclamation to the students and gave each a copy of it. At Tuskegee High School, DOJ attorney John Martin observed white children enter the school, but when the bus carrying African American children arrived, state troopers boarded the bus, which then drove away. He reported that there were no hostile crowds around the school, just newsmen.[69]

This was no longer just a school desegregation case. It had suddenly, like the Little Rock case, escalated into a law enforcement issue. Could a governor interfere with the efforts of these three school boards to comply with a federal court order? In response, the United States took two steps as soon as the troopers kept the Black students from attending the white schools. It filed a new suit that same day in Johnson's court, signed not only by the usual DOJ officials but also by Attorney General Robert Kennedy, against the governor, state law enforcement officials, and the State of Alabama, to enjoin the interference. The complaint began by saying that the United States brought this suit "in its sovereign capacity to safeguard the due administration of justice in its court and the integrity of its judicial process." Johnson's biographer, Jack Bass, reports that the judge objected to the department's request that, as he saw it, he do "the work for the judges in the Northern and Southern Districts" who had issued the Birmingham and Mobile orders. So Burke Marshall called those judges, and, in an unprecedented move, although the case had been filed in Johnson's judicial district, all the federal district judges from the three judicial districts in Alabama sat as a "five judge district court."[70] Johnson told Bass, "I presided in their presence and dictated the opinion, and they all signed it and went back home. There's no statutory basis or any other legal basis of which I'm aware that authorizes a five-judge District Court."[71] The Supreme Court seems to have later endorsed this procedure in those cases: "Because the two cases are interrelated, their limited consolidation for this purpose has a certain utility in avoiding conflicting decrees and aiding judicial consideration and enforcement."[72] Judge Rives denied the defendants' request to convene a statutory three-judge court, because the case raised no substantial constitutional issue.[73]

Second, the United States asked Johnson to issue a temporary restraining order against the interference with the desegregation in Macon County. At 5:15 p.m. on the same day, Johnson issued the order, enjoining the governor and the state troopers from further interference. Continuing the point-counterpoint movements, at 7:09 that evening, Wallace called up the Alabama National Guard to take the place of the now-enjoined state troopers. The following day, President Kennedy issued a proclamation forbidding any and all persons to interfere with the desegregation orders of the Alabama courts, and he also nationalized the Alabama National Guard, thus removing that force from Wallace's control.[74] Here the battle of executive orders ended, as President Kennedy asserted his willingness to use the superior force of the federal government against Alabama's racial caste system.

A hearing in the case two weeks later was anticlimactic. Wallace's lawyer, John Kohn, had filed papers attacking the court's jurisdiction and the authority of the United States to bring the suit, but the hearing focused on the merits of the case.[75] After presenting evidence of the role of the governor and state troopers in excluding African Americans from the white schools, Doar argued that there was no legitimate basis for interfering with the federal court desegregation orders. There was no substantial threat of violence, and even if there were, the Supreme Court had said in the case arising from desegregation of Central High School in Little Rock that the proper law enforcement response to threats of violence was to stop the violence, not to stop the desegregation. He argued that Wallace was using force "not to sustain law, but as an instrument for thwarting law."[76]

Kohn fell back on the well-worn segregationist argument that the

Fourteenth Amendment, upon which the desegregation order was based, was invalid. The amendment was "conceived in hate, born as an afterbirth of war, and apparently made legal at the point of a bayonet, and it has been a cancerous infestation of the Constitution since its inception."[77] After delivering this bald political appeal, Kohn went on to argue that there was no threat of further interference, and therefore the court should not issue an injunction. Doar responded that the only reason Wallace was not presently interfering was the federal temporary restraining order. The lawyers and judges made no mention of the murder of four children when a Ku Klux Klan member bombed the Sixteenth Street Baptist Church in Birmingham just a week after schools opened, but the link between the overheated racial atmosphere and their deaths surely lurked in the background. Indeed one of the five judges convened a grand jury to look into both the bombing and the obstruction of school desegregation.[78]

The court in this separate case, *United States v. Wallace*, recognized the interest of the United States and did not even mention the lack of statutory authority. It ruled: "The plaintiff [the United States] is suffering and, unless an injunction is entered, will continue to suffer immediate and irreparable injury as a consequence of the impairment of its judicial process, the obstruction of the due administration of justice in its courts, and the deprivation of rights under the Constitution and laws of the United States."[79] The court enjoined the governor and his subordinates from further interference and ordered that they maintain law and order so that desegregation could move forward. The concluding section of the order more generally enjoined them from "preventing, attempting to prevent, or interfering with the exercise of rights or the performance of duties under the orders of the United States District Courts for the Northern and Southern Districts of Alabama relating to the desegregation of public schools in the cities of Mobile and Birmingham, Alabama." This order became the first step toward the eventual statewide structural injunction that would come four years later.

Having also failed at halting the desegregation of the Macon County schools, Wallace and his allies would commit to undermining desegregation there by supporting the new school, private in theory but state-supported, for the white children of the county. The mayor of Notasulga, a small Macon County town, soon made his own unsuccessful stand in the schoolhouse door to stop integration. And State Superintendent of Education Austin Meadows became increasingly vocal in discouraging local school officials from desegregating.

The actions of Wallace and Meadows played into a rift that had developed between some white parents in Tuskegee who would acquiesce to token desegregation and those who called for defiance. Pete Johnson's story about the disbanding of the Tuskegee football team to avoid having Black teammates exemplified the deep divisions in the white community: the players voted to quit and dissolve the team, leaving the coach in tears. At the same time, members of the student council decided that they would attend the integrated school.[80] One parent willing to move forward with desegregation later said of a PTA meeting that she had "never seen such hatred and anger before."[81]

One white student related that when Tuskegee High finally reopened, only a few white students attended alongside Anthony Lee, Willie Wyatt, and the other Black children. The teachers tried to make desegregation work, she said, but finally her father withdrew her and moved her to Alexander City, where she lived with an aunt and finished high school.[82] Shortly after an African American girl entered his classroom for the first time, the vice president of the student council was called to the principal's office, where he was told that his father had called and that he was to come home immediately. He told historian Joe Bagley that he walked home, crying all the way because he knew he would "never set foot in that school again."[83]

4. New Year, New Schools, New Law

The Black students at Tuskegee High School soon found themselves in all-Black classes, as their white classmates of high school age either transferred to Macon County's two white high schools in Shorter and Notasulga or to the newly formed, private Macon Academy. Nonetheless, they felt that the teachers at Tuskegee High gave them a good education. The Tuskegee Civic Association praised the desegregating students for rendering a "civic service" and also thanked the DOJ lawyers "who worked diligently to see that the orders of the Court were obeyed, and that the lives of the children were protected."[1] Meanwhile, Governor Wallace helped raise money for the Macon Academy and, after the court had enjoined the school board from doing so, provided transportation for the white students from Tuskegee High to the other white public high schools in Shorter and Notasulga.

The first phase of desegregation had begun with emphasis on achieving token desegregation without saying much about the future. Would the pupil placement law still apply? What grades would be covered each year? How would the Black schools become desegregated? What about faculty and transportation? Until the interference by the governor and state school officials, most assumed that court-ordered desegregation must proceed school system by school system, rather than statewide. What in retrospect seems quite simple—the absorption of a few more students into a white school—was at the time a major, headline-grabbing issue.

Lawyers in the DOJ were well aware that Macon County faced the prospect of a one-race, African American school system. In October 1963 St. John Barrett outlined the issue to Doar. The "object to be achieved," he said, was "placement of at least some Negro children in white schools without precipitating: (1) Abandonment of the public school system; (2) Massive withdrawal of the white students." After detailing factors that might affect decisions by white parents, Barrett proposed collecting facts "to assess the relative value of the . . . factors." He then asked which factors "can be controlled or influenced in minimizing white student withdrawals?" He ended by posing three possible steps—publicizing the lack of alternatives to the Macon County public schools, entry of court orders that might "alleviate 'inundated' fears," and adopting a plan that would allow students to transfer from a school in which their race is in the minority.[2] Barrett's memo reflected a willingness to limit the number of African American transfers to white schools and to allow white students to transfer from a school if it became majority Black. This latter notion, Barrett conceded, would violate the Supreme Court's recent *Goss* decision from Knoxville, Tennessee.[3] While Barrett was careful not to recommend any particular course of action, his outline reflected deep concern that desegregation in Macon County would lead to white flight.

Then, in January 1964, the state Alabama Board of Education, exacerbating Wallace's prior missteps, violated former governor Patterson's strategy of leaving governance to local school authorities. The board ordered that Tuskegee High be closed for lack of adequate enrollment and that its students, all of whom were now Black, be sent back to their Black high school, Tuskegee Institute High. The order gave Fred Gray a path to turn a local case into a statewide case that became a model for desegregation cases across the South.

Wallace and Superintendent Austin Meadows were the two top officers of the state board. Meadows would soon join the governor as a central figure in *Lee*. Born in Alabama on Christmas Eve 1899, he had published his PhD dissertation in 1940 on safety and economy in school bus transportation. He was appointed state superintendent of education in 1946 and later elected to that office. A colorful figure, as a young educator he brought a White House conference on rural education to a halt by saying, "The folks back home really only wanted me to say hello to Fala." Eleanor Roosevelt responded by bringing in the White House First Dog to perform tricks.[4] A dedicated educator but a segregationist nonetheless, Meadows responded to *Brown* by urging the legislature to expand school funding; he believed this would persuade the "overwhelming majority" of African Americans in Alabama to stay in their own schools. As the *New York Times* reported, if "Negro schools [were brought] up to a par with those of white children. . . . there will be no great pressure for integration."[5] Meadows was also a member of the University of Alabama Board of Trustees which had voted, first, to temporarily exclude the university's first African American student, Autherine Lucy, in 1956, and later, to expel her.[6]

Gray knew what he was up against in Meadows and Wallace. He filed papers with the court, supported by the United States, adding the state officials and the rest of the state board as defendants, seeking a temporary restraining order (TRO), challenging the constitutionality of the forced closure of Tuskegee High, and challenging the state's tuition grant statute, which was designed to help fund segregation academies such as Macon Academy. The court entered the temporary restraining order and assigned the Black students to the white schools at Shorter and Notasulga. The DOJ had quietly prepared for violence: Attorney General Kennedy and President Johnson agreed that the department should develop paperwork to authorize use of the National Guard or regular Army to prevent interference with the desegregation at Shorter and Notasulga in case they were needed.[7]

Shorter High School desegregation occurred without incident, under guard of sixty Alabama state troopers. Notasulga did not go without violence. Anthony Lee and Willie Wyatt were among the students assigned to the school there, Macon County High. Wyatt recalls what was supposed to be his first day attending classes in Notasulga. Vernon Merritt III, a white photographer from the Black Star agency and a Birmingham native, was on the school bus. When it arrived at the school, the mayor of the small textile and farming community, James Rea, got on the bus "and told us about the overcrowding situation." Then Dallas County Sheriff Clark, whose normal field of racial violence was four counties and ninety miles away in Selma, boarded with an electric cattle prod and Wyatt could hear Merritt "screaming like a cow or a pig that you would hit with a prod. And after they pulled him off of the bus through the back door . . . I could see that he was laying on the grass, and they were kind of pummeling him." The bus then took the students back to Tuskegee.[8] According to the *New York Times*, Rea contended the presence of the six African Americans would have created a fire hazard; that evening, according to Rea, fire damaged the city's water plant, and Rea then ordered all schools closed. Rea claimed that the water shortage limited the school to 175 persons; he had previously ascertained that it had 165 students and nine teachers, for a total of 174. As with Wallace's exclusion of the students from Tuskegee High the preceding fall, the United States filed a separate suit against Rea, noting that he allowed whites but not Blacks to attend the high school and alleging that his conduct "interferes with and obstructs the performance of duties and the enjoyment of rights under the orders of this court in Lee." Rea responded that "he prevented the students from attending said school, one of the reasons being because of their race or color, but he alleges that said reason was occasioned by the temper of the local residents, and because of local conditions and traditions; that his action was consistent with the safety and welfare of said children." He added that the children were now free to attend the school.[9]

Johnson found that Rea's actions had no rational basis and were based on subterfuge to obstruct admission of the six African American students. He held that the federal court had the duty "not only to protect the rights of the original plaintiffs [in *Lee*], but to protect the authority and the integrity of the judicial process of [the federal court]." He therefore not only enjoined Rea from further interference but also ordered him to "maintain the peace and order . . . in and around the Macon County High School at Notasulga."[10]

Life at Notasulga settled down after this initial incident, according to Wyatt and Lee, who may have repressed some memories. On March 12, 1964, the Black children found graffiti on the school walls, such as "Leave before its [*sic*] too late," "Judge Johnson's school," and "Go home nigger." In May, Macon County Sheriff Preston Hornsby asked the DOJ to keep six US marshals in Macon County until school let out; he expressed deep concern in particular about Notasulga, where he thought "some sneak act of violence" could occur. The county superintendent opined, "The most upsetting thing to the whites in Notasulga appears to be that the Negroes will 'graduate' from 'their' school." However, after the state troopers agreed to watch the school, the sheriff and superintendent and Fred Gray agreed that the marshals could be withdrawn. The sheriff had a patrol car accompany the bus to the high school.[11] As at Tuskegee High, the whites left this high school. Then, toward the end of the semester an arson fire burned the high school building down, so that plans for a graduation ceremony were scrapped. Wyatt and Lee received their diplomas, however, and both then enrolled at Auburn University. Lee became the first African American to complete all four undergraduate years and graduate from Auburn.[12]

By contrast with Notasulga, the initial desegregation at Shorter High School was relatively smooth. White teachers and parents said they were not "integrationists" but believed in following the law. They also wanted to preserve the high school as a community resource. At a meeting of parents and teachers on February 4, most parents agreed to continue sending their children to the desegregated school. One of the teachers raised a new issue with DOJ attorney Jonathan Sutin: integrated athletic teams would not be able to play all-white schools. A white student told Sutin of resisting pressure to attend Macon Academy.[13] It appeared that where there was no official interference with desegregation, the enrollment of a few Black students would not lead to white abandonment of the public school system.

THE BURNING BUSH

In his latest filings in the case, Gray had not sought relief only for Macon County; nor had he confined his argument to challenging the tuition grant statute. Gray recalled, "I concluded that if Wallace, as governor of Alabama, had the authority under state law to close down a public school to prevent integration, then he must have the authority to use that same state power to further integration in all of the public elementary and secondary schools in Alabama."[14] He said the "realization hit me like the burning bush speaking to Moses" that if the governor had the power to close down a school in Macon County, "he should be compelled to use that same power to integrate all of the school systems in Alabama which were not already then under court order."[15] So Gray added the governor and other state officials as defendants in the case and asked the court for statewide relief.

The DOJ sent two of its top litigators, St. John Barrett and Bob Owen, to collect facts relating to Gray's motion, prompting Meadows to urge Attorney General Kennedy to "call a halt to the judicial proceedings which are usurping the executive functions of duly constituted State and local executive officers."[16] Barrett and Owen had supported most of Gray's motion, but they took a different approach to statewide relief, asking only that the court "enjoin the State Board to perform its constitutional obligation, within the limits of its state authority, to accomplish or facilitate the elimination of racial discrimination from the state school system." However, the United States did not express a view as to the extent of the board's authority—a partial departure from the private plaintiffs' position. Attorney General Flowers, in a document that he alone signed, argued that the Macon County Board had complied with the court's orders and that the plaintiffs had no right to expand the case beyond Macon County. The Macon County board had asked Flowers to represent them, but as to the state defendants he could only assert that he was "by law required to represent some, if not all, of the defendants."[17] The governor and other state defendants desperately backed away from the state board resolutions ordering the closing of Tuskegee High School and payment of tuition grants, saying that "they misapprehended their powers of closing schools and ordering transportation . . . [and] have rescinded said resolutions."[18] The state defendants also argued that the named plaintiffs had no right "to represent persons residing outside of Macon County, Alabama."[19]

The February hearing considered the order to close Tuskegee High School, the state board's activities related to Macon Academy, the double standards employed in assigning students to white schools, and the transportation assistance students at Macon Academy received. Johnson, as was his habit, took copious notes of the proceedings, including questions that the proceedings raised in his mind. For example, his notes ask, "Do defts conceive the desegregation of a school system a condition precedent to use of Alabama Placement Law"? His notes on Superintendent Pruitt's testimony observe that "these transfers [of whites from Tuskegee High to Shorter and Notasulga] were allowed by Macon Bd. w/o following procedures." They also note that the school board furnished transportation for whites to those schools. He placed a big star next to the text of the telegram Meadows sent to Pruitt in January 1964 stating that the State Board of Education "directs and orders" that Tuskegee High be closed and that bus transportation be provided. He also highlighted his notes that "pupil placement law used for Negro but not for Whites." Testimony about Macon Academy, Johnson wrote, foreshadowing the court's ruling on this issue "shows potential use of grants-in-aid to avoid integration of races in Macon Co. Public School System." He was particularly interested in the state's hurried accreditation of Macon Academy, namely that the state's visit occurred the same day as the academy filed its application, that the academy did not meet the standards for accreditation, and that "accreditation was made 'effective' Feb. 12, 1964, for the year 1963–64." Finally, he underscored testimony by a former employee of the state Department of Education that the department "understood that H.E.W. wanted a response from the local school authorities in the impacted areas in Alabama." The judge, in bringing the hearing to a close, identified five issues that he wanted the parties to brief, including "Deseg. of schools throughout State of Ala."[20]

After the February hearing, the department filed a lengthy brief, signed by Burke Marshall, US Attorney Ben Hardeman, and four CRD attorneys. The brief argued that the temporary restraining order should be enlarged into a preliminary injunction running against both the Macon County officials and the defendant Alabama officials; that the grants-in-aid statute should be declared unconstitutional as applied to grants for students at racially segregated schools and should be enjoined in Macon County and throughout Alabama; that the governor, state superintendent of education, and State Board of Education should be enjoined from interfering with desegregation in school systems in Alabama; that the state superintendent and board should be ordered to take affirmative steps to eliminate the dual school system in Alabama, "based not only upon the assumption and usurpation of authority by these officials but also upon the legal authority that they presently possess under Alabama law; and that the Alabama pupil placement law is unconstitutional "until the dual system of schools in Alabama is eliminated." The brief described the evidence of the state's official policy of segregation and its maintenance of a dual system; the general control and supervision that the state superintendent and board had over the local school systems and over the administration of the Pupil Placement Act; state officials' threats to pay tuition grants to students at Macon Academy and their active support of the academy; and their interference with the federal court orders.[21] In all of this, the government was inching closer to the plaintiffs' position.

Because the case now challenged the constitutionality of a state law—the tuition grant statute—federal law at the time required that a three-judge district court be convened. At Johnson's request, Chief Judge Elbert Tuttle of the US Court of Appeals for the Fifth Circuit appointed two judges to serve on the court with Johnson: Judge Richard Rives of the Fifth Circuit, whose chambers were located in Montgomery, in the same courthouse as Johnson's, and Judge Hobart Grooms of the Northern District of Alabama, whose chambers were in Birmingham. The three-judge court held a hearing in late February and another in April. The April hearing considered an issue that did not require a three-judge court. After the fire at the high school in Notasulga, which the court said was "probably the result of criminal action intended to discourage the attendance of said Negro children at the Notasulga school," the school board had reassigned the six Black students to the Black high school in Tuskegee.[22] The court found that the school in Notasulga was still able to operate, and so the three judges ordered that the children be allowed to continue attending it.[23]

Although Johnson's files reflect some skepticism that state financing of the local schools would render the state liable for discrimination by a school district, nonetheless, in July 1964, the court entered a ruling that cautiously laid the foundation for sweeping statewide relief if the governor continued on his course of overreaching and interference. The court readily agreed that the governor and State Board of Education had repeatedly interfered with the good faith efforts of the Macon County School Board to comply with the desegregation orders. Not only had they adopted resolutions to thwart desegregation in Macon County and ordered the local school board to divert money to the segregated private school, the board of education had also pledged to defend the people of Alabama from all federal orders to desegregate the public schools. The governor's executive order in September had declared, "Integration of the public schools will totally disrupt and effectively destroy the educational process." And the state superintendent of education had celebrated that "teachers, administrators and parents have firmly held the line for our way-of-life and in opposition to misguided parents who have tried to force the entry of their children into schools for a different race."

While enjoining the governor and state board from interfering with the desegregation of Macon County schools, the court said Wallace was enjoined in his capacity as president ex officio of the state board and not as governor. This seems to have been a symbolic show of deference to the office of governor and also a warning that if he persisted in his actions, the injunction would run against him as governor as well. The court also held that the state tuition grant law could not be used to finance the Macon Academy, though once more it showed restraint and did not declare the statute unconstitutional in all circumstances. Finally, plaintiffs had challenged Alabama's pupil placement law as unconstitutional. While agreeing that the school authorities had applied the law in a discriminatory manner in Macon County, the court declined to hold it unconstitutional "at this time," instead enjoining discrimination in the application of the law.

The novel and most consequential question before the court was whether to grant the plaintiffs' plea that it "order desegregation of all the public schools of the State of Alabama at the elementary and secondary level based upon the assumption or usurpation of authority by the Governor, the State Superintendent of Education and the State Board of Education." The governor argued that the local plaintiffs had no viable claim with respect to school systems outside Macon County. Here, the order making the United States not just an amicus curiae but also a party became crucial. The court said that the United States had an interest in pursuing "the public interest in the due administration of justice in the Federal courts." Therefore, "the contention of the defendants that relief must be restricted only to these Negro plaintiffs borders on the frivolous." The court said that the state defendants' actions "place[d] them in an extremely weak position." However, the court declined to enter the statewide desegregation order, saying instead:

> For the present time this Court will proceed upon the assumption that the Governor, the State Superintendent of Education, and the State Board of

> Education will comply in good faith with the injunction of this Court prohibiting such interference with the local city and county school boards, and through the exercise of considerable judicial restraint, no statewide desegregation order will be ordered at this time.

The court thus simultaneously showed restraint and deference to the state officials while also enjoining them from interfering with school desegregation anywhere in the state.[24] To underscore the seriousness of its order, the court also required the state officials to use whatever control and supervision they exercised over local school districts "in such a manner as to promote and encourage the elimination of racial discrimination in the public schools."[25] Gray had essentially asked the court to treat school desegregation on a wholesale basis rather than retail. He had been inspired by the governor's intransigence to ask for a remedy that no court had to that time awarded. That remedy would have shifted the burden of desegregation from plaintiffs in each school district to the state. However, the court must have felt that the law and facts were not yet sufficiently clear to warrant inventing a new form of relief. Nonetheless, the court's decision would lay the foundation for the novel and sweeping relief that eventually emerged.

The court announced its ruling in July, eleven days after the effective date of the Civil Rights Act of 1964, but there is no indication of any linkage between the two. While the act, as scholars recognize, enlisted federal funding agencies in the quest for equal education, it gave no guidance to the court or to DOJ.[26] The court had already issued a temporary restraining order in February and held a hearing in April when the outcome of the legislation was still in doubt. In any event, the legislation added nothing of immediate relevance to the issues before the court, and the court did not mention the act in its opinion, though the judges obviously were aware of it. Instead, the opinion is squarely grounded on *Brown*, the case involving Governor Faubus's interference with school desegregation in Little Rock, on later Supreme Court cases implementing *Brown*, and on Fifth Circuit cases enforcing *Brown*.

The court rendered its decision in a time of increasing racial turmoil. The "Mississippi Summer" that the Student Nonviolent Coordinating Committee (SNCC) was devoting to voter registration activities had exploded with the disappearance in June of three civil rights workers, whose bodies were not discovered until August. SNCC was also active in Selma, where Black efforts to use public accommodations that the new Civil Rights Act had opened to them led to more lawless behavior by Sheriff Clark. At least, however, school openings in Alabama occurred without major incidents, with slight increases in desegregation both in 1964 and 1965. By 1965 thirty-two African Americans were attending formerly all-white schools and eight whites were attending formerly all-Black schools in Macon County.[27] Statewide, slightly more than one thousand African American students in Alabama (0.34 percent of Alabama's Black students) attended formerly all-white schools.

NEW CIVIL RIGHTS LAW—CONGRESS STILL CAUTIOUS ABOUT SCHOOLS

Lyndon Johnson had been president about one week when he made his first move to dislodge the civil rights legislation sponsored by President Kennedy that was stuck in the House of Representatives. The new president inquired about a procedural maneuver aimed to freeing the bill from the Rules Committee, where it was blocked by its chairman, eighty-year-old Rep. Howard Smith of Virginia.[28] Such bills routinely died in Smith's committee without a whimper. One profile of the Virginia congressman explained, "A dedicated conservative, Smith has killed, watered down or postponed more progressive legislation than any other Congressman in modern times."[29] But Johnson, the former majority leader of the Senate, installed by Southern Democrats who thought he would always side with them to oppose such legislation, wore Smith down and then worked for months in the Senate, overcoming the fifty-seven-day filibuster, to win passage of what became the Civil Rights Bill of 1964.

The bill contained two provisions that would strengthen the federal government's hand in forcing desegregation of schools in the South. First, under Title IV, the DOJ would no longer have to wait for parents to file lawsuits before it could enter desegregation cases. Second, Title VI required federal agencies to withhold federal financial aid from any state or local government entity, including public schools, that discriminated based on "race, color or national origin" in the federally assisted program. With enactment of $350 million in federal aid for Southern and border states via the Elementary and Secondary Education Act, this was a powerful incentive for school districts to comply.[30] Alabama schools were to receive $34.6 million (equivalent to $285 million in 2020).[31] HEW issued "guidelines" to help school districts meet the nondiscriminatory stricture of Title VI. School systems could effectively insulate themselves from HEW fund-termination proceedings under Title VI and from federal court orders by complying with the guidelines.

The tortuous path to enactment had begun in 1962 when the DOJ responded to requests from Congress for its views on a variety of bills that had been introduced to deal with school segregation. Burke Marshall skeptically told Attorney General Kennedy that most "traditional civil rights legislation thinking . . . has centered on creating an issue rather than making an accomplishment." He thought the basic "national long-range problem with the Negro is economic" and suggested that Congress was more likely to enact economic or social legislation than civil rights legislation, a position he would change by the following year.[32] Nonetheless the department began to review pending bills that would adopt a modified version of the failed part III of the 1957 Civil Rights Bill, provide technical and financial help to desegregating school systems, authorize HEW to require desegregation, or authorize the DOJ to file school desegregation cases or authorize DOJ to intervene in private school desegregation cases.

In spring 1963 Marshall returned to Washington from Birmingham, where he had worked to bring about a peaceful settlement to the conflict between African Americans and white leaders of the city. He immediately initiated serious talks with Attorney General Kennedy and others about the need for legislation. Earlier in April, the attorney general had proposed new voting rights legislation, which he presented at a press conference.[33] However, now Marshall pushed for a broader legislative proposal. As Nicholas Katzenbach—deputy attorney general in 1963—described the conversations, "Our feeling was (I think Burke Marshall primarily really is the architect of the idea) we should attempt to deal with the causes of this rather than with the manifestations of the difficulties."[34] Conversation initially focused on desegregation of public accommodations, but "the President was anxious to put it all together in an omnibus bill."[35]

A few weeks after Marshall's return from Birmingham, President Kennedy met with Attorney General Kennedy, Marshall, and White House aides Ted Sorenson and Lee White to discuss a civil rights bill. The president did not want to revive the part III fight from 1957 and 1960 but expressed strong support for banning racial segregation in public accommodations and for authorizing federal enforcement of the school desegregation requirement. However, notably missing in Burke Marshall's and Nicholas Katzenbach's oral history discussions of the 1963 bill is any mention of school desegregation. An unsigned memorandum in White House files speaks of drafting a school desegregation bill but adds, "It need not be necessary to make an effort to have the bill passed this year."[36] This memorandum, from the day of the meeting, explains:

> We are attempting to draft a bill which would treat the school desegregation as a major educational problem, in which the federal government would have a responsibility for the stimulation of school desegregation plans. The bill will contain power for the Department of Justice to bring suit upon the recommendation of the educational authorities charged with administration of the bill in the event that school districts are completely uncooperative in the development of the bill.[37]

While this document reflects the administration's preference at that time for judicial rather than administrative action to desegregate the schools, it also reflects recognition of the ratchet principle—that there could be no turning back—along with a new willingness to complete the job and impose revolutionary change on the Deep South.

In June 1963 President Kennedy proposed on national radio and television that Congress enact a civil rights bill. He noted that both the courts and the executive branch had made a commitment "to the proposition . . . that race has no place in American life" and that it was now time for Congress to act. He asked that Congress "authorize the Federal Government to participate more fully in lawsuits designed to end segregation in public education."[38] Two days later, the leaders of the Republican and Democratic Parties in the Senate met to work out an agreement on a joint civil rights bill. They agreed, without any detail, that the bill should cover school desegregation. They added that it should include a "Powell amendment" forbidding race discrimination in federally assisted programs, something not mentioned in the May 20 White House paper on legislation. Representative Adam Clayton Powell, a New York Democrat, had been pressing since the Eisenhower administration for a ban on federal funding for segregated facilities, via a rider to school construction legislation that Congress had repeatedly defeated. Powell's proposal, as revised, became Title VI of the 1964 Act and became an important tool for bringing about school desegregation

The House of Representatives was first to consider the bill, and a House subcommittee drafted a substitute bill, which revived part III of the 1957 proposal.

Attorney General Kennedy, testifying before the Senate Judiciary Committee in July, noted that progress in school desegregation since the *Brown* decision "has been painfully slow." Although "education is basic to the future of this nation," he pointed out that more than a third of African American adults in Alabama had not even completed the fifth grade. While acknowledging that the proposed legislation "will not wipe out school segregation," he urged that "the time has come for Congress to act to prevent further delays" in school desegregation.[39] At a lengthy press conference in October, Marshall argued that the legislation should deal in separate sections with voting, employment discrimination, public accommodations, and schools instead of following the much broader Title III omnibus approach of the subcommittee.[40] The administration proposal initially allowed but did not require termination of federal funds for racially discriminatory activities, thus reflecting the administration's preference for resolving school desegregation issues in court.

With the assassination of President Kennedy on November 22, the political landscape shifted dramatically. His successor, Lyndon Johnson, had overcome desperate poverty to rise in politics. He had given "hints that he possessed a true, deep compassion for the downtrodden, and particularly for poor people of color, along with a true, deep desire to raise them up."[41]

As president, he used all the tools at his disposal to bring about passage of the Civil Rights Act of 1964, the Voting Rights Act of 1965, and the Civil Rights Act of 1968. In doing so, he outmaneuvered the Southern committee chairs who had used their seniority to block such legislation while Kennedy was still alive. "We could have beaten John Kennedy on civil rights, but not Lyndon Johnson," said Senator Richard Russell, the Georgia Democrat and master tactician of the Southern bloc. "That man will twist your arm off at the shoulder and beat your head with it."[42]

Russell and other members of Congress from the Deep South aggressively opposed civil rights legislation. Senator Sam Ervin of North Carolina took the lead in the initial Senate Judiciary Committee hearings on the Kennedy bill, arguing that it gave the attorney general too much discretion. Ervin entered into the record editorials charging that the bill would "open the door to a form of busy-body interferences with local authority as it deals with the ticklish problems of desegregation," and that, according to Mississippi lawyer John Satterfield, it would lead to "control by the federal government of both state and local governments in the educational field." Satterfield would soon represent George Wallace in *Lee*.[43]

Southern critics of Title IV's authorization of attorney general lawsuits to desegregate schools claimed that Title IV was regional legislation: "The only section of the United States that will be affected by this pernicious bill will be the South."[44] Senator Russell, in the closing days of the filibuster, bitterly expanded on the claim that the bill discriminated against the South: "The bill is aimed at what has become the most despised and mistreated minority in the country—namely, the white people of the Southern States."[45] A Northern supporter of Title IV noted that African American parents had "tragically few resources" to carry on expensive and protracted school desegregation litigation.[46] The result, he added, was that private litigation "has not made significant inroads on the established patterns of segregation."[47]

Southern politicians understood that the whites of the North were not so different from those of the South. Their common refrain was that standards and enforcement should apply equally in both regions of the country. They characterized the act as hypocritical—requiring the South but not the North to desegregate. But they also knew that if school desegregation were to be extended to the North, a backlash would ensue and enforcement would be weakened—which is exactly what happened.

President Kennedy's proposal took a circuitous path through House Judiciary Committee hearings and stalled in the Rules Committee until Johnson intervened. Debate in the Senate began on March 9 and ignited a Southern filibuster with Russell launching the attack, which went on for twelve weeks before the Senate voted for cloture.[48] Opposition to attorney general authority to sue for school desegregation generally avoided challenging *Brown v. Board of Education* and relied instead on federalism and separation of powers.

Most Northern Democrats and Republicans supported the bill, with almost all Southern senators voting against the measure. The act, as approved, authorized the attorney general to bring school desegregation cases, provided for technical assistance to desegregating schools, banned federal financial assistance to programs that discriminate on account of race, and authorized the attorney general to intervene in private race discrimination suits against public officials. It specifically defined "desegregation" as "assignment of students to public schools and within such schools without regard to their race," though it included the provision that "'desegregation' shall not mean the assignment of students to public schools in order to overcome racial imbalance."[49] This simplistic definition, focused solely on student assignments, did nothing to advance understanding of school desegregation requirements and ignored the systemic nature of school segregation: segregation determined where schools were built, who taught in them, how the children got to school, and to what athletic league school teams belonged. The caveat protected so-called "de facto" racially segregated school districts outside the South, but Southern school systems would also invoke it as they opposed systemic relief.

The act is notable for the many ways it hedged the federal role in school desegregation. A Civil Rights Commission attorney later observed, "As Congress took its first positive steps toward assisting desegregation, it was already becoming embroiled in disputes which would change the posture of the majority to one of hostility toward the courts and school desegregation."[50] Title IV of the act authorized the attorney general to sue for school desegregation only where he personally certified that he had received a written complaint from a parent who was unable to maintain legal proceedings. The attorney general could intervene in private suits only where he personally certified that the case was of "general public importance."[51] By contrast, there were no such limits to DOJ suits against discrimination in voting, public accommodations, or employment.

Adding to the confusion created by the act's definition of desegregation, Congress also provided:

> That nothing herein shall empower any official or court of the United States to issue any order seeking to achieve a racial balance in any school by requiring the transportation of pupils or students from one school to another or one school district to another in order to achieve such racial balance, or otherwise enlarge the existing power of the court to insure [*sic*] compliance with constitutional standards.[52]

These limits were also designed to mollify Northern protests against plans to remedy "de facto" segregation. Senator James Eastland of Mississippi observed dryly, "the two Senators from New York are, at heart, pretty good segregationists."[53]

The act blurs the distinction between private clients, like those of the NAACP LDF, and the United States, which is the client of the DOJ. It allows the attorney general to sue to remedy racial discrimination in the schools only when he has received a written complaint from a parent who is unable to bring litigation on her own. The narrowest reading would suggest that the attorney general is suing only on behalf of the complainant, with respect only to the matters raised in the written complaint. There is no indication, however, that this is the reading Congress intended. After all, the attorney general is also required to certify that the lawsuit "will materially further the orderly achievement of desegregation in public education."[54]

The DOJ eventually gave a much broader reading to the statute in order to take advantage of *Lee v. Macon County Board of Education*: one complaint from a parent in a state, in other words, could justify a statewide school desegregation suit to benefit all the children in the state. The complainant would remain anonymous and therefore free from retaliation, unlike plaintiffs in private suits, whose names would be public.[55] Still, the department had to verify that the complaint was valid. For example, two written complaints about school segregation in a city school district proved inadequate because one complainant had moved from the state and the other lived in the county school district, not in the district that prompted the complaint.[56]

In 1966 President Johnson proposed legislation "to broaden the Attorney General's authority to bring suit for the desegregation of schools and public facilities—enabling him to commit the government's legal resources where they are most critically needed." The president pointed out that

> although the Attorney General can move directly against discrimination in voting, in employment or in public accommodations, with respect to school discrimination he must first receive a complaint before acting. In communities where the atmosphere of intimidation and ignorance of the law's protection is most severe, the filing of a complaint is most unlikely. Thus where the need of the Attorney General's intervention is the greatest, his help is least likely to become available.[57]

Although the House Committee on the Judiciary quickly approved the proposed legislation, it died in the Senate. Toward the end of the Johnson Administration, an education task force concluded that the complaint requirement should be eliminated.[58] Not until 1974 would Congress finally authorize the attorney general to sue for school desegregation without a written complaint.

The Congress that passed the 1964 Act spent most of its deliberations on the fair employment and public accommodations provisions. But the provision that most significantly affected school desegregation proved to be Title VI, which prohibited racial discrimination in federally assisted programs and implicitly gave HEW responsibility over school desegregation. Title VI's ban on federal funding of discriminatory programs did not mention schools or desegregation, nor did it explicitly provide for suit to enforce it; instead, the only explicit remedy was the "nuclear option" of cutting off federal financial assistance to the racially discriminatory program, which would likely harm the very students whom the funding was supposed to help. For example, Representative Donald Matthews from Florida alleged that "the bill would deprive schoolchildren of milk money and basic education if there appears to be discrimination because of race."[59] The DOJ responded to this type of criticism by stating that as the department would be able to sue for desegregation under Title IV "it is not expected that such termination would occur."[60]

Thus, ten years after *Brown*, the Congress finally joined the other branches with a fairly strong civil rights act. The public accommodations section, which had been the most controversial provision, met with token initial resistance to compliance, but once the Supreme Court upheld it, most restaurants and hotels desegregated without difficulty, fulfilling William Faulkner's 1955 prophecy at a meeting of the Southern Historical Association: "We speak now against the day when our Southern people who will resist to the last these inevitable changes in social relations, will, when they have been forced to accept what they at one time might have accepted with dignity and goodwill, will say 'Why didn't someone tell us this before? Tell us this in time?'"[61]

While Congress had authorized DOJ suits to desegregate schools and had required federal agencies to ensure that federal assistance did not flow to racially discriminatory programs, Congress failed to specify how school systems should comply. It simply required federal agencies to adopt regulations to enforce the ban on federal assistance to discriminatory programs. In effect, it left the question of remedy to HEW and the courts. Only bold judicial and executive action would overcome the many limitations of the legislation. After initially publishing regulations under Title VI, HEW began requiring school systems to submit desegregation plans to show that they were in compliance. The regulation requires the commissioner of education to ensure that desegregation plans are "adequate" under Title VI but does not define "adequate."[62] By April 1965 HEW had received over five hundred plans that it deemed inadequate. Local school officials had requested that HEW "tell them the least they had to do in order to qualify for continued federal funding."[63] A state superintendent of education wrote to the commissioner of education expressing "our honest conviction that your office is obligated to provide official guidelines to school districts desperately seeking official answers."[64]

HEW faced both procedural and substantive questions in deciding how to provide guidance to school systems. Guidance could come case by case, school system by school system, through a series of decisions. This had been the practice in the courts. Carl A. Auerbach, a law professor at the University of Minnesota, wrote an influential memorandum pointing out that the case-by-case approach would "make it difficult to achieve uniformity" of application to school systems. He, along with another consultant to HEW, Professor Gordon W. Foster Jr., recommended the adoption of standards for public school desegregation. To be binding and authoritative, as Auerbach recommended, the standards would require the president's signature.[65] HEW decided, instead, to issue "Guidelines," which described HEW's expectations for desegregation plans but were not signed by the president and were therefore not formally binding.

After discussion with DOJ and clearing them with White House officials, HEW adopted guidelines that explained what would be deemed adequate, in hopes that this would eliminate the need to evaluate plans one by one.[66] A leading study of Title VI enforcement opines that the guidelines were "much more a response to bureaucratic need for certainty and predictability than to any civil rights impulse within the Office [of Education]."[67] In a letter to members of Congress, school superintendents, and other interested parties, HEW explained "that the guidelines are of general applicability while the courts fashion their orders on a case-by-case basis."[68] The guidelines were "adopted in the context of a body of desegregation law which inevitably influenced administrative choices."[69] The courts had developed few legal standards, so the guidelines necessarily expanded on prior court decisions. The "all deliberate speed" formula adopted by the Supreme Court ten years earlier remained the sole guidance on speed of desegregation, and the courts had yet to define the content of the desegregation. In the second *Brown* decision the Supreme Court had suggested that the lower courts "may consider problems related to administration" in devising plans for desegregation. These problems, the court said, arise from "the physical condition of the school plant, the school transportation system, personnel, revision of school districts and attendance areas into compact units."[70] Yet the focus of the decisions of the next ten years had been on opening white schools to a few Black students. Not until the barriers to Black enrollment in white schools had fallen did the other "problems related to administration" receive much judicial attention. Implicit in *Brown II* was the recognition that desegregation was a systemic issue, but the cases since then had primarily treated desegregation as simply involving opening doors to individuals. This was about to change.

NEW SCHOOL YEARS, NEW COMPLEXITIES

Judge Johnson called Doar a month before the 1964 school year began and told him that the Macon County schools had a new superintendent and the Tuskegee High School had a new principal. Both had "good" attitudes and planned to send their own children to the desegregated school.[71] In preparation for school opening, DOJ attorney Jonathan Sutin contacted school authorities, civic leaders, law enforcement authorities, and Black leaders. Tuskegee High School was to be reopened, but it was unclear how many whites would show up; only a handful had signed up for the desegregated grades. Rumors were flying in the white community about a flood of Black students enrolling, but in fact only fourteen were expected in grades 9–11.

Sheriff Preston Hornsby would use his limited force of two or three men to watch the school, but there was concern that the chief of police could not be trusted. The school board hired a night watchman, who resigned after receiving threats; a second resigned, also citing threats; a third had then been hired. Although not expecting trouble, Attorney General Katzenbach alerted President Johnson; as his assistant, Lee White, reported to him, "The Justice Department appears to have taken the necessary proper precautions and either National Guard or federal troops can be called into action if needed." The department had twenty US marshals in the area, and the Army made plans for a backup emergency force of eighteen hundred Alabama National Guardsmen. The president wrote, "Do I need to do anything," and White responded that he did not.[72]

In the spring the FBI had reported that no white teachers were expected to teach in the desegregated school in the fall. Nonetheless, by September Jonathan Sutin reported that nineteen white teachers were assigned to teach at the K–12 Tuskegee High School. It was reported that the all-white private school, Macon Academy, had more than three hundred enrollees and that Wallace had donated $6,000 from his campaign funds. Sutin returned on the eve of school opening, with Doar, and attended a meeting of white and Black parents and school children that had been organized by Mrs. Sullins, whose daughter had been among the Black pupils who integrated the school in 1963.

Among the few whites attending were Sheriff Hornsby and Allan Parker, the local banker and Chamber of Commerce president, both of whom had children at Tuskegee High. The next day, Labor Day, was a shortened school day; Doar and Sutin observed no problems. By late October, Doar reported that white enrollment had slightly risen and that some students from the academy had transferred back to Tuskegee High School because of concerns about educational quality, costs, and the atmosphere of hate at Macon Academy. Tuskegee High School again had enough students to field an all-white football team. However, the school appears not to have fielded a team in 1964 or 1965, according to the Alabama State Football Historical Association. Macon Academy fielded its first football team that year. Doar reported that the superintendent's greatest concern was that the lowered enrollment would lead to less state funding. By the second semester, white enrollment had stopped rising amid rumored pressure on forty Macon Academy students not to transfer back to the integrated school. Still, ninety-five whites were attending Tuskegee High.[73]

MOVING FROM WHETHER TO DESEGREGATE TO HOW TO DESEGREGATE

The question in 1963 had been whether the schools would desegregate. Neither the private plaintiffs nor the United States had suggested what that would finally mean. It is not clear what the African American community wanted: access to the white school or a more systemic and complete desegregation. By 1965, however, the question was not whether but how and how much? What grades would desegregate? How would the school authorities assign students to the desegregated grades? Would the students have to apply to transfer from a Black school to a white school? Would all students be given freedom to choose what school to attend? Would the students be assigned based on geography rather than race?

During the ten years since *Brown*, the Supreme Court had provided little guidance on the "how" and "how much" questions, and the executive branch and Congress had provided none. Instead, the lower courts were largely left to their own devices. The Southern states had, in reaction to *Brown*, adopted so-called pupil placement laws, based on the premise that "somebody must enroll the pupils in schools. They cannot enroll themselves; and we can think of no one better qualified to undertake the task than the officials of the schools and the school boards having the schools in charge."[74]

As late as 1964 when Alabama school districts were ordered to desegregate, they turned to the state's pupil placement law that, as Judge Rives noted, was "passed in an effort to meet and solve problems presented by the School Segregation Cases."[75] The Alabama law required the school authorities to consider a long list of criteria in making student assignments. Among them were "the psychological qualification of the pupil for the type of teaching and association involved," "the possibility or threat of friction or disorder among pupils or others," and "the maintenance or severance of established social and psychological relationships with other pupils and with teachers."[76] Implicit in such criteria was the assumption that Black students should attend Black schools and white students should attend white schools.

The question the school desegregation cases presented to the DOJ was whether simply to apply the Supreme Court cases or to argue in favor of more robust relief that would completely desegregate the school system. As a law enforcement agency, not a civil rights organization, what should guide the department in making that decision: the rather vague Supreme Court rulings or some vision of a desired final result? This question was not yet a burning one, as the NAACP LDF, the main civil rights organization litigating school desegregation claims, had been content to settle initially for the enrollment of a few African Americans in formerly white schools in the Deep South. But was that the ultimate goal or simply the first step?

Although upholding pupil placement plans in the abstract, the courts rejected them when they lacked standards, denied African American students "reasonable and conscious opportunity to have their choice of school considered by the enrolling authorities," or required students to apply to transfer after they were assigned to one-race schools based on their race. The Macon County School Board had proposed a desegregation plan in 1964 under which desegregation would not be complete until the 1969–1970 school year. Moreover, desegregation would be accomplished by allowing students to transfer schools, rather than by nonracial initial assignments. The court approved only the proposal for 1964–1965.[77]

In April 1965 DOJ attorney Jonathan Sutin and Fred Gray had another desegregation case before Johnson. After the hearing, the three of them repaired to the judge's chambers and discussed Macon County. Johnson asked Sutin to check on the plans for next year. Sutin did so and returned to report to the judge that the school board proposed to add only the second grade to the list of desegregated grades. Johnson and Sutin agreed that that was too slow, and the judge directed Sutin to prepare a plan desegregating three more grades in the fall and to cover all grades in 1966–1967. Johnson's proactive stance included asking the department to investigate Macon Academy.

In May the school district began distributing free choice forms on which students were required to choose which school they wished to attend in the fall. The school superintendent expressed concern that if too many Blacks enrolled in the white schools, whites would flee. At the time he expected forty-seven Blacks to enroll at Tuskegee High and two at the newly rebuilt high school in Notasulga. That summer the superintendent denied without explanation two requests for desegregated assignments. The superintendent also expected to place some white teachers in Black schools, though there was no mention of Black teachers in white schools. Another issue arose: two Black students played on the Tuskegee High School basketball team, and the other teams in the previously all-white league refused to play Tuskegee High. Moreover, whites who had transferred back to Tuskegee High School from Macon Academy were held disqualified to play. In an ironic twist, Tuskegee High School was scheduled to play Macon Academy in an upcoming tournament.[78] It was becoming increasingly clear that school desegregation was more complex than simply allowing a few students to transfer from one school to another and that the DOJ would play a role in systemic change to unravel the complexity.

Two years after the first African American students enrolled in white public schools in Alabama, there were signs that resistance to desegregation was weakening. At a meeting of the Alabama Association of Secondary School Principals, a panel of speakers from desegregated districts advised "that integration can be orderly and not detrimental to the school program if enough planning is done beforehand."[79] In August, Auburn University sponsored a conference of school board members and school superintendents to discuss desegregation. The keynote speaker, Atlanta school superintendent John Letson, observed that there was no longer a question whether the schools would be integrated and that "the fear of this problem is much greater than the reality." He added, "students are students," regardless of their race.[80] The *Birmingham News* editorialized that "the only sensible course is to insure [*sic*] that transition [to desegregation] is handled with a minimum of disruption to the education of all young people, both white and Negro."[81] A common theme at the conference was that "we are not here to discuss whether to desegregate but how to desegregate."[82]

The Voting Rights Act had ordered the attorney general to bring suits challenging the constitutionality of the poll tax. Judges Rives and Johnson were on the panel that heard the Alabama challenge. In the course of holding the Alabama poll tax unconstitutional, Judge Rives wrote, "from the Constitutional Convention of 1901 to the present, the State of Alabama has consistently devoted its official resources to maintaining white supremacy and a segregated society."[83] This recognition of the depth of state complicity suggested that Gray's idea that the court should order statewide relief in *Lee* had merit. Meanwhile, though the opening of school in 1965 was relatively peaceful when compared with the prior two years, more storm clouds were gathering.

5. The Case Goes Statewide

> President Johnson: "Why don't you just desegregate all your schools?"
> George Wallace: "Oh, Mr. President, I can't do that. You know, the schools have got school boards. They're locally run. I haven't got the political power to do that."
> President Johnson: "Don't you shit me, George Wallace."
> —*Jon Meacham,* The Soul of America: The Battle for Our Better Angels

Ever since he had ordered state troopers to bar Black students from the white school in Tuskegee in 1963, George Wallace had unintentionally threatened to expand the Macon County case into something more. In 1966 Wallace's term as governor was about to expire, and he had failed in his effort to repeal Alabama's term limits. He enlisted his wife, Lurleen Wallace, to enter the fray, and she defeated former governors Patterson and Folsom in the primary and then won the general election. Thus, the next chapter of the Macon County case would unfold largely on her watch, with George in the immediate background as Alabama's first gentleman.

While the DOJ decided to intervene with a complaint limited to the tuition grant issue, Fred Gray filed a bold and sweeping motion for the plaintiffs in September 1966, singling out George Wallace and seeking to hold him in contempt for violating the injunction against interfering with school desegregation in Alabama. As a backup, Gray's motion asked the court to require Wallace, Meadows, and the state board of education to desegregate all the public schools of Alabama. The plaintiffs alleged that Wallace had been instrumental in the Alabama legislature's passage of an anti-guidelines law, which "was enacted with the sole purpose and effect of nullifying school desegregation efforts by local public school officials" under Title VI of the Civil Rights Act of 1964.[1]

It was the HEW guidelines that provoked the Alabama legislation and infuriated Wallace. In his response, the pugilist governor ignored the anti-guidelines law issue and instead complained about the federal courts—"Communist tactics have no place in America"—virtually inviting the court to a contempt fight. He seemed to borrow a tactic from Governor Ross Barnett of Mississippi, who had tied the federal courts in knots over contempt charges related to his efforts to exclude James Meredith from the University of Mississippi.[2]

No doubt wishing to avoid providing Wallace with free publicity, the court promptly denied the contempt motion because "the primary purpose of this litigation . . . is the desegregation of the public schools in the State of Alabama and not punitive action." The court instead decided to concentrate on the motion for statewide desegregation, setting it on a fast track with a hearing scheduled for November 30, 1966.[3]

The day after the plaintiffs filed their motion, Johnson wrote to Doar asking that he "make known, as early as possible, the position of the United States on this matter."[4] Doar engaged in a lengthy decision-making process; however, while his answer was not formally made known until the United States filed its post-trial brief, "the CRD [position] was apparent to all before the post trial filing."[5] The plaintiffs had filed the motion and actively participated in the trial, with DOJ giving its full support. Nonetheless, when I presented our pleadings challenging the tuition grant statute to Judge Johnson on August 30, the judge responded, "What about the statewide desegregation relief?" Doar wrote and then crossed out a note on Barrett's memo that he was not happy that I had been sent in without being fully prepared to respond to Johnson's question.[6]

What followed demonstrated the importance of detailed fact analysis to shape the relief. It underscored the role of the federal government and the trust that the DOJ had established with the three judges. The department deployed the kind of factual analysis and legal theory that had so successfully laid the foundation for the Voting Rights Act.[7]

Doar quickly mobilized a large trial team, under the supervision of St. John Barrett, the division's most experienced litigator. When Barrett left his job as an assistant district attorney in California to work at the DOJ in 1954, shortly after the decision in *Brown*, he felt he "was mounting a surfboard on the leading edge of a new wave of history." Barrett had been chief of the Civil Rights Section before the 1957 Civil Rights Act created the CRD. He had deep experience in civil rights litigation, had worked on the Little Rock and New Orleans school cases, and had overseen the impact aid school desegregation suits.[8]

In a meeting the following week, Doar spoke with staff about the need for complete desegregation of schools in Alabama and about the difficulties he saw. He said that desegregation would have to comply with the latest rulings of the appellate courts and should be as uniform as possible. He noted as well that free choice plans for desegregation had sent some African American students to white schools, but no whites to Black schools. And while the need for statewide desegregation was apparent, he worried whether the three-judge court would be able to enforce compliance.[9]

The setting of the hearing date triggered a flurry of activity in the CRD. Although the division had taken no position on the plaintiffs' motion, it immediately began planning how to develop evidence on the role of the state officials in the racial segregation of local schools. It could have confined its case to proving their acts of interference but instead opted to enlarge the scope of the case to encompass the state's role in every aspect of school segregation. Division staff had to become experts in the nuts and bolts of Alabama school law. The case would not only have to show that the state officials had violated the Constitution but would have to develop evidence on how to remedy the violation. If all they had done was interfere with local desegregation efforts, the remedy might have been limited to banning future interference. The division set out to prove that Alabama state officials were deeply involved in every aspect of school segregation. Experience in the voting rights cases had demonstrated that detailed exposition of how the state pursued its racial discrimination program would help shape judicial relief to eradicate the discrimination, leading to a more encompassing remedy.

Division attorneys set up an intense program of evidence discovery. They would need to inspect and photograph Alabama Department of Education files, which would require filing a motion for discovery. They would also need to learn about the impact of the state officials' actions on the local school boards. This meant taking the depositions of school superintendents and subpoenaing their records—more copying. Moreover, they had to divide the analysis of the information gathered to encompass a variety of topics: school finance, school construction, teachers, transportation, and curriculum. A case of this magnitude would ordinarily take an army of lawyers and paralegals a year or more to develop. The term "paralegal," however, did not yet exist; neither the *Lee* plaintiffs nor the plaintiffs in a companion case brought by the Alabama NAACP branch had an army of lawyers; and the CRD had only a few lawyers assigned to Alabama. Displaying his willingness to breach organizational lines, Doar diverted to the *Lee* case several lawyers from their work in Mississippi and Louisiana. And displaying his inventiveness, he had created a cadre of "research analysts," recent college graduates performing what would now be considered paralegal duties; he assigned several of them to the *Lee* case. In 1966 almost all lawyers in the division were men; all the research analysts were women.

Barrett assigned me the task of organizing the efforts of the very talented trial team. Some of the lawyers and paralegals would later become partners in top-notch law firms or law professors. Some would move to public interest organizations. Only one of the lawyers and one of the research analysts were African Americans. Indeed, the CRD employed only a few African American lawyers and research analysts. The division had successfully recruited a large number of African American secretaries, but African American law graduates were in short supply and the DOJ had not developed an effective affirmative action program. Division staff was able to establish relationships with African American leaders in Alabama, but there was undoubtedly a racial divide that hindered trust. Nonetheless, years later, SNCC leader Robert Moses would refer to Doar as having been "our lawyer."[10] The NAACP LDF and the NAACP did assign some African American lawyers to the *Lee* case, and Fred Gray continued to represent the plaintiffs. The positions of the department and the LDF were closely aligned on most issues over the course of many years.

THE NAACP'S SUIT

To complicate an already complex case, the Alabama NAACP State Conference of Branches filed a separate suit against George Wallace and Superintendent Meadows, as well as the Tuscaloosa City school board and other state officials. The plaintiffs asked the court to hold the Alabama anti-guidelines law unconstitutional and to enjoin the defendants from interfering with compliance with the HEW guidelines. They were represented by the national NAACP counsel, Robert Carter; Howard Law School professor Frank Reeves; and by several African American lawyers from the Birmingham area. Because the suit challenged the constitutionality of the anti-guidelines law, a three-judge federal district court was required by law. Judges Rives, Johnson, and a new federal judge, Virgil Pittman, were named to handle the case. In October, the court consolidated for hearing the new suit with *Lee v. Macon County Board of Education*, so that four rather than three judges would hear the two suits. It is not clear why the NAACP filed a separate suit. There was, to be sure, rivalry between the national LDF and NAACP lawyers; perhaps there was rivalry between Fred Gray and the local NAACP attorneys. As it turned out, the local NAACP lawyers did not work well together; nor did Robert Carter and Frank Reeves. The NAACP case became a diversion from the main issue presented by the *Lee* plaintiffs, but the United States felt compelled to intervene to defend the HEW guidelines.[11]

Wallace and Meadows, adopting the view that the best defense lies in a good offense, treated the NAACP suit as an opportunity to join the United States and HEW officials as defendants to a "third party complaint." They acknowledged that the validity of the guidelines was at issue and asked the court to declare them invalid. The DOJ objected to the complaint against the United States but acquiesced in joining Secretary of HEW John Gardner and Commissioner of Education Harold Howe as defendants, so that the court could decide on whether the guidelines were valid. The court dismissed the United States but kept Gardner and Howe as defendants. The United States almost simultaneously filed a complaint in the NAACP suit, as amicus and plaintiff, asking the court to declare the anti-guidelines law invalid. This complaint was signed by Ramsey Clark, the son of Supreme Court Justice Tom Clark, who had succeeded Katzenbach as attorney general but who had not yet been confirmed by the Senate.[12] The United States not only complained of the interference with HEW's guidelines but portrayed the interference as targeting *Brown* itself: "The purpose and effect of H.446 is to facilitate and perpetuate maintenance of dual school systems based upon race in the State of Alabama and to impede and interfere with efforts of local school boards to transform dual structures based upon race into single non-racial school systems."[13]

The defendants took Howe's deposition, attempting to show that the guidelines were unlawful. They sought to show that the provisions regarding the percentage of students who transferred from segregated schools required "racial balance," in violation of the Civil Rights Act of 1964. Howe's responses refuted that contention but reflected a very ambiguous policy. While conceding that the guidelines said "the best indicator of whether a free choice plan is actually working to eliminate the dual school structure is the extent to which students have transferred from segregated schools," Howe added that a "low rate of transfers or the lack of any transfers does not directly result in a decision that the free choice plan is not being properly administered." In other words: "The percentage figures contained in the Guidelines act as administrative guides which are helpful in determining where we will focus our limited staff for the purpose of examining plans. These percentages are not automatic determinates related to compliance. In reviewing the plan we would look at all of its aspects, not just at the transfer of Negro students to white schools."[14]

HEARING ON THE TUITION GRANT ISSUE

The court also held a hearing on September 30 to consider the department's request to hold the latest tuition grant statute unconstitutional. I represented the United States at this hearing. It had been quite a month for me. With almost three years of practice in the CRD under my belt, I had developed knowledge of Alabama's schools through work on voting rights cases. The division had argued in Alabama voter registration cases that Alabama's literacy requirement could not be applied where the schools had failed to provide Black students with basic literacy skills.[15] I had handled hearings in school desegregation cases involving Bay County, Florida, and Crenshaw, Perry, and Hale Counties, Alabama, and had prepared the tuition grant case, taking depositions of private school administrators throughout the Alabama Black Belt. These were congenial depositions, as the defendants were represented by Maury Smith and Joe Goodwyn, highly capable and professional lawyers. Smith, who had worked in the Alabama attorney general's office before entering private practice, was a World War II veteran and a civic leader in Montgomery. Goodwyn was a member of the Alabama senate from Montgomery, where the Black registration had increased sufficiently to make him a moderate on race issues. He described his visit to an African American church to seek the vote of congregants: Before being allowed to speak with them, he spoke with the ministers about why he should receive the "Nigra" vote. They told him that would not do. They instructed him to pat his knee and pronounce the word "knee," then to slowly raise his hand and say "grow." Then they had him combine the two words and repeat several times "knee grow." Only then could he talk with the congregants.

In advance of the September hearing, Goodwyn, Smith, and I decided that we could agree on the facts of the case and that the only issue was one of law, so we spent considerable time working out a written stipulation of facts. On Friday, September 30, as the lawyer representing the moving party, I was to be first to present the case to the three judges. As the hearing began, I informed the court that the parties had agreed on the facts and offered our stipulation as an exhibit. I had expected the court to be pleased that it would not have to sit through a long factual hearing. Instead, the presiding judge expressed displeasure that we had taken the court's time and required Judge Grooms to drive ninety miles from Birmingham to Montgomery to hear the case. The court set a briefing schedule and adjourned, having set a hearing on the plaintiffs' motion for statewide relief for November 30, just two months away. I flew back to Washington, tail between my legs. Still, the challenge to the tuition grant statute ultimately prevailed.

PPREPARING FOR THE TRIAL

The team had only six weeks until trial, but during that brief time the CRD conducted extensive discovery, taking depositions of seven state officials and thirty-eight local school superintendents, inspecting records at state and local levels, and serving interrogatories on the defendants.[16] The team divided the state into quadrants, with two lawyers assigned to each one, thus making it possible for depositions to be conducted in several locations at the same time. Private plaintiffs participated in some of this discovery but did not have the resources to do so in full.

Why mobilize such a large force to prove the obvious? A respectable argument could have been made that since the state had required the creation of racially segregated school systems, the state had an affirmative obligation to dismantle them. After all, of 294,737 African American children in Alabama public schools, only 1,009 attended school with whites.[17] However, logic unadorned by facts often fails in court. No court had issued statewide relief in a school desegregation case, and it seemed prudent to present proof supporting the liability of the state officials. The nature of the state control might also prove useful in fashioning relief.

Doar had inculcated his staff in the romance of the records. As later described by author Jimmie Breslin, Doar had relied heavily on voter registration records in developing the foundational cases of the Voting Rights Act. In voting rights litigation, the division had needed to prove that voter registrars had accepted voter applications of less qualified whites while rejecting those of equally or more qualified African Americans. Division lawyers analyzed the registration records, and secretaries typed five-ply index cards reflecting the analysis. Breslin explained, "by cross-filing index cards of white and black voters, the lawyers were able to prove that if a black man and a white man gave exactly the same answers to the questions, the black man failed and the white man passed."[18] Even before the statewide case, records had played an important role in school desegregation cases. While it was easy enough to prove that the school boards had strictly enforced Alabama's school segregation laws, the records reflected both the methods and extremity of the disparate treatment of Blacks and whites, which proved essential to developing remedies for the segregation.

When it came time to develop the statewide suit in *Lee*, discovery revealed a treasure trove of records. Division lawyers had some knowledge of the extent of statewide school discrimination because that had been a basis for its suit attacking the Alabama poll tax. A book from the 1930s revealed the extent to which Alabama's schools were not only segregated but also unequal. The author, the distinguished Black educator Dr. Horace Mann Bond, had based much of his study on the records of the Alabama Department of Education. So the trial team embarked on a detailed inspection of state records, which came to form the backbone of the case for statewide relief. The records also provided invaluable information that would inform remedy proceedings. CRD lawyer Chad Quaintance had presciently outlined in a memo how the department of education's records would reflect state complicity in every aspect of system of racial segregation.[19] Although the broad outlines of the extent to which the state officials had interfered with school desegregation and the scope of their legal authority over local school districts may have been known, the details exposed through discovery underscored the pervasiveness of the state controlled system of racial segregation. The state exercised broad authority in school construction, assignment of faculty and staff, and transportation, always favoring racial segregation. A few examples make the point.

Upon request from local school systems across the state, the Alabama Department of Education conducted periodic school surveys, inspecting school sites, buildings, and transportation systems. The department reports that followed the surveys included recommendations on the future use of school sites and buildings. The FBI created exhibits to graphically show how state school surveys, ostensibly undertaken to improve education in the surveyed school systems, perpetuated the racially dual school system. Some surveys failed to suggest the consolidation of Black and white schools in order to eliminate schools that the surveyors found subminimal. Some suggested consolidation along racial lines. Some suggested locating new schools in a manner that perpetuated segregation. In response to this pattern, HEW experts showed how the schools could be integrated.

Specifically, two government exhibits contrasted the segregative recommendations for school use in Calhoun County with the more compact and desegregated alternatives that were available. The exhibits, on large posterboard,

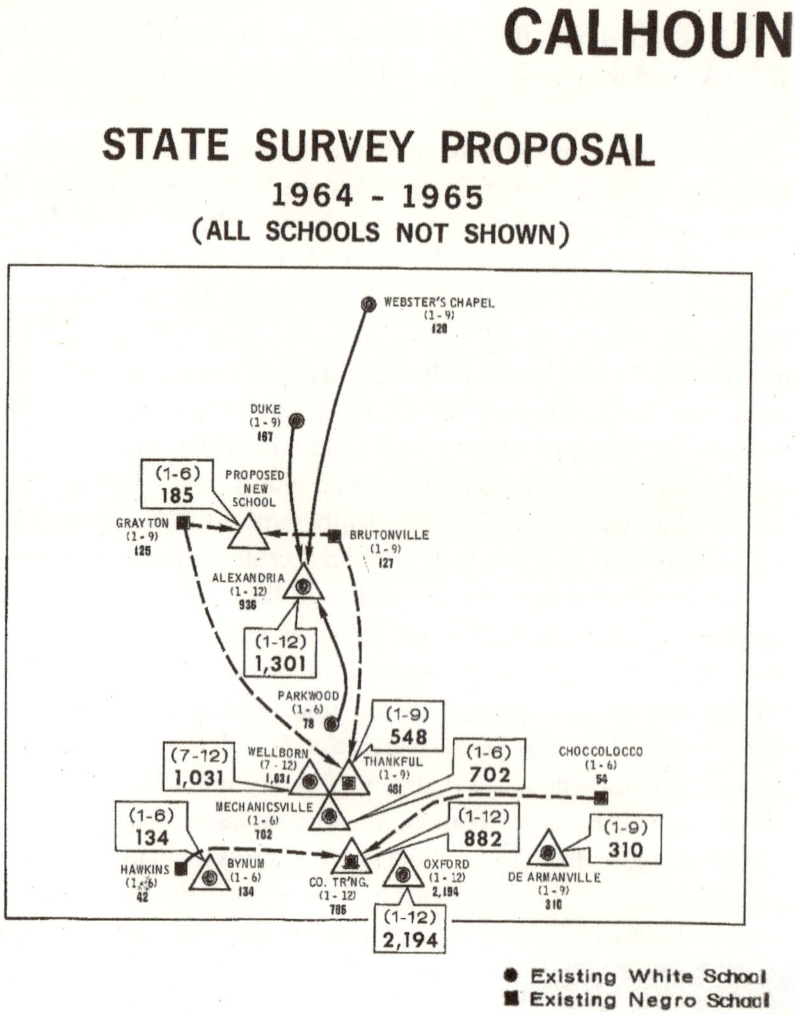

Figure 1. Exhibit 144A, Alabama State Board of Education Report for Calhoun County 1964–1965, Survey no. 196.

used triangles, squares, colors, and lines to explain how Alabama's department of education had acted as if there were two school systems, one white and one Black, underscoring the fact that the survey recommendations ignored the possibility of treating all the schools as part of one racially neutral system. The first exhibit showed that the state school survey recommended building a new Black elementary school for only 185 students living in the north part of the county and busing the students in grades 7 through 9 to the all-Black Thankful

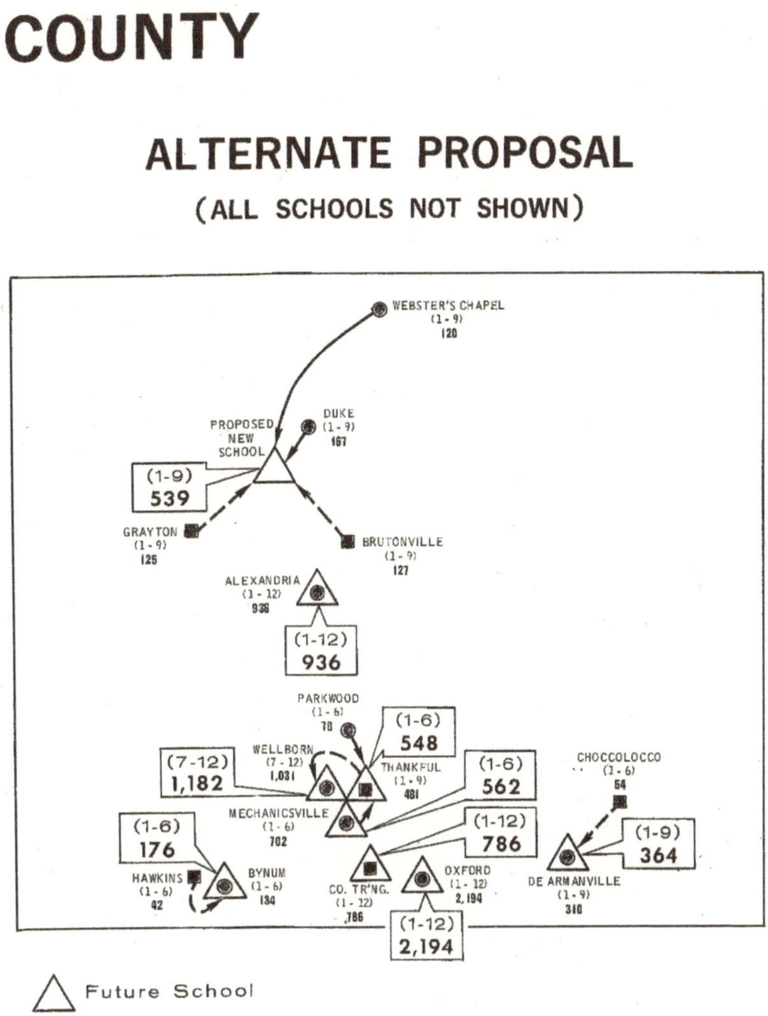

Figure 2. HEW's "Alternate Proposal" for Calhoun County, Alabama.
Source: Government Exhibit 144A.

school in the southern part of the county. The only Black high school was in the southern part as well. The survey proposed consolidating white schools in the northern part of the county and sending all 1,301 white students to Alexandria, a 1 through 12 school. A companion exhibit prepared with help from HEW showed how school consolidation could be achieved with less busing, sending 539 students of both races to the new elementary school and 936 students of both races to Alexandria. Yet, the surveys recommended school construction separately for each race and segregated transportation routes for students. While the exhibits may seem difficult to follow, the court got the message: "Such a method of consolidation was for no purpose other than to perpetuate segregation of the races."[20]

Deposition of the Tuscaloosa County school superintendent revealed that the governor and state superintendent used extraordinary measures to carry out "the public policy of the State that Negro teachers not teach white children."[21] The statistics confirmed the policy: of more than twenty-eight thousand teachers in the state, only seventy-six were teaching in schools of the other race.[22] Traditionally the state department of education would allocate funds to school systems based on "teacher units," calculated separately for each race. A school superintendent from a heavily Black school system pointed out to Austin Meadows that a merger of the two sets of teacher units would enable the system to direct more money to the white schools. Meadows responded that directing money this way would "result in the courts assigning the Negro children to said white schools." Moreover, such a change would show "that the white people in official positions do not intend to treat Negro pupils either justly or fairly."[23] Yet the very next year saw Meadows adopt a rule that resulted in funding a 28:1 pupil teacher ratio in white schools and a 30:1 ratio in Black schools, shorting the Black schools by 617 teaching slots. Even teacher training institutes continued to be racially segregated.[24] Discovery also revealed that the department of education viewed a college degree as essential; hiring a teacher without a degree "cuts at the very heart of a school." Nonetheless, the department approved filling vacancies at Black schools with Black teachers without a college degree rather than hiring white teachers with a college degree to fill those positions.[25]

Discovery also revealed egregious segregation at the postsecondary level, in Alabama's growing network of trade schools and junior colleges. The state maintained six trade schools and two junior colleges for Black students and twenty-one trade schools and twelve junior colleges for white students. As late as 1965 Meadows, seemingly oblivious to the requirements of the Constitution and Title VI, proudly hailed plans to establish two trade schools and a new junior college for the "minority race."[26]

Plaintiffs and the United States were aware of some of the state defendants' deliberate interference with school desegregation. Discovery and legal research revealed that the interference was ubiquitous, constant, and both general and targeted, and that it began even before the Supreme Court's decision in *Brown*.

In 1953 the Alabama legislature appointed a committee to prepare legislation in the event that the court's decision "destroys or impairs the principle of separation of the races in the public schools of this State."[27] In 1956 the legislature declared the *Brown* decision null and void. And, of course, the governor had deployed state troopers to stop desegregation in 1963. These early actions served as backdrop to the state defendants' continued interference with school desegregation after the 1964 order in *Lee* enjoined them from further interference in this area. They helped explain why, despite the Civil Rights Act and enforcement by HEW, only about 4,200 of the more than 294,000 African American students in Alabama public schools attended school with whites. By the time of the trial, only 17 of Alabama's 118 school systems were under court order to desegregate.[28] The rest fell squarely within HEW's enforcement authority.

THE TRIAL

The plaintiffs in *Lee* were asking the court to do something that had never been done before on such a scale. The court's answer would determine whether school desegregation litigation would continue to proceed laboriously one school system at a time. A whole generation of school children had graduated from segregated schools throughout much of the South since *Brown*, as regional politicians' strategy of forcing system-by-system litigation had succeeded in delaying compliance with the Fourteenth Amendment. The three judges had hitherto been reluctant to issue a sweeping statewide order and were unlikely to issue one if they could not enforce it. Most probably they wanted the force of the federal executive behind any such order. The Supreme Court in *Brown II* had placed on the shoulders of the local federal judges the task of supervising school desegregation. But how could the court master the details of ninety-nine school systems? And what if the state officials refused to comply? The task would become partly bureaucratic and partly one of law enforcement.

I flew to Montgomery on Saturday, November 20, and stayed there for the next two weeks. I took the depositions of Superintendent Meadows and his assistant, Dr. George Layton, on Wednesday. The next day was Thanksgiving. The trial began the following Wednesday, with Fred Gray, representing Anthony Lee and his co-plaintiffs, questioning Meadows. Not only did the discovery establish the extent of state control of local school districts and the pervasive pressure to resist the HEW desegregation requirements, it also revealed an absence. The court's 1964 order had not only enjoined the state defendants from interference but had also ordered them to use their authority "to devote every effort toward initiating desegregation and bringing about the elimination of racial discrimination in the public school system."[29] Much like the case of the dog who didn't bark, the records of the Alabama Department of Education revealed no efforts to eliminate racial discrimination. This led to the following colloquy between Gray and Meadows:

> Q: Can you relate to this court or refer to this court any written document in your office or release of any sort that you have sent to City and County Boards of Education in which you encouraged or promoted the elimination of segregated school systems in this State?
> A: No. I approach it from nondiscrimination viewpoint.[30]

Meadows's defense was that he had been ordered to encourage the elimination of racial discrimination but not racial segregation:

> I have never encouraged anybody to initiate desegregation plans. I have urged . . . that they not discriminate against any individuals, and if that required desegregation, then they would have to follow desegregation, but only to prevent discrimination has been my recommendation, prior to the Civil Rights Act and the U.S. Office of Education guidelines.[31]

Meadows's belief that segregation was not discrimination led him to write an astonishing paean to segregation and send it to local school superintendents throughout Alabama, which became an exhibit at trial. The government brief mentioned it but, in an apparent effort not to appear to be seeking to embarrass Meadows, left out such passages as "Birds of a feather truly flock together. Wild geese fly across this continent in 'V' formation, but they never join any other flock of birds. . . . Red birds mate with red birds, the beautiful blue birds mate with other blue birds, and so on through bird life." The district court, however, quoted Meadows's "parable" at length, beginning with "'Segregation' is a perfectly good word. It has been practiced down through the ages for good results. The Lord set aside or segregated fruit from the apple tree in the Garden of Eden from Adam and Eve."[32]

Barrett presented the government's case, armed with information from his trial team about his exhibits and lines of witness questioning. The evidence established that the state officials had not only failed to promote desegregation of the schools but had actively promoted segregation and had interfered with those school systems that were willing to desegregate, allowing Wallace and Meadows to largely succeed in fending off desegregation. Alabama, with only 2.4 percent of its Black students attending school with whites, had less desegregation than any other Southern state, less even than Mississippi.[33] Wallace's attack on the HEW guidelines may have helped his wife's campaign to succeed him in office but became an important part of the proof in *Lee*. Forty-five Alabama school districts had neither a court-ordered desegregation plan nor a plan approved by HEW.

The question then became how to fashion relief against the state officials. In one of his anti-guidelines speeches, Wallace had charged that desegregation decrees reflected "the collusion which exists between the Executive Branch of government and the federal court system."[34] While Wallace overstated the case, Judge Johnson and his colleagues did rely on the government drafts when preparing their decrees. In cases involving individual districts that task had been simplified by the existence of the guidelines and by the Fifth Circuit's holdings that the courts should follow them. But how to design a statewide decree?

DESIGNING A REMEDY

Establishing a violation of the Constitution and of prior court orders would prove much easier than designing an effective, workable, and fair remedy. The success of any statewide desegregation order against those who had so vehemently opposed desegregation seemed doubtful. Alabama public officials had shown themselves adept at defying, stalling, and distorting orders to desegregate schools or register qualified African Americans to vote. Such intransigence had led to the Voting Rights Act of 1965, which had abandoned flexibility and deference to local officials and had empowered federal employees to register voters. *Brown*, at the remedy stage, had left "primary responsibility" for desegregation to "good faith implementation" by "school authorities." District courts reviewing desegregation plans were to "be guided by equitable principles." The court had told the lower courts to ensure that the school board plans would "effectuate a transition to a racially nondiscriminatory school system."[35] In response Alabama school systems had refused to comply. When ordered by federal courts to do so they had delayed and, when desegregation became inevitable, they had sought to minimize it. Continued flexibility in designing a remedy seemed fruitless.

In August 1966 Doar had raised with the *Lee* team the question of appointing a special master to take over the desegregation responsibilities of the state superintendent of schools, after receiving a staff proposal that the state superintendent "be ordered to require as a prerequisite to payment of state money that the recipient school board provide education on a desegregated, non-racial basis."[36] By October Doar expressed a goal of complete desegregation of Alabama schools, based on the latest rulings of the higher courts. He also noted the difficulties of a cookie-cutter approach, as it would be difficult to attain uniformity between the rural, 80 percent Black Lowndes County and the predominantly white urban system in Tuscaloosa. He also acknowledged that no one had the answer to the fact that free choice ran only from Black schools to white schools and not in the other direction. Finally, he expressed concern that a three-judge court could not effectively enforce compliance.

In earlier phases of the case, the relief had been shaped by reference to the experiences of individual students. Doar, Jonathan Sutin, and other CRD lawyers had spent time with the students and their parents and had learned about their hopes for equal education. The focus on the experience of individuals had been shaped by the way in which the division had approached voting rights litigation. Individual African Americans had testified about their unsuccessful efforts to register to vote, which contrasted with the testimony of individual whites about their effortless registration experience.

Working through the December holidays, a team of ten attorneys, five paralegals, and eight secretaries produced a 133-page "brief," plus voluminous statistical appendices and a detailed proposed decree. The CRD team was unusually introspective in its discussion of relief. It mused about "what specific form of relief against the defendant state officials can be effective to accomplish the desegregation of public schools throughout the State." It worried "whether the court [could] effectively control [each state Department of Education] program or function through its order to further compliance with constitutional standards at both the state and local levels." And it urged the court to fashion relief that desegregated the schools rather than punishing the defendants. But it acknowledged that the issues "admit[ed] of no simple, and perhaps of no single, answer."[37]

The government brief then addressed what the decree ought to include. The division attorneys had concluded that it should strengthen the 1964 decree against state interference and discrimination and seek to bring into initial paper compliance the school districts without court-approved or HEW-approved desegregation plans.[38] The question then became how to bring about this compliance. The brief suggested alternatives: add these districts as defendants and issue an injunction against them; ask the United States to obtain approved plans from these districts; require the state superintendent to obtain plans from the districts; and only add the districts as defendants if they failed to submit adequate plans. The brief expressed the "hope that whatever method is used to seek commitments of compliance from local school districts, the great majority of these districts would give a commitment to abide by current legal requirements once those requirements had been clearly enunciated by this court in its judgment in this case."[39] The brief assumed that the court would spell out the criteria that each plan must meet.

The government brief in *Lee* had, of course, addressed the issue of actual compliance—that is, how to ensure nondiscriminatory implementation of the desegregation plans. It urged the court to order the state superintendent to report to the court and the plaintiffs on implementation by each school system and by the state. In February 1967 we filed a supplemental brief laying out a proposed decree. Johnson's file contains a heavily annotated copy of that proposal, which became the basis of the court's order, but with many changes.[40] The supplemental brief proposed that the court require the state superintendent of education to notify forty-two listed school systems that they are required to adopt a desegregation plan that either met criteria for a freedom of choice plan or met the criteria of the revised HEW guidelines. Instead, the court ordered the state Superintendent to notify ninety-nine listed school systems that they must meet the standards "embodied in the plan attached to this decree."[41] In twelve pages, the plan detailed affirmative steps that school systems must take to disestablish state-enforced or -encouraged school segregation and eliminate the effects of the state's past race discrimination in supervising the public schools. The steps included student and faculty desegregation, nondiscrimination in every aspect of the school system, and equalization, construction, and consolidation of schools to promote desegregation. The decree and plan included extensive reporting requirements.

On December 29, 1966, a panel of the Fifth Circuit issued a decision that, in the words of the future chief judge of the United States Court of Appeals for the Fourth Circuit, J. Harvie Wilkinson III, "transformed the face of school desegregation law."[42] The opinion in *United States v. Jefferson County Board of Education* was the third and most thoroughly developed of a trilogy of opinions written by Judge John Minor Wisdom. Emphasizing with italics, Wisdom articulated a pragmatic rule: "*The only school desegregation plan that meets constitutional standards is one that works.*" To implement that rule he turned to the HEW guidelines, which "offer new hope to Negro school children long denied their constitutional rights." Noting that "the courts alone have failed," he hailed the possibility that the three branches of the federal government, acting together, "may be able to make meaningful the right of Negro children to equal educational opportunities." The court rejected the defendants' claim that the guidelines were unlawful. The lower courts had approved desegregation plans that had resulted in 110 (0.019 percent) of the 59,361 African American students attending white schools in 1965. Faculties were completely segregated. In the eleven states of the former Confederacy 2.25 percent of the African American students attended white schools. Wisdom's opinion concluded that the experience recited in the DOJ brief—128 lower court cases leading to 513 district court orders and 76 court of appeals orders in ten years—"argues strongly for uniform standards in court-supervised desegregation." He attached to his opinion a decree, primarily based on the HEW guidelines, "to apply uniformly throughout this circuit in cases involving plans based on free choice of schools." Using words that would, less than two years later, be adopted by the Supreme Court, Wisdom explained the objective: "a bona fide unitary system where schools are not white schools or Negro schools—just schools."[43] Doar ordered copies of the 153-page decision and dissent printed for all the lawyers in the CRD. The question then became whether, because of its significance and bold relief, the decision would be reviewed by all the judges of the Fifth Circuit, sitting en banc.

ORAL ARGUMENT IN LEE AND JEFFERSON COUNTY

The court heard oral argument in *Lee* and *NAACP v. Wallace* for eight hours on February 3, 1967. Judge Rives presided. Although as a judge who had taken senior status, he would be ineligible to participate in any en banc proceedings in the *Jefferson County* case, he presumably had some notion that led him to say that the *Lee* court was disposed to await the outcome of any en banc hearing that might be held in *Jefferson County* before issuing a decision in *Lee*, though it did plan to rule in time to be effective for the fall 1967 school opening.

The court turned first to *NAACP v. Wallace*. Rives dominated the lively questioning of the NAACP lawyer, Joan Franklin, and Barrett. He expressed several concerns: Could HEW issue the guidelines without the president's signature? Could HEW require faculty desegregation? Does free choice take a back seat to integration? May the courts require racial balance? When John Satterfield took the lectern to argue on behalf of Wallace and Meadows, Judges Johnson and Pittman jumped in with similar questions.

Most of these questions arose because of Congress's ambiguity in the new Civil Rights Act. Title VI required HEW to adopt "rules, regulations, or orders of general applicability," but they were not to become effective "unless and until approved by the President."[44] HEW had adopted regulations approved by the president, but Satterfield argued that this language also applied to the guidelines. Barrett argued that, unlike rules, regulations, or orders of general applicability, the guidelines did not have the force of law; they simply advised school districts about policies. Title VI said it did not apply to employment practices "except where a primary objective of the Federal financial assistance is to provide employment."[45] In addition, the employment provisions of the Civil Rights Act, Title VII, did not, as originally enacted, apply to educational institutions.[46] Here, however, court decisions carrying out *Brown* came to the rescue; the statute might not apply to faculty employment, but the Constitution did.

The Supreme Court had suggested and the Fifth Circuit had held that, at the very least, if free choice was inhibited by faculty segregation, the faculty must be desegregated. Title IV, which authorized school desegregation suits by the attorney general, provided that "'desegregation' shall not mean the assignment of students in public schools in order to overcome racial imbalance."[47] A related provision said the act did not "empower any official or court of the United States to issue any order seeking to achieve a racial balance in any school by requiring the transportation of pupils or students from one school to another or one school district to another in order to achieve such racial balance."[48] Satterfield argued that the HEW guidelines violated these provisions, both by requiring race-based student assignments where free choice was ineffective and by unfairly targeting Southern dual school systems while allowing so-called de facto segregation in the North. Rives seemed attracted to this argument, but Franklin responded that the Constitution recognized a distinction between segregation intentionally imposed by the state and de facto segregation. Barrett added, relying on *Jefferson County*, that an order taking race into account in order to remedy state-imposed segregation was not inconsistent with the ban on orders to achieve racial balance.[49]

Moving on to the *Lee* case, the court first heard from LDF lawyer Henry Aronson, representing the plaintiffs. Aronson's boss, Jack Greenberg, described him as "unlike any other LDF lawyer" because his "chutzpah knew no bounds."[50] After reciting the evidence that had overwhelmingly showed the culpability of Wallace and Meadows, Aronson turned to the main question: what to do about it? Aronson argued that free choice was not a constitutional right and that there is no right to associate with students only of your own race. When Rives expressed concern about that argument, Aronson responded "I disagree." He said a free choice plan must "work," prompting Rives to ask what "work" means. Judge Grooms jumped in to ask whether Aronson wanted "forced integration" and Aronson responded, "Yes, that is the only way to end years of segregation; there is no middle ground."[51] The remainder of Aronson's argument discussed details of a proposed decree, culminating with ruminations from Rives that while a new decree could be more specific than the prior one, it was still hard to see what more the court could do than stop the state from becoming a party to discrimination. He thought perhaps state funds to segregated school systems could be terminated, but then the school systems would have to be joined as parties to the case. Maury Smith, arguing for the defendants, said that they had simply exercised their right to dissent and to disagree with the guidelines and that the pressure they exerted on local school officials was required to balance pressure from HEW. Argument by Hugh Maddox, legal advisor to George and Lurleen Wallace, touched on the alleged invalidity of the ratification of the Fourteenth Amendment, the question whether *Brown* was valid, and the lack of any individual claiming he is being discriminated against. Finally, Fred Gray, in his rebuttal argument, urged that the court decide the case promptly and not wait for *Jefferson County.*

Soon after the oral argument in *Lee*, the Court of Appeals granted en banc review of the panel decision in the *Jefferson County* case. Doar again assembled a team of lawyers and paralegals to prepare for the oral argument to the twelve judges of the Fifth Circuit. Discussions and papers the team prepared for Doar focused on free choice, faculty desegregation, and school construction policies. While Doar reviewed the transcript of the *Lee* argument, his top assistant on the *Jefferson County* case, David L. Norman, noted that the freedom of choice remedy "brought to the surface an apparent controversy over the issue whether the Constitution requires desegregation or integration." Norman was referring to a much-cited 1955 ruling by North Carolina US District Judge John J. Parker that school districts were not required to mix students of different races but were only forbidden to treat students differently because of race.[52] Norman told Doar that school boards "must be guided by the principle 'but for the difference of race of student A and student B would they, by logic or by sound educational principles, be attending the same school;' and if they would be, the board must take affirmative action to bring about that result."[53] This meant that freedom of choice suffices only if it leads to students A and B attending the same school.

Argument took place the following month, in Jacksonville, Florida, where the General Services Administration had to build a facility that could accommodate the twelve judges of what was then the nation's largest court. The *Jacksonville Journal* predicted that the case would be "historic not only for the number of judges involved, but for the importance of the decision."[54] Ten lawyers participated in the five-hour hearing, but the arguments of two stood out. John Satterfield, representing some of the defendant school systems, said the issue was "whether . . . the illegal compulsion of the federal government will be substituted for the illegal compulsion of the states."[55] He argued that a uniform decree based on the HEW guidelines would destroy freedom of choice: "Students will be assigned and reassigned on the basis of race. . . . Teachers will be under federal inspection."[56]

For his part, Doar began by departing from the outline he had prepared of his argument and answering a question that had been posed to counsel for the private plaintiffs: what did the plaintiffs and government want in this case? The "simple answer," he said, riffing from Judge Wisdom's opinion, "is that the Government wants not white schools, or not schools for white children and not schools for Negro children, but just plain schools."[57] Doar's argument then stressed Congress's intent in the Civil Rights Act of 1964 to ensure racial equality in voting, public accommodations, employment, and education. Enlarging on the language of the act, he said that as to education the act "meant the elimination of the dual school system."[58] He pointed out that the act had not only empowered the attorney general to sue or intervene in school desegregation cases to "materially further the orderly achievement of desegregation"—it had created parallel enforcement by HEW in Title VI.[59] Doar promised that the DOJ and HEW would "try to speak with one voice."[60]

The judges, listening to Doar "with an intensity that was attributable to their respect for John's integrity and sense of fairness,"[61] grilled him on what "just plain schools" meant. Judge Griffin Bell, who later became attorney general in the Carter administration, pressed the question whether the ultimate goal was racial balance. Doar responded that he was less concerned about "where we are heading than where we are" and that, while not seeking racial balance, "I am not satisfied with a system that doesn't provide fairness to Negro children and results in not 123 of 60,000 children being in white schools, but 59,860 Negro children being in Negro schools with Negro faculties in a Negro environment, put there by the School Boards for one reason, race."[62] Doar stressed the systemic nature of the racial segregation regime and the need to "deal with not just the formerly white school but all schools."[63] Turning to the HEW guidelines, Doar urged the court to recognize "that this Court and HEW, under the very nature of things, are like two engines on an airplane. . . . and to the extent that it's possible . . . we ought to try to keep those two engines in synchronization because, if we don't, we're going to have all of the School boards coming into this Court."[64] The en banc court modified the panel's decree in minor ways but otherwise approved the panel decision. It paraphrased Judge Wisdom's language and explained that the desegregation plan must lead to "integrated, unitary school system in which there are no Negro schools and no white schools—just schools."[65]

HEW MOVES FORWARD

While the parties were litigating *Lee*, HEW was busy enforcing Title VI. In a discussion memorandum for Douglass Cater, a special assistant to President Johnson, HEW noted "an urgent need now to enforce" the guidelines. The memorandum pointed out that in several Southern states, including Alabama, more than half the school districts failed to comply with the guidelines. Therefore, HEW planned to increase the number of enforcement actions and begin reviewing compliance by school districts under federal court orders. While planning to continue allowing use of freedom of choice, "there is growing evidence that it is rarely an effective means of eliminating the dual school system." Therefore, it may later "have to be abolished generally across the board by administrative action."[66] Harold Howe reported in December 1966 that HEW had begun formal enforcement proceedings against forty-eight Alabama school systems for failure to submit an acceptable desegregation plan and another four because of poor performance under a free choice plan. HEW cited examples of an African American parent losing a job with a white family after her son began attending a white school; Black children forced to ride the African American bus to the white school; and parents approached by school board members to discourage their children's attendance at a white school.[67]

HEW was also reconsidering whether to seek the president's signature on the guidelines. HEW's David Seeley wrote that the lack of formal presidential approval provided opponents of desegregation "openings . . . to sow seeds of doubt about the legality or integrity of our operation" and placed "our field staff in such a vulnerable position and exposes them to such vituperative and hostile opposition and causes unwarranted complaints."[68] Barrett, fresh from arguing the statewide desegregation issue in *Lee*, agreed that it was desirable for the president to formally approve the guidelines, as did Doar's special assistant, Owen Fiss, who sent Doar Carl Auerbach's 1965 memorandum. Fiss said the memorandum "belies the prevailing HEW dogma that the guidelines were intended to be nothing more than an 'internal set of rules' for use by the Commissioner's own staff."[69]

THE COURT ORDERS STATEWIDE DESEGREGATION

The *Lee* court issued its unanimous decision on March 22, 1967, a week before the Fifth Circuit's en banc decision in *Jefferson County*. Judge Rives, who presided in *Lee*, probably had some advance notice of the *Jefferson County* decision, and the *Lee* opinion adopted some aspects of the Fifth Circuit ruling. By then the two principal defendants, George Wallace and Austin Meadows, were no longer in office. So the court began by substituting the newly elected Governor Lurleen Wallace and State Superintendent of Education Ernest Stone, who had been sworn into office in January, as defendants.[70] Although the new Governor Wallace acted much the same as her husband had, the new state superintendent, in a break from Austin Meadows, was to become a cooperative partner in enforcing the decree.

The court's lengthy opinion develops the facts to conclude:

> Not only have these defendants, through their control and influence over the local school boards, flouted every effort to make the Fourteenth Amendment a meaningful reality to Negro school children in Alabama; they have apparently dedicated themselves and . . . have committed the powers and resources of their offices to the continuation of a dual school system such as that condemned by Brown v. Board of Education. . . . As a result of such efforts . . . today only a very small percentage of students in Alabama are enrolled in desegregated schools.[71]

The court noted that the defendants' segregative activities had infected virtually every aspect of public education and that, accordingly, the remedy "must be designed to reach the limits of the defendants' activities in these several areas and must be designed to require the defendants to . . . disestablish" the racial dual system in school systems covered by the decree. The decree, eleven pages in the reported decision, detailed the required methods of desegregation.[72] The court somewhat optimistically suggested that once the state coercion to resist desegregation was removed, local school systems would comply with orders from the state superintendent directing them to comply with the uniform state plan, and it rejected the defense argument that these school systems were indispensable parties. The court did agree that it might be necessary to bring a few districts into the litigation if they continued to operate in an unconstitutional manner. In the companion case, *NAACP v. Wallace*, the court held Alabama's anti-guidelines law unconstitutional and that HEW's 1966 Revised Guidelines were constitutional and did not violate the 1964 Civil Rights Act. The opinion concluded with "Ancillary Declarations and Observations," noting that while the act did not require racial balance, it did require "eliminating a dual structure of separate schools for students of different races and removing every vestige of legal discrimination."[73] As Johnson's biographer Jack Bass noted, "The court order [in *Lee*] provided local school boards and superintendents throughout Alabama with a collective sigh of relief. Coming under court order gave them breathing room at home, where they could blame what had to be done on the courts and provided shelter from pressure by the Wallaces."[74]

In a preview of the way in which the case would continue to expand, the court also ordered the defendants to eliminate discrimination in Alabama's trade schools, junior colleges, and state colleges. Although the plaintiffs' motions in the case had not specifically referred to higher education, they had referred more generally to "public education," which apparently sufficed. The DOJ trial brief devoted a few pages to the two race-based systems of trade schools and junior colleges under the control of the state board of education but did not mention the state colleges. And there was no evidence that any plaintiff had even expressed an interest in attending any of these institutions. Nonetheless, the court believed that "the plaintiffs are also clearly entitled to relief in this area," because the defendants were responsible for these schools, which "have been and continue to be operated as if Brown v. Board of Education were inapplicable in these areas."[75]

When the court issued its statewide order, a member of Alabama's state board of education thought it meant that "HEW . . . is out of it now" and that "now we'll be dealing with judges and not a bunch of (federal) bureaucrats." He thought that "the whole school system will be better off under a federal judge."[76] US Commissioner of Education Harold Howe was not so sure, simply noting that the court had "taken a position that supports the Office of Education requirements for school desegregation." Howe added that Alabama "has the largest proportion of compliance problems of any state, and this action will serve to give local school districts a chance to take the responsibility that is theirs to bring desegregation about."[77] The relation between the court order and HEW requirements would become an early point of contention.

Reaction in Alabama was swift. The leading newspaper in Montgomery editorialized that the decision would mean that "Alabama will likely have far more desegregation at the opening of school next fall than any other state." The editorial added that the court's decision "became inevitable when former Gov. George Wallace sent armed troopers to Tuskegee on that sad morning in September of 1963 to prevent children and teachers from entering school, even though the community—albeit reluctantly—was prepared to carry out the orders of the court as gracefully as it could in desegregating its schools."[78] The *Montgomery Advertiser* chimed in that Alabama's public schools "were *totally federalized* yesterday" and also blamed "the granitic stupidity of Wallace Administration I, which continued to intimidate local boards, to cannonade against the law and to urge defiance, even to the point of public intimidation of local officials doing what they considered to be their duty."[79]

A prescient law review note observed a few months later that the court's insistence in *Lee* "that the state had an affirmative duty to insure [*sic*] that local school boards had adopted successful desegregation plans" could "be applicable to all the states in the South."[80] While a Delaware case ten years earlier could have also served as a precedent, *Lee* would become the case other courts would look to in ordering statewide relief.[81]

6. Aftermath: Response to the Statewide Decree

One week after the March 22 decision, Governor Lurleen Wallace, addressing the Alabama legislature, declared that the decree created "an emergency which threatens our state," calling it "a decree with which compliance is a physical impossibility." It "was rendered in malice and animosity." Apparently not trusting the new state superintendent of education, Ernest Stone, the way her husband had trusted Austin Meadows, Governor Wallace asked the legislature to place in her hands "all powers heretofore vested . . . in the State Superintendent of Education." She also asked the legislature to issue a cease-and-desist order to the three federal judges "advising them that their actions are beyond the police power of the State of Alabama."[1] The speech was full of bluster and indignation, and although a news report called it "exceptionally sophisticated,"[2] the *Lee v. Macon County Board of Education* judges found it riddled with many factual errors. While pledging to "win the battle, day by day, inch by inch, and decree by decree," she modified the pledge by adding "within the law."[3] An editorial in the state's largest newspaper, while urging an appeal of the court order, criticized the governor's "spirit of defiance and disrespect for law and orderly processes."[4] Another paper called the speech "a new binge of defiance which comes close to a declaration of Civil War II."[5] The governor appeared on *Meet the Press* in April and indicated the state would make additional challenges to the court orders. And the legislature held hearings where Lieutenant Governor Albert Brewer charged the decree would "absolutely destroy public education in Alabama," while John Satterfield advised that the local school boards were not legally bound to comply with the court's order since they were not parties to the suit.[6] Governor Wallace also called a "summit" meeting of Southern governors to protest the school desegregation orders, but most of her colleagues snubbed the meeting; the three who did attend (from Georgia, Louisiana and Mississippi) simply vowed to resist the orders "within the law."[7] All that came of the sound and fury, though, were unsuccessful stay motions in the trial court and the Supreme Court, an unsuccessful appeal to the Supreme Court, and two more unconstitutional state laws. The attorney general of Alabama supported his stay motion with a very weak resolution from the Alabama Association of School Administrators that expressed "hopes that some extension may be granted to the 20-day period allowed local boards of education in preparing to carry out the provisions of the court order and decree" but said nothing about the requirement to desegregate. Several trade school administrators also supported the stay, but not the state superintendent of education or any local school boards.[8] As a headline in the *Birmingham News* pointed out, "School boards, judges join to defy governor." The accompanying story said that at least ninety-seven of the ninety-nine school systems listed in the decree were trying to comply.[9] The Supreme Court's summary affirmance of the three-judge court's decision established *Lee* as a solid precedent for future statewide desegregation orders in other states. The affirmance also meant that the district court could confidently enforce its order, free of legal doubt.

Enforcement would entail two intersecting activities. First, it required looking at each school system to determine whether it was complying. This first activity depended on the second: determining the content of compliance. In 1967 school systems would have to adopt a freedom of choice plan and begin desegregating their faculties. As we will see, though, the meaning of *compliance* would change, and the court would increasingly rely upon the federal government to help navigate the changes.

With so many school systems now involved in the case, the plaintiffs and the federal government faced a fluid scenario. Stone, a segregationist but committed to complying with the law, filed his first report to the court on April 17, with attached reports from individual school systems. Two days later, Doar and St. John Barrett discussed whether the systems should be joined as defendants or whether to direct Stone to act. The following day the DOJ submitted a report to the court stipulating that thirty-nine districts had adopted the model plan, another eight would have no Negro schools in the coming school year and had adopted relevant portions of the model plan, twenty-seven systems had submitted 1965 or 1966 plans, and five had submitted plans that failed to meet the court's model.[10] The report listed each district and explained how its plan met or failed to meet the court's requirements.

HEW COLLIDES WITH THE COURT

The school systems' initial revisions of their desegregation plans seemed to vindicate the workability of the court's decision to direct the state superintendent to enforce the order. In a subsequent order the court directed the superintendent to inform forty-eight systems that their plans were inadequate, and issued, for the first time, show cause orders to four school systems that had failed to present adequate desegregation plans. The order marked the beginning of a further expansion of the number of parties in the case and expanded the reach of the District Court for the Middle District of Alabama to the other two federal judicial districts. The following month the DOJ reported to the court that thirty-eight of the forty-eight school systems had satisfactorily amended their plans and five more were in process of doing so. Only five school systems had failed to present compliant plans. The court added those systems as defendants in the case. In June, the court ordered two of the five systems to amend their plans but withheld an order as to the other three based on assurances from those systems that they would comply. By late July, the court noted that ninety-eight of the ninety-nine school systems listed in the March decree had adopted plans that complied with the decree.[11]

Title VI and the decree presented Alabama school systems listed in the decree with differing requirements. Title VI required them to satisfy HEW that they were not engaging in discrimination; the decree required the state superintendent to make this determination. The HEW guidelines favored a geographic zoning plan for student assignment; the decree provided for a freedom of choice plan. Some provisions of the guidelines were missing from the decree. The dates for the freedom of choice period under the guidelines differed from the dates under the decree. Finally, the guidelines arguably required more teacher desegregation than the decree. The school districts, with the late exception of those just added as defendants, were not parties to the case, so the question became how to reconcile these differences. More broadly, how would these latter affect relations among the federal actors—the court, HEW, and the DOJ? HEW regulations provided that if a school system under a court order to desegregate gave HEW assurance that it would comply with the order, the school system would not have to file an additional assurance that it would comply with the guidelines.[12]

The possibility of a conflict between court standards and HEW's standards had concerned the DOJ for the prior two years. In a June 1965 meeting, DOJ attorneys had noted the problems stemming from Title VI as including "the roles of the various agencies in handling complaints, investigations, and dealing with other agencies must be made clear."[13] The potential for agency conflict meant that clarification of the respective roles of the department and HEW was sorely needed.

At the same meeting, DOJ attorney David Rubin listed questions regarding the department's role based on Title VI. Among the concerns was whether the department should "assume or attempt to assume responsibility for coordinating federal policy and interpretation under Title VI." The underlying considerations included (1) the need to have a unified and single government voice; (2) the tendency of federal agencies to focus on giving out money rather than on desegregation; and (3) the desire to have the department participate in agency decisions that might spark litigation. "For example, HEW's guidelines affect what we can do in school suits and determinations or procedural questions will affect our posture in suits to enforce assurances under Title VI."[14] This presentation specifically addressed concern about how HEW's enforcement might draw the DOJ into litigation and the pressing need to have the roles of the agencies clarified.

The DOJ's position with respect to HEW's authority remained fluid from 1965 until the issue was decided in 1967. CRD attorney Reuben Ortenberg described enforcement of Title VI as "a responsibility shared by the Department of Justice and many other agencies."[15] Ortenberg's concern was focused on inconsistent action under the authority given by Title VI—"for example on the basis of negotiations with School Board officials, HEW might approve a plan which we [the DOJ], on the basis of our contact with Negro leaders, might feel obliged to attack in the Courts, either in the same or different school districts."[16] Paul Rilling, a former HEW official, later explained to a congressional committee that coordination between the two agencies on school desegregation had "never been too effective" and that there had "always been too much of a feeling that each Department has its own job to do and does it pretty much without close coordination with the other."[17]

These descriptions of the relationship between the two departments omitted mention of some sources of friction. DOJ attorneys were litigation focused, with experience forged in voting rights cases and in their early efforts in school desegregation cases in Southern courts. HEW relied on educators to enforce Title VI, with advice from HEW lawyers. At the outset, neither the educators nor the HEW attorneys had experience in race discrimination matters, though they would develop that expertise over time. DOJ efforts were concentrated in the CRD, while at the outset HEW confused enforcement by spreading responsibilities among the secretary's office, the Office of Education, and the general counsel's office. As a leading school desegregation scholar, Gary Orfield, describes the structure, the secretary's office and the commissioner of education backed strong enforcement, but lower-ranking officials in the Office of Education feared damage to their relationships with local educators and the general counsel focused on paper compliance rather than actual desegregation.[18]

The structure of civil rights enforcement at HEW remained in flux at least until the creation of the Office for Civil Rights in 1967.[19] HEW's reliance on regional offices resulted in loose control of day-to-day enforcement actions, in contrast to the highly centralized control exercised by Burke Marshall and John Doar and their successors over CRD attorneys. The division's litigation orientation led to some preference for individuated fact-dependent review of school desegregation efforts. HEW had responsibility for Title VI compliance by thousands of school districts and needed clear administrative standards. The DOJ controlled all litigation, represented HEW when school districts challenged enforcement actions, and brought school desegregation cases. This control effectively gave DOJ the final word on Title VI enforcement, leading to resentment by HEW officials and perhaps a little arrogance by CRD attorneys. Doar viewed DOJ litigation as "the primary tool in the fight against discrimination," with litigation and the guidelines as "the two blades of a scissors, a scissors that was operated by the head of the Civil Rights Division."[20] Meanwhile, the Civil Rights Commission criticized the department's "narrow focus on law enforcement through litigation" and its failure "to enlist the aid of others in its effort to assure equal rights."[21]

Despite these sources of tension, the DOJ and HEW managed to set some differences aside. Doar formed an effective working relationship with Peter Libassi, who had taken charge of HEW civil rights enforcement.[22] The department urged the courts to follow HEW guidelines. HEW educators served as expert witnesses in DOJ cases and drafted desegregation plans for recalcitrant school districts. Department lawyers defended HEW in court.

In 1967, though, the role of HEW was still being worked out. The department and the *Lee* court proceeded down separate enforcement tracks toward an inevitable collision. By April 1967 HEW administrative proceedings had found eleven Alabama school districts in violation of Title VI. Peter Libassi wrote to White House officials Douglass Cater and Joseph Califano that he had conferred with Doar, who agreed that the *Lee* order "does not affect our proceedings" and that "HEW should continue processing Alabama cases in an orderly and routine fashion without interruption."[23] David Seeley, head of the Office of Education's Equal Educational Opportunities Branch, sent letters to Alabama school systems pointing out that the HEW requirements were similar to federal court requirements. He followed up with a trip to Alabama, where he met with Superintendent Stone, answered questions on a Birmingham radio station, and debated Alabama lawyer Maury Smith at the University of Alabama.[24]

Later that week St. John Barrett responded in oral argument to the defendants' contention that HEW should be joined as a party in the case. He told the court that "insofar as there may be differences between this Court's plan and the Commissioner's [of Education] guidelines, [the Commissioner] will accept compliance with this Court's plan as meeting the Title VI requirements." Barrett added, however, that the commissioner had an obligation to start proceedings to terminate financial assistance if districts failed to meet "the standard that this Court has adopted."[25]

A few days later, DOJ lawyers met with Derrick Bell, deputy director of HEW's Office for Civil Rights, and other HEW staff to coordinate enforcement in Alabama. They first discussed the impact of the court order on HEW enforcement of Title VI. The HEW regulation provided that school systems "subject to a final order of a court of the United States for the desegregation of such . . . [a] school system" would be treated as having an acceptable plan if they agreed to comply with the order.[26] The *Lee* decree did not directly place school systems under a court order; they were not defendants in the case. The government lawyers, however, knew that Judge Johnson viewed the matter differently. DOJ lawyer Sandy Ross agreed that the *Lee* systems did not fall within the literal terms of the HEW regulation but suggested that "HEW should consider . . . that because of the *Lee* decree, Alabama school systems are not in the same category as school systems in other states." Another CRD lawyer suggested that "school systems whose performance is unsatisfactory may have to be made parties to the *Lee* case."[27] Bell took the position that the two departments should try to make school systems feel under two sets of pressure toward one set of standards and should avoid interdepartmental fighting. He agreed that the DOJ would have to take the worst systems before the court and thought HEW would not be getting to the stage of cutting off money. But, he emphasized, this did not mean that HEW should get out of Alabama. Ross stressed that the measure of performance is whether the system has complied with the *Lee* plan, and Ruby Martin, director of HEW's Office for Civil Rights, closed by saying that there should be joint review, using standards she hoped were the same as HEW requires elsewhere.[28] The following week the court sent a warning shot to HEW, saying, "As courts attempt to cooperate with executive and legislative policies, so too the Department must respect a court order for the desegregation of a school or school system."[29]

The issue came to a head in the summer of 1967. CRD attorney Alexander Ross reported that his department and HEW were negotiating with fifteen Alabama school systems whose funds had been terminated under Title VI and another twenty-three systems for which there has been an initial decision recommending termination of funds. One of those systems, Lanett, a small city in eastern Alabama with two schools—a white school enrolling 1,309 students and a Black one enrolling 606 students—had adopted a freedom of choice plan in 1966. Free choice had led to minimal desegregation by the fall of 1967, with six Black students going to the white school and five whites going to the Black school.[30] HEW's Bell observed that there had been "insufficient progress in desegregating the schools in freedom of choice and because of this fact the proposal is unacceptable."[31] He noted that not only was "the present pupil performance . . . poor" but "prospects for future improvement are practically nonexistent," with fear of economic reprisal undoubtedly chilling Blacks from choosing the white school.[32] However, the plan complied with the standards established by the order in *Lee.* The Lanett superintendent wrote to Johnson, HEW officials, and Stone, describing the twelve teachers who would be teaching across racial lines, as well as steps to upgrade the Black high school. The superintendent met with Johnson and DOJ attorney Merle Loper and later with HEW representative Jim Dunn.[33] The discussions failed to allay HEW concerns and HEW terminated funds. The three-judge court held a hearing on Lanett's motion to enjoin HEW from doing so. At the hearing, St. John Barrett put HEW's Peter Libassi on the stand. Libassi argued that Lanett was not under a court order, because the *Lee* order was against the state officials, not the local school systems. Judge Rives responded, "We've gone about our limit in trying to work with HEW." Johnson, for his part, thought the local districts had become de facto parties to *Lee.*[34]

The court granted the motion to enjoin HEW and held that because Lanett had agreed to comply with the *Lee* order, the department could not cut off funds based on noncompliance with its guidelines; instead, HEW should have first brought its findings and views to the court's attention. It was up to the court, not HEW, to make a final determination whether Lanett was in compliance. The March 22 court order "had the effect of restoring each of the 99 school systems listed therein to an 'in compliance' status insofar as being eligible to receive federal financial assistance is concerned."[35] In granting the motion to enjoin HEW, the court noted that rather than terminating funds, HEW should bring noncompliance to the court's attention.[36] Thus, the statewide desegregation order moved the responsibility for enforcement from Washington to Montgomery, insulating school districts from what they considered to be bureaucratic interference with local autonomy. HEW remained in the picture, as an assistant to the federal court, but lost its previous power to unilaterally decide who was in compliance and who was not.

The order against HEW triggered concern in Washington. HEW general counsel Alanson Willcox sent Doar a lengthy analysis in which he concluded that the injunction was wrongly issued but that "policy and practical considerations militate against appeal." Willcox argued that the court was wrong in saying that HEW had interfered with the court order. Moreover, the effect of the court's ruling was to require judicial review before rather than after HEW termination proceedings. However, he concluded that the *Lee* precedent would "not impede administrative enforcement of standards that are also subject to court-ordered enforcement." He closed by suggesting that Doar consider whether the decision "might be troublesome in other areas of government."[37]

Doar treated the issue as one of great importance, sending a copy of Willcox's letter to Attorney General Ramsey Clark and instructing the head of the division's appeals and research section, David L. Norman, to give it "your most careful and immediate consideration." Doar thought "the decision is so wrong" in several regards.[38] Nonetheless, one of the section's attorneys recommended to Norman against an appeal because it was not at all clear that the court order was wrong and the government had more to lose than to win from an appeal.[39] Norman disagreed, because he thought the federal court should defer to HEW, which had more resources at its command to enforce desegregation requirements. He believed that the court's decision would "set a dangerous precedent that would impair the federal enforcement program."[40] In the end, there was no appeal and the order's consequences went beyond *Lee*, serving as a precedent in all court order cases—by the 1970–1971 school year "approximately 400 Southern school districts demonstrated their compliance with Title VI by filing final court orders with the Office of Education."[41]

The DOJ and HEW began jointly reviewing school system compliance with the court order and not the HEW guidelines. Survey teams created reports for HEW, which would write letters to the systems with desegregation deficiencies under the court order and the steps needed to conform to the court order.[42]

MORE ENFORCEMENT ISSUES

Most school systems complied with the decree by filing freedom of choice plans that followed the court's detailed requirements. Some systems with few Black students complied by closing their Black school and assigning its students and teachers to white schools. When a few systems failed to submit satisfactory plans, the United States moved to add them as defendants and to order a satisfactory plan. This resulted in further expanding the suit brought by Anthony Lee, by then a senior at Auburn University. The court ordered some school systems to close small Black schools and assign their students and teachers to white schools and ordered others to adopt the plan set forth in the March 27 decree. In one district ordered to close its Black schools, a state court ordered the school district to reopen them; on motion of the United States, the *Lee* court joined the school district as a party and held that the state court injunction unlawfully interfered with the district's compliance with the statewide court order.[43]

In anticipation of the first school year under a statewide school desegregation order in Alabama, rumors flowed—George Wallace would form an Alabama Citizens' Militia, an effort would be made to frustrate the court's orders, the legislature would interpose itself between the court and the school systems.[44] The DOJ considered the possibility that it might need to bring criminal actions "in the event of private or official interference with school desegregation." One question was whether the interference with desegregation in local school systems that were not parties in *Lee* would be covered by federal laws against interfering with a court order.[45]

Once again, on the eve of the fall semester, Judge Johnson wrote to Doar asking that the DOJ take "some planning and preliminary steps" to "secure the enforcement of our court order and the orderly desegregation of the schools involved in our March 22 order, without either private or official interference." Johnson referred to information "indicating that there may possibly be some official state interference and quite probably will be interference by private individuals and groups . . . when the schools open."[46] When Doar called Johnson, he learned that the judge was relying on information from Alabama legislators. Johnson and Doar discussed a bill being pushed by Governor Wallace and her husband that would give students free choice of the race of their teachers and empower the governor to terminate state funding to noncomplying school districts. Johnson wanted the DOJ to seek an injunction if the bill passed. When Doar objected that he "did not like to enjoin the statutes without any facts," Johnson replied that this statute was unconstitutional on its face and was designed to interfere with the court's faculty desegregation order.[47] While a growing number of Alabamians objected to Wallace's continuing racial demagoguery, the legislature passed both the teacher choice law and yet another tuition grant law.[48] The *Lee* court held both laws unconstitutional, finding that the tuition grant statute "contains all of the malignant coloring which so fatally marked its two predecessors" and that it was "an evasive scheme to circumvent Brown v. Board of Education." It found that the teacher choice statute "promotes and encourages discrimination" and constituted "nothing less than affirmative state enforcement of private racial discrimination."[49]

By September, most school districts had adopted compliant plans, and Frank Dunbaugh, the section chief in charge of the case, reported that "our job will be to enforce present commitments and to seek modifications and refinements as they become appropriate."[50] Some districts adopted satisfactory plans but failed to achieve the required faculty desegregation in the fall of 1967. The United States sought to join them as defendants and asked the court to order further faculty desegregation. The court said it would deny relief because the United States had known about the shortfalls in faculty desegregation well in advance but had not filed its motion until school opened. However, the court went on to explain in detail what the school districts should do and said it was "apparent" that they must do it before the January semester began.[51]

As the process continued, Superintendent Stone became more involved, particularly after a county superintendent entered his office with a noncompliance letter from HEW that he had not yet seen. The process was soon revised in the name of efficiency and HEW began sending Stone directly its communications with local superintendents, including letters stemming from field surveys conducted by the department.[52]

When school opened in the fall of 1967, the percentage of Black students in Alabama enrolled in white schools had increased from 2.4 percent to 6.3 percent, and 871 teachers were teaching in faculties in which their race was in the minority. While this was far from full desegregation, Alabama in three and a half years had come a long way from George Wallace's inaugural promise of "segregation forever."

Schools opened in relative peace, despite the bluster from the Wallaces and the passage of the teacher choice and tuition assistance acts. However, school opening also brought to the surface issues that would continue to expand the scope of the case. Until then, cases had focused primarily on making it possible for African American children to attend white schools, with little attention to desegregating Black schools or to so-called second-generation desegregation issues, such as in-school discrimination, dismissal and demotion of African American teachers, principals, and coaches, and discrimination in extracurricular activities such as athletics. White parents chose only white schools for their children, evincing a belief that Black schools were inferior; and they resisted allowing Black teachers to teach their children. It seemed clear that the free choice system perpetuated the prior system of separate but equal for all but a handful of African American children.

African American teachers were growing increasingly concerned that when schools were consolidated and teachers reassigned, the burden would fall on them, not on white teachers. The court had ordered that the burdens be equally shared, but history suggested that African Americans would bear the brunt. The teachers hired Fred Gray to represent them, and Gray, though still representing Anthony Lee and other students, filed a motion asking that the teachers association be allowed to intervene as plaintiffs in the case. The court granted the motion, so that Gray was now representing two sets of plaintiffs with similar interests he hoped would not come into conflict. In his view, "it was very important that ASTA be made party-plaintiffs so that as the rights of parents and students were being litigated, the rights of African American teachers, principals, coaches, and administrators would also be litigated."[53] It is not clear how Gray would represent both if, for example, students would benefit from the closing of a substandard school but faculty would benefit from keeping the school open.

A few months later, the United States moved to order the ninety-nine school districts not to participate in any athletic conference that discriminated based on race, and the court then added the athletic associations as defendants. It held that "Alabama's dual athletic system has led to inadequate athletic programs in the various Negro schools" and ordered the two segregated associations to be merged into one. HEW then set about monitoring compliance, holding a briefing session with Alabama survey teams in October before they fanned out initially to investigate current compliance in seven of the districts with past compliance issues.[54] The trainers at the session explained the March statewide desegregation decree and the July order against HEW.[55]

Meantime, the CRD had reorganized, combining the section responsible for Alabama and Georgia with the section responsible for Mississippi and Louisiana, among other states. The short-term effect was that "the Southern Section [was] forced to operate on a day-by-day basis responding to crises as they arise, instead of carrying out an orderly program."[56] I was no longer in the new section, which retained responsibility for the *Lee* case. Doar's special assistant, Owen Fiss, expressed concern about the management of the case, based on letters he received from Johnson.[57]

In November 1967 Doar left the CRD to head the Bedford Stuyvesant Corporation in New York, created by Robert Kennedy—then a US senator from New York—to address urban issues in Brooklyn. Would the special relationship between the division and Johnson continue under Doar's successor, Stephen J. Pollak? Pollak had served in the solicitor general's office and as an assistant to President Johnson responsible for bringing about home rule in the District of Columbia. He was no stranger to Judge Johnson, having served as Doar's top deputy and as the lead lawyer in a case in Johnson's court challenging Alabama's poll tax. At the end of 1967, the DOJ filed a detailed report with the court, analyzing reports from Superintendent Stone and summarizing the extent of desegregation in each of the ninety-nine districts.[58] The court then wrote to Pollak, pointing out compliance deficiencies in forty school systems covered by the March 1967 decree and asking the department to confer with Superintendent Stone and each school system "and make specific suggestions and recommendations to the officials concerning the areas where they must secure additional faculty desegregation and where they must close inferior schools." Reflecting the hybrid status of the DOJ—amicus and plaintiff intervenor—the court specified to Pollak that it was asking the department to act in its capacity "as amicus" and "to speak for this Court in this regard."[59]

Although the department promptly formed an enforcement program for the spring and summer, Pollak did not fully agree with portions of Johnson's letter. His response explained that he did not believe that the division could speak for the court in its conferences with school systems because it was not acting as amicus in the usual sense of the word. Rather, the DOJ "has been representing the interest of the United States as an active litigant in this case," a role incompatible "with a role in which we act as a representative of the court." Johnson's letter had also said that the court believed that the only theory for requiring faculty desegregation under a free choice plan was "to remove one of the influencing factors in a free choice plan." Pollak responded that "we must respectfully disagree" with the court, but he did agree that the extent of student desegregation "provides a helpful measuring stick for deciding priorities for action." Pollak noted that HEW was conducting field reviews of the school systems listed in the court's letter, though the reviews would not be completed by the April 1, 1968, deadline which the court had set. The DOJ would maintain an attorney in Montgomery to "confer with Stone and with local school systems, and unresolved issues of non-compliance would be brought to the court, not to a HEW administrative hearing."[60] In short, Pollak made clear that the CRD would continue to enforce the court's decree vigorously but would do so as an independent actor.

In a thirty-two-page letter to Stone the following month, Pollak detailed deficiencies in compliance by many school systems in the conduct of free choice and in faculty desegregation, equalization of facilities and educational materials, construction, and consolidation of schools. He suggested that the decree obligated Stone to seek detailed proposals from each school system "setting forth exactly how and by what date the system will eliminate the vestiges of the dual school system."[61] Later that spring, when asked about a Black school in Bellamy, Alabama, with no indoor plumbing, only one outdoor faucet, and mud surrounding the outhouse, Stone responded that the Black children had the option of exercising free choice to attend a white school.[62]

THE TRANSITION TO "JUST SCHOOLS" BEGINS

That spring the Civil Rights Commission conducted hearings in Montgomery, which brought public attention to the operation of desegregation plans. Witnesses described the ineffectiveness of free choice in one of the *Lee* counties. One African American couple decided not to let their child attend a white school because "Greenville is a small community, and we somewhat depend on the white people for our living."[63] The commission also quoted an African American tenant farmer from the Greenville area whose landlord told him to move after his daughters exercised their choice to attend a white school, saying, "I'm just not up for colored children going to a white school." Similarly, white employers in Crenshaw County described being pressured to fire African American employees whose children chose white schools. The commission reported that in another county the school superintendent had contacted African American parents who had chosen white schools for their children and had encouraged them to rethink their choice.[64] Many similar stories came to the attention of DOJ attorneys. Summarizing his interviews in Monroe County, the setting for *To Kill a Mockingbird*, a CRD lawyer wrote, "Freedom of choice does not seem to be working very well in Monroe County." His interviews reflected intimidation by whites, both physical and economic.[65]

At the same time as it was preparing its report to the *Lee* court, the department was also drafting a Supreme Court amicus brief in perhaps the most consequential school desegregation case to come to the court on the merits since *Brown*, a case that would lead to another round of litigation in *Lee* and other desegregation cases. The court had agreed to hear cases in which plaintiffs were challenging the adequacy of freedom of choice plans in school districts in Virginia, Tennessee, and Arkansas, grouped under the name *Green v. County School Board of New Kent County, Virginia.* Broadly speaking, the issue in the cases was whether *Brown* required integration or desegregation. Integration would require that white students attend formerly all-Black schools, while desegregation would only require that Black students be allowed to choose to attend formerly all-white schools. There was broad agreement within the government that all schools must be integrated, but the case nevertheless prompted vigorous debate within the CRD and with the Office of the Solicitor General, which represents the United States in Supreme Court litigation.

Division lawyers were always aware that free choice was a chimera. Public schools had traditionally not been organized based on free choice. Alabama's pupil placement law, adopted as a method of resisting *Brown*, had been a primitive forerunner to the HEW version of free choice. Even if stripped of the baggage of the Alabama law, free choice was unlikely to bring significant levels of desegregation to white schools and was never going to desegregate Black schools. In 1958 the Supreme Court had refused to say that Alabama's pupil placement law was per se unconstitutional, and the following year the Civil Rights Commission approved laws of this type as a "possible method by which compliance may be achieved."[66] From 1963 until 1968 the United States had sought to impose free choice plans on Alabama school systems.

So a frontal attack on free choice lacked case law support. Free choice did serve as a means of breaking ground against the complete segregation that prevailed until 1963. The division's experience in the voting cases taught that the defendants would hang themselves if the CRD established a factual basis, not just an abstract one, for changing the case law. In this case, letting the placement law operate would demonstrate its ineffectiveness.

In September 1967 Doar agreed with HEW that the DOJ would work toward developing the law "to the point where free choice would not be permitted unless it achieved 'complete desegregation.'"[67] One division attorney wanted to argue in *Green* that free choice was not a reasonable vehicle for disestablishing the dual school system and eliminating the racial identity of schools. He also reported on a more sophisticated argument proposed by St. John Barrett, by then deputy general counsel at HEW. Barrett likened the case to the early voting rights case from Tuskegee, *Gomillion v. Lightfoot*, where the Supreme Court had looked at the statistics showing the number of African Americans who had been residents of Tuskegee before the legislature redrew the boundary lines and compared them with the number of African Americans who had been removed from the city by the new lines. Barrett thought that "the outcome of [free choice] is as predetermined, and intended, as the facially non-racial device in *Gomillion*."[68] Four years after joining the CRD, I undertook my first assignment to draft a Supreme Court brief, in *Green v. County School Board of New Kent County*, along with my colleagues Gary Greenberg and Merle Loper. We sent the solicitor general our lengthy draft arguing, quoting *Jefferson County*, that the school authorities had the obligation to "bring about an integrated, unitary school system in which there are no Negro schools and no white schools—just schools." While free choice may be a suitable interim desegregation tool, the draft argued, it "makes no sense in New Kent County." It was "the only facially neutral system of assignment that would inevitably keep the Negro school all black." The choice presented to students was whether to choose a Black school or a school designed for whites, rather than a race-neutral choice.[69]

The solicitor general opted initially to argue that freedom of choice plans were per se unconstitutional. Pollak, hewing to the position that Doar and HEW's Libassi had adopted, objected to the argument that freedom of choice could never be a constitutional method of desegregation. Pollak argued that the division's experience suggested that completely ruling out freedom of choice would place the Supreme Court "out on a limb . . . that neither the Fifth Circuit nor the Federal Executive . . . had previously been prepared to climb out to." Per se invalidity of free choice was "inconsistent with the Department's established enforcement program," he wrote, and it would unduly tax the enforcement staffs of the DOJ and HEW. If a school system created a non-discriminatory climate, free choice could work, because "Negroes have the gumption to choose what they truly want."[70] Although the question whether free choice was per se invalid seemed important at the time, more important was the agreement of the division and the solicitor general that *Brown* required more than allowing a few Black students to attend white schools. They agreed that the problem was systemic and that to eradicate the dual school system it was necessary to desegregate the Black schools as well. The effect of this argument was the same as the per se argument, as few if any white students would choose to attend a Black school.

The solicitor general agreed to abandon the argument that free choice was per se invalid. Instead the government's brief focused on results and the need for a "comprehensive program which actually achieves desegregation" and noted that the continued existence of "all-Negro schools, attended by an overwhelming majority of the Negro children" marked the desegregation plan as ineffective. Relying on cases where the government sought to remedy racial discrimination in voter registration, the solicitor general argued that "affirmative measures must be taken to overcome the effects of past discrimination and reverse the direction." The brief quoted *Jefferson County* and argued that traditionally dual school systems had the duty to convert to "a unitary, nonracial (nondiscriminatory) system—lock, stock, and barrel." Finally, the brief noted that in the context of the three small school systems before the court, the effect of free choice was twofold: "The apparent official sanction given to the preference of the white students aggravates the injury to the Negro children; and, at the same time, it lends encouragement to the separation of the white students and tends to stiffen those very attitudes that desegregation might relax."[71] The solicitor general's brief, written by Louis Claiborne, omitted the *Jefferson County* language quoted in the division's draft and in the plaintiffs' brief: "no Negro schools and no white schools—just schools."[72] However, it argued vigorously for disapproval of freedom of choice in a school system that continued to maintain an all-Black school where normal assignment methods, such as geographical zoning, would bring complete desegregation. Claiborne participated in the oral argument in early April, stressing that freedom of choice in these cases "is such a transparent device to enable the white students, primarily, and their parents to segregate or continue the segregation of the school system in a way that the State itself could not."[73]

An undercurrent of concern about white flight ran through some of the arguments in the Supreme Court. For example, the lawyer for the school board in the Tennessee case warned that zoning white students into the Black school would bring "the immediate reaction of resegregation."[74] Similarly, the brief for the school board in the Arkansas case explained that "the white parents in Gould would be no more willing than those in Chicago, Washington, or New York, to send their children to predominantly Negro schools,"[75] a point their lawyer reiterated in oral argument.[76] Justice Byron White asked Claiborne whether it would be relevant if the white students were to flee the school system if assigned to the Black school; Claiborne replied that it would be irrelevant.[77]

The Supreme Court decided *Green* in a year of turmoil and violence in the United States. President Johnson, mired in the war in Vietnam, announced that he would not run for reelection. In February, the Kerner Commission, which President Johnson had created in the wake of urban riots, prophesied, "Our nation is moving toward two societies, one black, one white—separate and unequal."[78] As if to validate the report's conclusion, Dr. Martin Luther King Jr. was assassinated in Memphis one day after the *Green* argument. While riots continued after the King assassination, Johnson signed the Fair Housing Act, which prohibited discrimination based on race, sex, national origin, or religion in sales, rental, or financing of housing. It appeared as if the courts, the Congress, and the executive branch might be united in seeking racial equal opportunity.

In May, the Supreme Court unanimously decided the *Green* trilogy of cases, requiring, for the first time, the desegregation of Black schools as well as white schools. The opinion rejected the claim that *Brown* did not require integration of formerly segregated school systems, noting that while "for the time immediately after Brown II the concern was with making an initial break in a long-established pattern of excluding Negro children from schools attended by white children . . . the transition to a unitary, nonracial system of public education was and is the ultimate end to be brought about." Henceforth, the court said, the school board bore the burden "to come forward with a plan that promises realistically to work and promises realistically to work now." Paraphrasing language from the Fifth Circuit panel's opinion in *Jefferson County*, the court concluded that the school board must "fashion steps which promise realistically to convert promptly to a system without a 'white' school and a 'Negro' school, but just schools."[79] Freedom of choice plans were acceptable only if they "worked." *Green* significantly developed the law of school desegregation in three ways: it recognized the systemic nature of maintaining a separate set of schools for each race; it therefore recognized that Black schools must also be desegregated if possible; and it required a terminal plan, not just interim desegregation measures. *Green* shifted the emphasis from how many Black students were attending white schools to removing the racial identity of schools. It meant that, for the first time, the burden of desegregation would not fall solely on African American students but would be spread to students of both races. For the first time, whites might be assigned to "Black" schools, as part of the transformation to "just schools."

Division attorneys were ecstatic. An anonymous wag wrote these lyrics (to the tune of Joy to the World), performed at a staff holiday party in 1968:

> Joy to the schools, free choice is dead,
> For Green is now the law;
> Your system please reformulate
> For now's the time to integrate;
> Let zoning be your plan,
> Or pairing if you can.
> Rejoice, free choice, free choice is dead.[80]

In his influential chronicle, *The Civil Rights Era*, historian Hugh Davis Graham characterized *Jefferson County* and *Green* as articulating an "inchoate" compensatory theory, "an evolving, proportional theory of compensatory justice, together with its necessary handmaiden, statistics."[81] Graham's elegant language, based on a phrase coined by J. Harvey Wilkinson, misstates the theory of those cases. Dismantling the dual school system does not "compensate" students for past wrongs. It does not restore lost educational opportunity. Rather, it eliminates the ongoing wrong of deliberately maintaining two sets of schools, one for Blacks and the other primarily for whites. The goal is schools as they would have looked had there never been a dual school system in the first place. The reliance on statistics stems from the transitional use of freedom of choice to desegregate schools. Simply put, if freedom of choice resulted in continuation of racially separate schools, it failed to meet the goal of school desegregation.

Shortly before the Supreme Court decided *Green*, Lurleen Wallace died and Lieutenant Governor Albert Brewer became governor. According to one historian, Brewer was committed to improving education in Alabama, which spent less on schools than any state except Mississippi.[82] He announced his intention to "abide by any court order," adding, "I won't like so many decide which ones."[83] However, Brewer, like Wallace, "understood the supreme value of racial politics, and . . . sought to protect white privilege and white rights."[84] He called freedom of choice "one of the principles of a democratic society" and warned that abandoning freedom of choice would cause "public indignation, chaos, and loss of public support for education."[85] As one news article put it, "the state of Alabama—which once fought against freedom-of-choice plans—is now planning a legal battle to preserve them."[86] The parties in *Lee* disagreed about next steps, however, and both the plaintiffs and the DOJ filed motions to require school systems where free choice had not desegregated the Black schools to take further steps.[87] The Alabama state board of education resolved to fight the motions, on the ground "that the freedom of choice plan even though involuntarily accepted by each board, had been implemented in good faith by each . . . school system."[88]

Soon after the plaintiffs filed their motion, a deposition of the Talladega County school superintendent showed that despite *Green*, school systems would continue to argue for freedom of choice, even when most Black students remained in Black schools. The superintendent opined that white parents would not permit their children to go to formerly all-Black schools:

> The people have somewhat accepted freedom of choice, they don't like all aspects of it, but at least they are living with it; but if we are forced to move to some other kind of system, such as zoning or pairing, I think the people are going to resent an arbitrary action such as that; you can push people up to a certain point, but there finally is a breaking point at which you cannot push people.[89]

Governor Brewer, too, continued to champion freedom of choice. He told members of the Alabama Bar Association that they must help "preserve public education—not a discriminatory education, but a quality education" and defend freedom of choice.[90] He urged school boards not to enforce truancy laws against parents who objected, as one newspaper put it, "to situations created by federal court desegregation orders."[91]

The Talladega superintendent said that abandoning free choice would lead to less desegregation and would threaten the community's financial support of the schools. This sort of doomsday prophecy was common. However, fifteen years later, the school system was 42.6 percent Black, virtually the same as when the superintendent delivered his prophecy.[92]

Early in his career, author James M. Fallows, writing for the *Southern Courier*, largely staffed by *Harvard Crimson* reporters and editors, wrote about the hearing on the DOJ desegregation motions, using language that generally did not appear in the mainstream newspapers: Alabama opposed freedom of choice and was "struggling to preserve quality education for our white children and our nigras [*sic*]." Alabama Assistant Attorney General Gordon Madison told the court, "The people of Alabama are never going to send their white children to nigra [*sic*] schools." More elliptically, defense attorney Maury Smith argued that the DOJ's statistical case against freedom of choice "takes no account of the many complexities involved." While Pollak argued that freedom of choice "has been a miserable failure in ending the dual school system," the court was not so sure. However, the three judges indicated that school systems would have to ramp up their faculty desegregation and close more inadequate black schools.[93]

Preparation for the 1966 hearing had required a large commitment of resources. One of the research analysts assigned to the case, MaryLee Campbell, a young John Doar protégé from New Richmond, Wisconsin, had compiled the statistical evidence and the case files. The follow-up enforcement monitoring and litigation continued to consume resources, and in 1968 Campbell again gathered evidence to support further relief in light of *Green*. After the hearing, Judge Rives, the senior judge on the *Lee* panel, wrote to Assistant Attorney General Pollak, "I must say the Department of Justice has done a splendid job in this case, somewhat assumed the burden of the boards of education in presenting a concrete plan . . . I very seldom have even seen a case in which the lawyers have been of more aid to the court than this case." Pollak wrote to Campbell, quoting Judge Rives, and telling her that she "did a magnificent job in the development, preparation and presentment of the Department's case. . . . You may take true personal pride in the comments of Circuit Judge Rives."[94]

Although the three judges showed a strong commitment to enforcing the law against racial discrimination, they knew their fellow Alabamians and displayed caution in fashioning decrees. They must have thought that conditions in the Black schools must change before one could require school systems to assign white students to traditionally Black schools. Indeed, Judge Johnson had noted in another case that "white students will not elect to attend and will not, if any other choice is available, attend a predominantly Negro school."[95] Many Black schools were housed in deplorably inadequate facilities and would have to be closed. As the faculties in Black schools remained almost all Black, assigning more white teachers to them would make the schools more attractive to white students. The court of appeals had held in August, in another of Judge Johnson's school desegregation cases, that he was correct in requiring "progress" in desegregation and in ordering more faculty desegregation.[96] In the words of some of the appellate judges, it was time for "the tell-tale mark of segregated faculties to pass away."[97] Johnson had, however, left freedom of choice in place in that case, simply warning that "unless the 'freedom-of-choice' plan is more effectively and less dilatorily used by the defendants in this case, this Court will have no alternative except to order some other plan used."[98] He later explained his reluctance to order far-reaching changes in student assignment: "In the school cases that I heard during the years of desegregation, the prime concern came down to the welfare of the children. In my mind, busing to achieve racial balance is simply not worth the price of the potential disruption both to the school system and the students themselves."[99]

The *Lee* court in August issued a remarkably detailed order directed at Superintendent Stone, specifying the number of teachers to be assigned across racial lines in each school in each school system by the beginning of the 1968–1969 school year. For example, in Autauga County the court ordered that the assignment of full-time teachers reach not less than:

Autauga County High School	4 Negro teachers
Autauga County Training School	6 white teachers
Billingsley High School	2 Negro teachers
Hicks Memorial School	2 Negro teachers

And so on, for six more named schools. The order also listed schools or grade levels that must be closed by the beginning of the 1969–1970 school year. These schools "either have fewer students than required under the minimum-student standards set by the State of Alabama Department of Education, or the continued operation of which will have the inevitable effect of thwarting the success of the freedom-of-choice plans for desegregating the school systems."[100] Thus, Autauga County must close grades 10–12 of two of the Black high schools. Baldwin County was to close not only grades 7–12 in one Black school but also all grades in two others. The court was aware that closing the schools endangered the jobs of teachers, so it ordered that "all teachers assigned to the schools or grades being closed, be absorbed by transfer to other public schools within the system."[101]

Even before entry of this decree, Alabama school systems under the prior *Lee* orders had already closed 151 substandard Black schools, leaving 267 functioning Black schools. Noting the good faith of Governor Brewer and State Superintendent Stone, the court said that even though freedom of choice had not yet disestablished the dual school system, "the members of this Court are unanimous in the belief that the freedom of choice method is the most feasible method to pursue," because "there simply are no other or more effective means reasonably available at this time that promise a speedier conversion to a unitary system." The court denied the motion to order the abandonment of freedom of choice; it said the faculty desegregation and school closing order were "the minimum necessary . . . in order to justify the continued use of the freedom-of-choice method for disestablishing its dual school system."[102]

Although he could have claimed the decision as a victory upholding freedom of choice, Brewer instead charged the court with carrying out the "socialistic claims the Justice Department asked it to" and called the order a "devious and roundabout means" of "requiring busing without the formality of busing." Early the next year, he told Alabama school board members they had no "obligation to obey any orders which you receive from the Justice Department." In the same Wallace-like speech, he bemoaned the "havoc" that a "federal judge—sitting in his ivory tower" had wrought on education.[103]

The *Lee* plans and the plans in the other school systems under court order in Alabama led to 8.3 percent of the state's Black students enrolling in majority white schools in 1968, an improvement but lower than in most other Deep South states.[104] It soon became apparent, too, that some school systems were not complying with the court's order to desegregate faculty and close inadequate Black schools. The United States filed a motion for clarification of the court's order, the governor and superintendent moved to modify the order, and the Alabama Education Association (representing white teachers) was allowed to enter the case as an amicus curiae. The judges reiterated that they were "dedicated to 'freedom of choice' as the most feasible method" to desegregate Alabama schools but added, "the Court cannot make freedom of choice work without good faith and effective efforts on the part of the school authorities." Expressing concern that "the education and future welfare of our children can be wrecked by petty politics and by racial prejudice," the court added the school board members and superintendents of nineteen school systems as defendants and ordered them to show cause why they should not be required "to adopt and follow some plan other than 'freedom of choice' as a method for desegregating said system and converting it to a unitary nonracial school system."[105] Nine days later, the court ordered the nineteen districts to show cause why the court should not notify HEW that they were no longer in compliance with the court's order, thus freeing HEW to terminate federal funds to them.[106] Pollak told Dunbaugh, the section chief responsible for *Lee*, that "as before, *Lee v. Macon* continues to roll on and make major demands upon us for review of the actions of the schools and for possible new filings in the court." Pollak added that he looked to Dunbaugh "to make certain that this review work goes ahead and that we meet our responsibilities."[107] Within a few weeks of these orders, the court dissolved them, based on commitments from the school districts to "take action with regard to faculty desegregation and school closings."[108]

The Doar-Pollak era at the CRD was about to end. On November 5, Republican Richard Nixon defeated Hubert Humphrey and George Wallace to become the president. Wallace, running as the candidate of the American Independent Party, won five states in the Deep South—something for Nixon and his campaign manager and former law partner, John Mitchell, to ponder as they looked ahead to the next election. Nixon nominated Mitchell, a pipe-smoking, gruff-voiced New York municipal bond lawyer, as the new attorney general. Pollak set his resignation effective at noon on January 20, the moment Richard Nixon would become president. In an interview, Pollak recalled, "My last act was to identify my successor, Jerris Leonard, to the guards who were denying him entry to the building."[109]

7. "Watch What We Do"

President Nixon took office in the midst of the civil rights revolution. He was no revolutionary, and civil rights groups feared a counterrevolution. True, as President Eisenhower's vice president, Nixon had supported civil rights for African Americans. According to his assistant for domestic affairs, John Ehrlichman, his 1968 campaign for president sought the "racist" vote by making a "subliminal appeal to the anti-black voter."[1] In part of that appeal, he inveighed against "forced busing," around the same time as Governor Brewer was using similar language. Both were no doubt influenced by the rhetoric of George Wallace.[2] Nixon argued that the "federal government and the federal courts" should not "act as local school districts in determining how" to carry out the mandate of *Brown v. Board of Education.*[3] During the campaign Nixon had met with segregationist Senator Strom Thurmond of South Carolina, the Dixiecrat presidential candidate in 1948 who became a Republican in 1964, and told him he opposed busing to desegregate. An article about the meeting opined, "Presumably, Nixon may endorse the 'freedom of choice' approach to school desegregation."[4] But Nixon advisor Robert Ellsworth, who rode with Nixon and Thurmond as they spoke during a limousine ride, gives a different account. He says Nixon feared that Thurmond would ask him to support freedom of choice and told Ellsworth "I can't do that," because it would cost him the election.[5]

We have already seen the impact a change in presidential administrations may have: While President Truman's DOJ strenuously argued for desegregation in the *Brown* case, President Eisenhower took a much more restrained approach. The desegregation phase of enforcement began under the Kennedy and Johnson administrations, but it had yet to reach most African American school children in the Deep South. Would it continue under Richard M. Nixon, the first lawyer-president since Franklin D. Roosevelt? Nixon was also the first Republican to make significant inroads into the South, seen in his 1968 victory over Hubert Humphrey. He won in Virginia, Florida, North Carolina, South Carolina, and Tennessee and outpolled Humphrey in Georgia and Arkansas, where Wallace was the top vote-getter. He could see the potential for carrying the South in the next presidential election, and in 1972 his sweep of most of the nation was led by very high percentages in the Deep South. Given the hostility of most white Southerners to school desegregation, critics believed that Nixon, pursuing his "Southern strategy," determined to change course from the policies of the Johnson administration.[6] Yet more desegregation occurred under the Nixon presidency than under any president before or since. This is perhaps the strongest evidence of the power of the courts to bring about social change. And passage of the 1964 Civil Rights Act had brought the executive branch into more school desegregation cases, which the courts were then deciding.

Before the 1968 election, a series of judicial decisions had signaled the end of freedom of choice and had announced a rule requiring an end to separate Black schools and white schools and a transition to "just schools": the Fifth Circuit's decision in *Jefferson County*, the district court's decision in *Lee v. Macon County Board of Education*, and the Supreme Court decision in *Green v. County School Board*.

The Nixon administration initially went forward with litigation to enforce *Green* but then dramatically reversed itself in a set of Mississippi cases, claiming that immediate desegregation of those schools would cause "confusion and a catastrophic educational setback" to more than one hundred thousand children in thirty-three school districts. The lower courts granted a delay of desegregation, but the Supreme Court, in an expedited ruling in October, held that the time for delay had passed and school districts must desegregate "at once."[7] That ruling created a dilemma for the Nixon administration: how to preserve its political standing with Southern whites in the face of the demands of the court. Should it ignore the court or enforce its decision?

The dilemma became more profound the following April when the court, in the *Swann* case, held that one-race schools in formerly de jure segregated school systems were presumptively in violation of the Fourteenth Amendment and that busing might be required to desegregate them.[8] In the absence of *Swann* and the Mississippi decisions, the Nixon administration might easily have settled for minimal freedom of choice desegregation, with a few African American children attending white schools. In these circumstances, though, the ratchet principle came into play. The administration seems to have decided that it would be best to put the task of desegregation behind it as quickly as possible.

Jack Greenberg, who then headed the NAACP Legal Defense Fund, believed Nixon "had no ideological convictions about this" and simply "wanted to do what would work for him."[9] Meanwhile, Nixon received conflicting advice. One advisor, Lamar Alexander, urged that the DOJ "step up a program of judicial enforcement," while another, Patrick Buchanan, argued that the federal government should seek to reverse the *Green* decision.[10] Nixon followed Alexander's advice. The department established an Education Section in the CRD; created an interagency task force composed of HEW, the DOJ, and White House representatives; and held a conference to explain to Southern United States attorneys the need for immediate desegregation. George P. Shultz, then the secretary of labor, later described the Nixon administration's reaction to the Supreme Court's 1969 order bringing "all deliberate speed" to an end. Nixon declared *Brown* to be correct "and expressed his intention to enforce the law." He created a cabinet committee to manage the transition to desegregated schools, with George Schultz as the de facto chairman. His co-chair, Vice President Spiro Agnew, "wanted no part of this effort." Schultz describes bringing Black and white leaders to Washington and, later, meeting with them in Louisiana. When Attorney General Mitchell met with the leaders, he told them, "I will enforce the law." The president met with each group and urged them to help make the transition to unitary school systems orderly and peaceful. Years later, Schultz quoted *New York Times* writer Tom Wicker's statement, "The Nixon administration accomplished more in 1970 to desegregate Southern school systems than had been done in the 16 previous years, or probably since." At the same time, civil rights leaders in the 1970s took a much different view of the Nixon administration's stance on school desegregation. One wrote in 1974 that the administration had decided "in the field of school desegregation to subordinate specific constitutional and statutory responsibilities to what it considered to be its vital political interests."[11]

Finally, in 1972, Nixon's frustration at being boxed in by the Supreme Court decisions led him to decide that the only solution was to seek a constitutional amendment enshrining freedom of choice. Stating "that education requiring excessive transportation for students is definitely inferior," he believed that "this country is not ready at this time for either forcibly integrated housing or forcibly integrated education."[12] Nothing came of these plans, however.

The Nixon record on school desegregation has drawn varied descriptions, ranging from strong criticism for blocking desegregation to strong praise for successfully desegregating the schools of the Deep South. On the one hand, desegregation scholar Gary Orfield has alleged that Nixon issued "directives to staff to do as little as possible to enforce school desegregation."[13] Orfield charges that "HEW had given up its mission of bringing the nation's public schools into compliance with constitutional requirements" for desegregation and that the DOJ "gave low priority to school cases."[14] Another scholar, Rosemary C. Salamone, writes that "immediately upon taking office, the Nixon Administration started whittling away at the gains made" and adopted a "posture of 'benign neglect.'"[15] As noted historian James T. Patterson explains, "Nixon's calculated policies did not please staunch advocates of desegregation. Many branded him a racist." Yet, Patterson continues, "his request that Southerners obey the rulings of the Court did help to prevent a resurgence of massive resistance in the 1970s. Indeed, the changes that soon occurred in the South were extraordinary and dramatic."[16] Similarly, leading constitutional scholar Bruce Ackerman concludes, "Nixon's strategy played a key role in gaining political support for another large advance in southern desegregation." Ackerman notes that by 1970 the South had become "the most integrated region in the nation."[17] And a 2009 study of Nixon's civil rights policies explains how "Nixon quietly ended de jure segregation in the South."[18] Yet another study holds that "Nixon did indeed play a decisive role in breaking massive resistance to school desegregation."[19] A biographer lists "desegregating the Southern schools" as one of Nixon's great accomplishments, along with such actions as opening up China and creating the Environmental Protection Agency.[20] Many of these studies discuss Nixon's politics and his policy views, but they do not reveal the interaction of the White House, DOJ, and HEW or the role *Lee v. Macon County Board of Education* played in desegregating Southern schools.

Nixon's views reflected both bias and commitment to the law. A revealing memorandum he wrote late in his first term, for the eyes only of his top assistants John Ehrlichman and Bob Haldeman, espoused a libertarian approach of freedom of choice in major human decisions, "in the deepest philosophical sense and not in the narrow obstructionist sense that the term was used in fighting the school cases in the South in 1966, '67, and '68." He said he opposed both legal segregation and forced integration but added, "it is only segregated black education which is inferior and that actually segregated white education is probably superior to education in which there is too great a degree of integration of inferior black students with the white students." Today it may seem incredible, but the memo nonetheless goes on to say, "My feelings on race, as you know, are, if anything, ultra-liberal." Although espousing enforcement of *Brown*, Nixon worried, "we simply have to face the hard fact the law cannot go beyond what the people are willing to support."[21] These private thoughts written in 1972, as he was running for a second term, are consistent with his mixed record starting with his inauguration in 1969.

Upon taking office, the new administration found motions filed by the DOJ pending, along with HEW administrative hearings under Title VI to enforce the *Green* decision. Orfield has fed the myth that by the time Nixon took office, "the task was largely completed."[22] However, while the Johnson administration had ended the systematic exclusion of Black children from white schools, it had barely begun the process of eliminating the dual racial system of schools, including especially the continued maintenance of white schools and Black schools. As a Nixon advisor later put it, "There hadn't been that much desegregation. There was a lot of law but there was very little action."[23] During the last year of the Johnson administration 78.8 percent of African American students in the Deep South attended Black schools.[24] Orfield might more accurately have said that the courts, private plaintiffs, the DOJ, and HEW had initiated an irreversible process and cemented the rule of *Brown*. The South had successfully resisted enrolling Black children in white schools for more than ten years after the *Brown* decision. The *Green* decision, though, meant that white children would have to be assigned to Black schools, not just that Black children should be allowed to enroll in white schools. The outgoing administration's motions to enforce *Green* confronted Nixon with an explosive and unwelcome issue.

Would the Nixon administration take up the challenge and continue to press for unitary school systems, or would it follow "forced busing" rhetoric of the campaign? Nixon had also campaigned as the "law and order" candidate, a phrase which seemed to require following court rulings even if the president disagreed with them. Nixon struggled with these internal contradictions throughout his ill-fated presidency. An early victim of that struggle, Leon Panetta, Nixon's first head of the Office of Civil Rights at HEW, begins his recounting of his experiences at HEW by quoting Nixon's statement the day after the election: the theme of his administration would be "Bring us together again."[25] Panetta would have to deal with the HEW guidelines, which called for complete desegregation by the fall of 1969. The next few years would reflect the fact that the policies of the new administration were constrained by the actions of its predecessors and of the courts.

Southern school boards and politicians were emboldened by Nixon's campaign slogans and assumed that enforcement policies would change.

Nixon's designee to head HEW, Robert Finch, reinforced that assumption at his confirmation hearing. Although stating that the government should employ "pressure and conciliation" to push school desegregation, Finch added, "You don't just come in with a meat-axe and bludgeon someone into compliance."[26] An HEW official opined that Finch's statements "have set us back tremendously. . . . Everyone believes there's going to be a change."[27] However, the DOJ "continued after the inauguration to perform as if there had been no change in the White House."[28]

Most lawyers in the CRD had been hired during the Kennedy-Johnson administrations, and this was their first experience with change from one political party leading the country to the other. But most regarded themselves as law enforcers, not political partisans. While understanding that policies might change with a new administration, their overarching job was to enforce the law. Policy would come into play where the law was ambiguous or where priorities were being set. But the *Green* case seemed unambiguous. Division lawyers took a wary wait-and-see view of the new administration, hoping that, in the optimistic words of a high-ranking CRD attorney, "In a place like this, the self-perpetuating mechanism of the law makes any basic change unlikely."[29] Later events would prove him wrong in the short run but correct in the long run. The lawyers found themselves viewed with suspicion by both the president and his detractors. They needed to respect the policy positions of the duly elected president, while also remaining true to the law they were sworn to enforce.

During prior administrations civil rights groups and the press had been mildly critical of the DOJ. During the summer of 1964, SNCC picketers had come to the DOJ building with signs reading, "In Mississippi there is a town called Liberty; in Washington there is a department called Justice." Civil rights groups had wanted faster desegregation of the schools and tougher enforcement by the DOJ and HEW. Still, the tensions between civil rights groups and the department were ameliorated by the fact that they were pursuing a common goal. Civil rights groups and the press, however, evinced deep suspicion of the Nixon administration. As a Nixon biographer notes, "The press largely missed the real story of how Nixon desegregated the schools. Instead, they focused on [Vice President] Agnew as salesman of Nixon's so-called Southern Strategy to win white votes in the South."[30] The often-shrill voices viewing with distrust every move of the DOJ made in school desegregation cases had their impact on morale in the CRD, an effect compounded by some actions of the attorney general and HEW secretary. Yet most of the career staff stayed on to complete the work they had begun under Presidents Kennedy and Johnson.

Though the president's nomination of an assistant attorney general for civil rights can often signal the direction the division is to take, the selection of Jerris Leonard for that position did little to clarify what the lawyers could expect. Leonard, whose nomination was quickly approved by the Senate, had been the leader of the Wisconsin state senate. He had been elected to the legislature at the age of twenty-five, shortly after graduation from law school. On one hand, he had sponsored fair housing legislation in the Wisconsin senate; on the other, he had belonged to a segregated private club in Milwaukee. He had promoted funding of various programs for African American youth. However, he had no experience with school desegregation.[31] Leonard would later report that when he met the president, Nixon said, "Jerris, enforce the law but use your head, and get that damn school desegregation over before the 1972 election."[32]

Every new presidential administration confronts the reality that law enforcement is more complex than campaign slogans. It is common to make mistakes early in a presidential term, and the real test of the presidency is whether the president learns from those mistakes. And, as one observer noted, "Nixon was the first president to enter the completely remade civil rights landscape."[33] So it should not be surprising that the early days of the Nixon administration's enforcement of the Civil Rights Act's provisions on school desegregation were marked by twists and turns and contradictions, with the administration not finding a steady path until 1970. Ultimately, though, as historians have noted, Nixon's "posturing over school desegregation and busing disguised a pattern of quiet and effective cooperation by executive agencies with the toughening judicial mandate in the South."[34] Indeed, Attorney General Mitchell's assistant, Kevin Phillips, harbored the view that enforcement of civil rights would drive white Southern Democrats to become Republicans. For example, Phillips believed "The more Negroes who register as Democrats in the South, the sooner the Negrophobe whites will quit the Democrats and become Republicans."[35]

After his inauguration, President Nixon, asked for his position on school desegregation, responded, "If freedom of choice is found to be simply a subterfuge to perpetuate segregation, then funds should be denied to such a school system. If a freedom of choice plan, however, is found to be one which actually is bringing an end to segregation, then a freedom of choice plan, in my opinion, is appropriate."[36] Career staff was encouraged by these statements and by the early actions of the administration. One high-ranking holdover from the Johnson administration said of the first month, "I haven't seen even minor, let alone major, shifts in civil rights policies here."[37] Alabama school systems wasted no time in testing the new administration's resolve, however, and the results revealed both the more reticent nature of the president in his public statements and his private acceptance of the position bequeathed to him.

The Russellville City, Alabama, school superintendent asked for further delay of the planned closing of an all-Black school, because promised construction of a new integrated school had not yet begun. Similarly, the city of Guntersville, where Marshall County operated an all-Black school that was to be closed by fall 1969, proposed to create its own separate school system. While the DOJ filed no immediate motions in *Lee*, Leonard wrote Judge Johnson objecting to delay in Russellville and insisting that the new Guntersville system must assume the obligations of Marshall County.[38] While more than a dozen motions had been filed by school systems in the first two months of the year,[39] the Nixon administration's first affirmative move came at the end of April 1969, when it asked the court to order further desegregation of the trade schools and junior colleges.[40]

Then, in June, the United States moved for a desegregation plan for Autauga County, followed by a more expansive motion in July, seeking relief against twenty-five school systems whose reports "reflect that substantial progress toward the elimination of the dual school system based on race . . . will not be achieved for . . . 1969–70 without the formulation and implementation of additional desegregation plans." The court added those systems as defendants and agreed that all but two of them continued to operate dual systems based on race. It ordered further relief as to the other twenty-three systems, analyzing each separately and tailoring the relief to each situation—closing of some African American schools, cessation of busing Black children past white schools, and assignment of at least 25 percent of faculty members "opposite from the race of the majority of the faculty in each school in the" system. In some systems the court required that in 1969–1970 at least 20 percent of the African American students attend white schools. While finding that the freedom of choice method "gives no realistic promise of being sufficiently effective in the reasonably near future," the court left freedom of choice in place "where possible" for the 1969–1970 school year, effectively punting to the next school year. The court ordered some systems to submit plans by December that promised to eradicate the dual system by the following September. In other cases, the court took the unusual step of directing its order to both the school system and the United States, ordering that the government send HEW educational experts to study the school system and submit a plan to the court for completely eliminating the dual school system by fall 1970.[41] While it must have been clear that such a plan would entail assigning some white students to historically Black schools, the court remained silent on that point.

Nixon had expressed particular discomfort with using federal fund termination as the vehicle for achieving compliance with *Brown.* Career lawyers at the DOJ lacked knowledge of the internal deliberations within the administration but assumed that school desegregation policies were the subject of discussion by the president and his staff. After a period of seeming continuity with the enforcement policies of the Johnson administration, a warning sign emerged in early July 1969. Mitchell joined with HEW Secretary Finch in a joint statement on school desegregation, announcing a preference for DOJ litigation rather than fund termination, calling for full compliance for 1969–1970 but leaving open the possibility for "some limited delay" if required by "bona fide educational and administrative problems."[42] They explained that they would seek to "achieve full compliance with the law in a manner that provides the most progress with the least disruption and friction."[43] Mitchell, meeting with African American leaders concerned about the administration's civil rights policies, told them they "would be better advised to watch what we do instead of what we say."[44]

An early and important memorandum from White House staffer Lamar Alexander to a top Nixon advisor, Bryce Harlow, explained how DOJ litigation could work. After arguing that Nixon's school desegregation policy must differ from President Johnson's for Nixon to carry the South and border states, Alexander proposed that the administration "phase out H.E.W. Guidelines and step up a program of judicial enforcement." He viewed guideline enforcement as "arbitrary" and HEW officials as entering school districts "only to gather facts and to support conclusions already reached." Noting a proposed suit against Georgia still under consideration by DOJ, he suggested that "in the South the major new weapon should be the state-wide suit like that now active against the state of Alabama. Lee v. Macon County."[45] On August 1, the department filed the Georgia case, seeking desegregation of eighty school districts.[46] It appeared as if the Nixon administration was proceeding to enforce

Green's requirement of full desegregation but was less firm as to timing and method. It is no wonder that the district court in Alabama was unwilling to grant complete relief for the coming school year. Moreover, the Georgia case would not be decided until December, and some saw the case as a move to delay desegregation rather than to enforce *Green*.[47]

In a speech to the American Bar Association that month, Attorney General John Mitchell explained the administration's policies on several controversial topics, including school desegregation. His speech repeatedly invoked terms from the common law—"reason" and the "reasonable man"—as the touchstones that would guide the DOJ. He explained the preference for court action rather than fund termination in segregated school districts, calling it "a totally responsible, moderate and practical way to achieve great progress in an extremely difficult problem area." Court action would allow federal funds that benefited children to continue to flow, would provide cover for school officials who wished to comply with the law, and would be based on the expertise of educators from HEW.[48] It would shift political blame away from the administration.

All this was consistent with the approach the DOJ and the court had taken in *Lee*. However, six days later, the Nixon administration abruptly reversed course in school desegregation cases in Mississippi. In a breach of normal protocol, the secretary of HEW (rather than the lawyers for the government) sent a letter to the chief judge of the Fifth Circuit Court of Appeals asking the court to delay school desegregation in twenty-three Mississippi school districts in order to avoid "chaos, confusion and a catastrophic educational setback to the 135,700 children, black and white alike" in those districts. Although the DOJ had earlier urged prompt relief, noting that no white child attended a formerly all-Black school and that segregation exceeded what was permissible under the HEW guidelines, it immediately filed a motion based on the HEW secretary's letter. It asked the court to delay desegregation in those districts, contradicting the division's prior position urging the court to order implementation of HEW plans in those districts.[49] This change would have profound consequences for school desegregation throughout the South and would, ironically, hasten the pace in *Lee* and in the later statewide cases that the department filed in other Southern states.

Desegregation in Mississippi had been proceeding at a much slower pace than in Alabama. No system would desegregate without a court order, and there was not yet a statewide school desegregation case. And unlike the *Lee* plaintiffs, African Americans in Mississippi almost always had to appeal to the court of appeals to get relief. The DOJ pushed hard for relief based on plans drawn by HEW. The Fifth Circuit had warned the districts the prior year that they must integrate or abandon Black schools by fall 1969.[50] Department attorneys and private plaintiffs went back to the Fifth Circuit in 1969, and it ordered that HEW plans be put in place that fall. However, in light of the government's turnabout, the court had little choice but to grant the delay. Lacking a sound legal justification for doing so, the court chose not to publish its decision. These events led to chaos and confusion, not in the affected school districts but in the DOJ and HEW. The private plaintiffs quickly sought relief in the Supreme Court, and the department found itself for the first time aligned with the Mississippi school districts, represented by the state attorney general and John Satterfield, and against the Black plaintiffs. Assistant Attorney General Jerris Leonard allowed as how he was "somewhat embarrassed."[51] The president, asked at a press conference about his desegregation policies, tried to place himself between two "extremes:"

> There are those who want instant integration and those who want segregation forever. I believe that we need to have a middle course between those two extremes. That is the course in which we are embarked. I think it is correct.
>
> As I evaluate the situation this year, I found that there are twice as many schools that are desegregated at the opening of this term as was the case at the opening of the term a year ago. I think that is progress.

He spoke of "two goals-to achieve the goal of desegregated schools without, at the same time, irreparably damaging the goal of education now for the hundreds of thousands of black and white students who otherwise would be harmed if the move toward desegregation closes their schools."[52]

For the first time in its twelve-year existence, the CRD plunged into an internal crisis. Career attorneys felt betrayed. Never before had such a blatant change in position been forced on them. And it was a change that they felt was unwarranted factually and legally. Their credibility in court suffered, as did their relations with lawyers for private plaintiffs. Many of the attorneys rose up in protest and some resigned.[53] Those who stayed faced choices: cooperate with the administration, ignore its policies, seek to change them, or ask to be taken off school desegregation cases and reassigned to other, less contentious areas. Over at HEW, Leon Panetta, who backed strong enforcement, was forced to resign his post. Former assistant attorney general Stephen J. Pollak, who had shaped the government's argument in *Green*, told the *New York Times*, "The United States Government has turned its back on all those elected officials who now have to answer to their constituencies about why they, too, didn't flout the law by stalling."[54] Jerris Leonard did not enhance the government's case when, a few weeks before oral argument in the Supreme Court, he told a press conference that "if the Court were to order instant integration nothing would change. Somebody would have to enforce that order." He added that the CRD did not have enough people to enforce that kind of decision.[55] The *New York Times* editorialized that Leonard's warning "strikes at the foundation of government by law."[56]

Nixon had retained President Johnson's solicitor general, Erwin Griswold, who dutifully opposed the private plaintiffs' request for immediate Supreme Court review, but once the court agreed to hear the case, Griswold left the unhappy task of representing the government in oral argument to Jerris Leonard. Trying to put the best face on the case, Leonard told the court, "I for one would like to be on the side of taking more optimistic point of view and I think those of us who deal daily with the problems of school desegregation can safely say to this Court that we have made some rather substantial breakthroughs in school desegregation and . . . the end of the road is in sight." The private plaintiffs had argued that—fifteen years from the *Brown* decision—delay in desegregation was no longer permissible. Leonard responded that the *Green* case had only been decided eighteen months earlier and great progress had been made since then, "so we are . . . a little disturbed about those who become frustrated and say it's been 15 years since *Brown*." When Leonard added that some of the districts in the case were "terribly complicated," Justice Hugo Black, a native Alabamian, peppered him with questions reflecting impatience with the government's position, asking, "what does that do . . . except delay?" Leonard urged that the court do nothing precipitous, to which Black rejoined, "Would anything be precipitous in this appeal now? With all the years gone by?"[57]

The court promptly and unanimously ruled in *Alexander v. Holmes County Board of Education* that the defendant school districts must "immediately" begin to operate a unitary school system.[58] Asked at a press conference what his school desegregation policy was in light of the court's decision, Nixon responded, "To carry out what the Supreme Court has laid down."[59] The Southern Regional Council, which had been mildly critical in characterizing as inadequate the Johnson administration's efforts to achieve desegregation, issued a scathing report tying the delays to the Nixon administration's "Southern strategy": "The segregationist South had come to think during the preceding ten months that the administration was genuinely going to succeed in preserving for a long time some semblance of 'separate but equal schools.'" The report charged that the DOJ "seemed determined to act as a 'conciliator' with white officials in the Deep South rather than take advantage of an unprecedented opportunity to spearhead civil rights enforcement."[60]

Leonard consulted with his top career advisors on how to respond internally to the uproar in the CRD. Based on their advice, in September, he restructured the division from a geographic to a subject matter organization, "giving each lawyer a choice of whether to work on school desegregation cases."[61] One of the new sections was to be devoted exclusively to school desegregation. Although he knew that I had deplored the Mississippi delay, Leonard asked me to head the new section, committing himself to fully staffing the section and vigorous enforcement of *Green.* The twenty-two lawyers and five research analysts (paralegals) assigned to the Education Section would include some who had signed a statement protesting the delay in Mississippi. My mentor since I began as a fledgling lawyer in 1964, David L. Norman, had been retained as a top assistant to Leonard; Norman, a brilliant legal strategist committed to ending the racial caste system, urged me to take the new job. In my five years of legal practice with the CRD, I had experience in school desegregation litigation, a strong working relationship with HEW officials, and good relations with lawyers for the NAACP Legal Defense Fund as well as with school board lawyers; I had also taken on administrative responsibilities in several sections of the division. The new section would be staffed by many lawyers with whom I had worked and whom I deeply respected. I agreed with former attorney general Ramsey Clark, who said the CRD lawyers had "intense devotion to the rule of law and . . . the will to bring equal justice if we give them the means."[62] Though many of my colleagues were skeptical, I believed both in Leonard's good faith and that the Nixon administration had little choice but to enforce the law, and ultimately accepted the appointment.

For the next five years, my time would be devoted almost exclusively to enforcing nondiscrimination in the public schools. *Lee* remained a major vehicle for doing the job, and not just in Alabama. By 1974, when I moved to a different job in the division, the schools of the South, including Alabama, had become the least segregated in the country. Critics of Nixon would argue that this progress came despite his policies, but arguably, like the opening to China, Nixon was better positioned than his predecessors to complete the job of desegregating the schools. Perhaps Nixon's biographer Stephen Ambrose was correct in concluding that Nixon "did what he did, not because it was right but because he had no choice."[63] During those five years the NAACP Legal Defense Fund continued its vigorous push for desegregation, sometimes disagreeing with CRD lawyers about how best to desegregate the schools.

By 1969 the ever-shifting rhetoric of opponents of desegregating Alabama's schools latched onto a new theme: the DOJ and HEW allegedly discriminated against the South in their enforcement of desegregation requirements. The critics were correct in pointing out that African American children in the North tended to attend virtually all-Black schools, while whites attended virtually all-white schools. Legally, however, Northern school systems claimed they were not violating *Brown* because they had not deliberately segregated the races, while segregation in Southern schools had been required by state laws. In order to desegregate Northern schools, the DOJ would have to prove that their racial isolation resulted from intentional acts designed to segregate the races. Proving a Northern desegregation case required considerable resources, but the new Education Section had only forty-five lawyers, paralegals, and secretaries.[64] Relying on *Lee* as a precedent to bring more statewide cases would address four problems, two political (the "Southern Strategy" and Title VI's mandate to terminate funds) and two practical (the written complaint requirement and the slow pace of litigating one district at a time).

"SCHOOL INTEGRATION ENTERING CRITICAL STAGE"

Politically, the Nixon Administration's so-called Southern strategy adopted the tactic of completing desegregation as soon as possible. Within a few years, the era of large-scale school desegregation would draw to a close.[65] But in late 1969, Supreme Court decisions, Nixon administration blunders, and public opinion left the DOJ and HEW with little choice but to tell the Southern school systems that there was no longer any excuse for delay. Building on *Lee*, statewide suits could hasten desegregation, so that it would not be as great an issue in the next presidential election. Paul Rilling, who had resigned from HEW a month after Panetta, testified to a congressional committee that the

Georgia statewide suit had brought about progress and implied that more statewide suits were desirable.[66] Even the Black leader Julian Bond tempered his highly critical verbal assault on the Nixon DOJ by acknowledging that in his home state of Georgia, department lawyers had "wrung agreements for fall integration from a large majority of the school districts."[67] Leonard argued that at long last the courts had defined what the law required, "so, today, as we look to this September [1970], school boards know what they have to do."[68] Leonard's belief that the law was now clear seems at odds with Nixon's view stated a few months earlier, that the "range of differences" in lower court rulings reflects "honest disagreements about what the law requires."[69]

Statewide court orders would also mean that HEW would largely be relieved of the need to terminate federal funding of Southern school systems. As the Civil Rights Commission explained, "In the South, OCR's (Office of Civil Rights') activity is being somewhat pre-empted by the courts. According to the head of the southern schools program, if the Justice Department brings state-wide suits throughout the southern and border states, HEW's review role will be substantially eliminated in the South, although it could conceivably play a role in reviewing the court orders."[70] Leonard suggested that HEW would monitor compliance.[71] Practically, the DOJ would not need to wait for written complaints from multiple school districts but could use one written complaint as the basis for bringing one suit to desegregate all the segregated districts in the state. In addition, one statewide suit would defeat the strategy that Southern officials had discussed in 1956 of decentralizing in order to slow down the inevitable desegregation of Southern schools; a single suit would require fewer CRD resources than multiple lawsuits. Lamar Alexander optimistically asserted that "one and one-half Justice Department attorneys can keep tabs on the administration of one state-wide suit."[72]

In December 1969 the department convened a conference in Atlanta "to focus on the problems of full compliance with the Supreme Court's mandate [in *Alexander v. Holmes County Board of Education*]." Never before had the DOJ gathered Southern US attorneys, US marshals, and FBI agents to meet with the CRD. Although the department later characterized the "main achievement of the meeting" as the "development of general enforcement policies as well as a clearer understanding of the enforcement functions of each agency represented," it would be more nearly accurate to say that the DOJ used the meeting to deliver marching orders and make it plain that desegregation must be completed by the fall of 1970.[73] To aid the United States attorneys during the transition to complete desegregation of the schools, we gave them a booklet of recent school desegregation cases, sample pleadings, enforcement statutes, and statistics showing the status of desegregation in nine Southern states.[74] Frank Dunbaugh, the deputy assistant attorney general to whom I reported, recalls, "When we were done with educating them, all of the career people (including me) were ushered out of the room. Deputy Attorney General Richard Kleindienst went in and (so I have been told) explained that the President wanted the major push on schools to occur in 1971, not in 1972. He advised these presidential appointees that if they had a problem with the plan, he would accept their resignations."[75]

In 1970 Nixon became the first president to issue a detailed statement on how to achieve school desegregation. Also for the first time in American history, a Senate select committee, chaired by Senator Walter Mondale, a Democrat from Minnesota, held extensive hearings on equal educational opportunity, including school desegregation. Nixon's statement set forth the policies his administration would follow, and it did follow them. The Senate hearings led to a report, but no desegregation legislation.

Underlying the litigation, the congressional hearings, and the president's tortuous path to writing his own policy statement was the disruptive nature of the new stage of school desegregation. Before *Green* the issue had been whether to admit a few African Americans to the all-white schools. When the issue became how to transform both white and Black schools to "just schools," the answer seemed simple at one level: reassign students, through grade restructuring, boundary changes, and other well-known educational methods. To lawyers steeped in voting rights litigation, proof of racial discrimination logically determined the relief—extirpating the racially dual school system and its effects, "root and branch." But the question of what the schools would have looked like in the absence of state-imposed racial segregation was unanswerable. In a predominantly white school system, might some schools have been all white even without the racially dual system? In a predominantly Black school system, might some schools have remained all Black? Nixon's former law partner Leonard Garment, who advised him on school desegregation matters, later explained that "the problem was developing at such a rate and with such intensity that I soon came to realize that this was one of the more critical issues confronting the President at the beginning of his administration."[76]

The problem was compounded by the existence of private racial discrimination. Until 1968 it had been lawful in most of the country for homeowners to discriminate based on race in selling or renting their homes. Racial discrimination had been the norm in real estate. While no longer lawful, the effects of this private discrimination pervasively determined geographic population patterns. And even after passage of federal fair housing legislation in 1968, real estate brokers continued to guide buyers to neighborhoods based on the reputation of the schools that served them. Most white parents avoided or were steered away from neighborhoods served by Black schools. Many white parents, even if willing to send their children to schools with some African Americans, harbored fear of sending them to majority Black schools, belying the claim of segregationists that the Black schools were equal to the white schools. Racially segregated private schools increasingly became a haven where white students could flee to escape desegregated public schools. In short, the theory of nondiscrimination law collided with practicalities caused by continued racial prejudice. No prior president had confronted this collision, and Nixon, with or without political considerations, faced a serious challenge. While Presidential Counselor Daniel Patrick Moynihan had suggested that "the issue of race could benefit from a period of 'benign neglect,'" fifteen years of neglect, arguably not at all benign, had destroyed that option for racially dual school systems.[77]

Nixon's statement on school desegregation reflected a desire to settle a period of turmoil and indecision in the White House and possibly, as one of his biographers suggests, "his occasionally well-concealed desire to do the right thing."[78] In September 1969 Leonard Garment, the chief civil rights official on the White House staff, had floated a "statement on bussing" reflecting the views of the Justice Department and HEW "as to current law and policy in this area."[79] The draft became the basis of a November 1969 letter to Representative Edward J. Derwinski (R-Illinois) explaining that where racial "segregation within a school system exists as a result of deliberate discrimination, the courts themselves have required affirmative action to correct that situation." Therefore, the letter added, school systems might have to reroute school buses or even add busing, but the administration would seek to ensure the "educational soundness" of any court ordered busing.[80]

Garment's draft statement had said that the administration would require affirmative action; the letter placed the onus on the courts instead. Garment sent a copy of the Derwinski letter to Vice President Agnew as background for Agnew's appearance on *Face the Nation.*[81] Patrick Buchanan then proposed to the president that Agnew give a speech announcing "the bill of particulars *against* any more compulsory integration, anywhere in the country at this point in time." Arguing that integration was harming education, Buchanan boldly asserted, "The second era of Re-Construction [*sic*] is over; the ship of Integration is going down; it is not our ship . . . we ought not to be aboard." Buchanan opined that the administration could live with a very limited interpretation of *Brown v. Board of Education* but needed to get *Green v. New Kent County* reversed, so that the courts would not require "the shifting of white children into black schools."[82] One draft of a proposed speech would have had the vice president proclaiming, "For the life of me, I cannot see ahead any benefits to justify the terrible costs we are paying and that we shall pay in the future, if we move toward racially unified school systems throughout this country."[83]

Nixon rejected Agnew's proposed speech, saying he would "continue along the current road," but Buchanan appealed. When Nixon assigned Garment to work with Buchanan on the speech, Garment responded, "I think the speech should be the President's," as it would serve to situate Nixon as a leader on the subject. Nixon decided he would write a statement (not a speech) himself, "in a sound way, on that fine line, representing the decent body of opinion, rejecting extremism on both sides." He added "that somewhere down the road I may have to carry out this law. I can't throw down the gauntlet to the Court." He told his chief of staff, H. R. Haldeman, that "a policy of moderation and steady progress would bring far greater and earlier success" than "pushing too hard and too fast."[84]

A battle royal ensued in the White House over the content of the president's statement. Bryce Harlow later told William Safire, a Nixon speechwriter and later *New York Times* columnist, "On no other document in the years I was there did the President deliberate more than on this one."[85] Not mentioned in Safire's account is the Lamar Alexander memorandum that had pushed statewide court enforcement in lieu of enforcement of HEW guidelines. Alexander argued that the order in *Lee* "gets results; progress under the order is superior to that in other districts." Alexander and Buchanan did agree on one point, succinctly expressed by Alexander: "In order to carry the South and border states—a necessity for reelection—the President must act decisively to rebut the [George] Wallace charge that Nixon and Humphrey-Johnson-Kennedy are the same on the school desegregation issue."[86]

During the internal battle that led to the issuance of the president's statement, the administration considered a variety of approaches. Through all the debates and drafts, one sees the centrality of the Supreme Court decisions. Ehrlichman, Nixon's domestic affairs assistant, suggested adopting a proposal from Harry Dent Sr., creator of the Southern Strategy, to appoint a blue ribbon panel of experts to " recommend ways in which decent education can be maintained while complying with the court orders."[87] Yale Law professor Alexander Bickel proposed a "school desegregation statute" that borrowed selectively from the HEW guidelines, raising the "question of whether the statute intends to nullify or otherwise to diminish the effect of the omitted provisions of the guidelines."[88] Bickel thought it should be possible to comply with *Brown* "without at the same time producing the absurd result of resegregation." The draft statute would find a school system "unitary" if it assigned students to the nearest school, so long as this was done in "good faith," even if that resulted in perpetuating all-Black schools. Unitariness could also be achieved by "mixing the races in the schools in a ratio that, within a substantial permissible range, bears a relation to the proportion of one race to the other in the total school population in a district."[89] A White House aide found Bickel's proposed enforcement and remedial provisions "confused and limited."[90]

William Rehnquist, the assistant attorney general for the Office of Legal Counsel and later chief justice of the Supreme Court, met with Bickel to discuss the professor's proposed bill but then apparently proposed a constitutional amendment. Garment thought that Rehnquist's legal analysis of the *Green* case was "way wide of the mark" and that the proposal "would be bitterly divisive." He thought it would drive African Americans to "an explosive surge not merely of discontent, but of real anger—a feeling of betrayal." African Americans would view the amendment as striking at the Fourteenth Amendment, "which has been at the heart of what progress" they have made in their "whole agonizing upward struggle." Moreover, so would it offend "a lot of whites who have . . . allied themselves with the black cause."[91]

Meanwhile, an ad hoc committee of high-ranking people from the White House, DOJ, and HEW began meeting to evaluate school desegregation plans for individual districts, drawn by HEW officials. The committee "would balance the legal and educational factors with the political considerations."[92] In February the committee morphed into the Cabinet Level Group on Desegregation, lasting until the end of 1972.[93] Nominally headed by Agnew "to satisfy the South," the committee assembled—under the leadership of Labor Secretary Schultz—cabinet members, high-ranking White House aides, and civil servants to carry out the president's policies, getting into the weeds of implementation.[94] One of the White House aides, Ed Morgan, visited the CRD daily, in the words of Frank M. Dunbaugh, "to get a report and to try to pressure AAG Jerris Leonard to let up on enforcement." Leonard, though, resisted. When Morgan's deputies tried to get him to modify the division's positions, Frank Dunbaugh "reminded the white house staffers that they worked for Ehrlichman and that we worked for AG Mitchell and AAG Leonard." Dunbaugh "suggested that they had to convince Morgan who had to convince Ehrlichman and he had to convince Mitchell. Then if Mitchell told Leonard what to do," Dunbaugh insisted, "we would follow orders. None of the white house suggestions ever made it back to me through these bureaucratic channels."[95]

Nixon and Agnew met with Georgia Senator Richard Russell, who transmitted the views of Southern governors and senators concerned about HEW's school desegregation efforts. A summary of the meeting reported:

> The President said that [the Cabinet Committee's] function was to work with the local elite—the State and community leaders throughout the South—in order to help them implement the law in the states and school districts in a way that would be least disruptive of the overriding goal of quality education. The Vice President said the committee is also to construe the law and to ameliorate the concerns of the individual school districts and perhaps help with obvious educational deficiencies. He said that his committee "might also be able to help mold public opinion in a way that would encourage the courts to be more responsive to public sentiment."[96]

Attesting to the importance the DOJ placed on completing school desegregation, Mitchell gave Dunbaugh the highest department employee award for his "design and implementation of a plan to enforce the desegregation of schools in the Fall of 1971."[97]

The policy review, Garment aide Brad Patterson observed, was not assigned to either of the cabinet members responsible for school desegregation enforcement. Rather than assigning the review to the attorney general or HEW secretary, Nixon relied on Garment, a "typical, archetypical, White House assistant, I've always felt, the kind of gentleman who fits the description in the [Charles E.] Merriam Report of 1937: a fellow who works quietly, emits no public statements, possessed of great physical vigor and a passion for anonymity."[98] Garment "spent nearly all his time for two months . . . assembling a lawyer's brief for the President on the whole question of school desegregation."[99]

Nixon chose not to appoint a blue-ribbon commission; not to change regulations; not to propose a change in the law; not to propose a change in the Constitution. Instead, he decided to "take on the integration problem directly."[100] He wrote a statement directed at the public, at school authorities, and at the lawyers and educators at the DOJ and HEW. The ad hoc committee would be expected to follow the policies established by Nixon's eight-thousand-word statement, which began by reaffirming his "personal belief that . . . Brown v. Board of Education was right in both constitutional and human terms." He set out to explain the existing law, explicate difficulties in implementation, and "suggest approaches that can mitigate such problems as we complete the process of compliance." He stressed that "the constitutional mandate will be enforced" but criticized lower court decisions requiring "wholesale compulsory busing." Noting the distinction between de facto and de jure segregation, he summarized, "There is a constitutional mandate that dual school systems and other forms of de jure segregation be eliminated totally. But . . . an area of flexibility—a 'rule of reason'—exists, in which school boards, acting in good faith, can formulate plans of desegregation which best suit the needs of their own localities." In contrast, school officials may, but are not required to, combat racial isolation in de facto segregated districts.

Nixon urged "realism." He worried that past policy had demanded "too much of our schools: They have been expected not only to educate, but also to accomplish a social transformation." Other institutions must "share the burden of breaking down racial barriers." After discussing educational issues associated with desegregation, he insisted that "if the essential element of good faith is present, it should ordinarily be possible to achieve legal compliance with a minimum of educational disruption." All this led up to a section of the statement labeled "Policies of This Administration," consisting of enforcement policies and "policies for progress." The latter included research, jawboning, and monetary assistance for desegregation. Nixon repeated that the government must enforce the law and eliminate deliberate racial segregation "root and branch." School districts must achieve substantial racial balance of faculties and equality of facilities and quality of education. He favored the neighborhood school system and, in the most debated idea in the statement, argued that some segregation in the South was the result of de facto rather than de jure segregation, with the duty to desegregate applying only to the latter. The Supreme Court would later endorse this idea but place on school boards the virtually impossible duty of proving that segregation was not the result of the dual school system.[101]

The president's muddled, poorly organized statement attempted to allay concerns of white Southerners while endorsing desegregation and enforcement of laws requiring an end to the dual school system. Those responsible for enforcement had to view the statement as their marching orders. But what did it mean? The statement drew strong criticism. Jack Greenberg, head of the NAACP LDF, responded to the notion that some segregation in the South could be de facto rather than de jure: "How can you have de facto segregation in Jackson, Miss.?"[102] Leon Panetta, freshly fired as head of HEW's Office for Civil Rights, called the statement "a cop-out." His colleague, Paul Rilling, charged that the president's statement "adopted much of the verbiage of the segregationists: we must preserve neighborhood schools; busing is bad; education is more important than integration; desegregation heightens racial tension; many Negroes don't want it, etc."[103] Tom Wicker of the *New York Times* read the statement as a signal "to the South that pressures against dual school systems will be perceptibly eased." Charging Nixon with sophism because of his emphasis on good faith, Wicker concluded, "A school board composed of P. T. Barnum, Harry Houdini and Richard M. Nixon would not be able to devise more dazzling escapes from the clanking chains of desegregation than almost any old Southern school board will be able to arrange through so generous a formula."[104] A more cautious assessment by the *Times*'s Robert B. Semple Jr. called the statement "one of the major documents of [Nixon's] Presidency." Characterizing it as "thorough but ambiguous," Semple observed that critics read the statement "as an endorsement of the status quo in racial matters," while friends viewed it as "a long overdue effort to set forth a strong Government commitment to desegregation but allow the courts and, preferably, local communities to work the problem out in their chosen ways and at their own pace."[105] The editorial cartoonist Paul Conrad of the *Los Angeles Times* drew an "Administration line" school bus, whose rear end bore the warning "Caution—This school bus equivocates at all stops," and with a left turn arrow reading "for integration" and a right turn arrow reading "against busing."[106]

Perhaps the attitude toward the president's message within the CRD was best summarized in an April Fools' Day edition of the weekly report of division activities: "School section attorneys were recalled from the field and from vacations to Washington for a special meeting last Monday in the Panetta

Room. The meeting was called to clarify President Nixon's 10,000 [*sic*]-word statement of clarification of school desegregation problems. Mr. Leonard thanked everyone for coming."[107] Of course, there was no Panetta Room in the DOJ.

The division's Education Section had been working on developing statewide school desegregation suits when the president issued his statement. After reading the statement I returned to those suits and, in the next few days worked on school issues in Iberville Parish, Louisiana; Accomack, Virginia; Coffeeville and Tunica, Mississippi; Crosby, Texas; Jefferson County, Alabama; Bay County, Florida; and Barnwell County, South Carolina. The following week the Education Section met with Leonard. Section lawyers had opted to interpret the president's statement as endorsing enforcement of *Green* and *Alexander*. But would they be allowed to act on this interpretation?

Leonard sent John Ehrlichman an implementation plan based on discussions with the attorney general, the secretary of HEW, Leonard Garment, and HEW officials, "in order that there be no misunderstanding." They agreed that Alabama and Georgia would be in compliance with desegregation requirements by fall 1970 because of the statewide suits. The plan focused on 215 noncompliant districts in Arkansas, Florida, Mississippi, North Carolina, and South Carolina. The DOJ and HEW would engage in negotiations with state officials to bring about maximum voluntary compliance, and the DOJ would bring suit by June 10 "against state superintendents or local districts depending upon the number of such districts not then in compliance." Leonard noted that the meeting with the division's Education Section had been "successful in that there was no question as to what the President expected nor was there any question with respect to his wishes being carried out."[108] While the president, even in the pre-Watergate climate, could not legitimately interfere with law enforcement, he had the right to set policy direction.

New desegregation plans would have to be drafted and the legal sufficiency of plans submitted by school districts would have to be reviewed. The administration created a joint HEW-Justice committee to review plans drafted by HEW experts or by school districts. In turn, the HEW-DOJ work was reviewed by the Cabinet Committee on School Desegregation (later renamed Cabinet Committee on Education), probably to keep in line "radical, intemperate elements within HEW and Justice."[109] Leonard claimed that the collaborative approach of Justice, HEW, the Cabinet Committee, the White House Staff, and state advisory councils to solve school desegregation problems "dramatically illustrates our nonlitigative and cooperative approach to this especially sensitive civil rights area."[110]

I served on the committee, along with J. Stanley Pottinger, who had succeeded Leon Panetta as head of HEW's Office for Civil Rights, the HEW general counsel, the head of Office of Civil Rights' Education Division, and my immediate boss, Frank Dunbaugh.[111] A reporter noted at the time that the committee reviewed "desegregation plans for compliance with the law," adding that the committee's goal was "to avoid having plans in which one school district is required to go further in breaking up its dual school system than a neighboring district."[112] In the run-up to the opening of school in the fall of 1970, HEW and the DOJ jointly reviewed more than 150 desegregation plans. In addition, joint negotiating teams visited seven Southern states.[113] The executive director of the committee, future Watergate defendant Robert Mardian, told Southern school board members, "The President said that segregation of pupils must be eliminated root and branch, and that it must be done at once. School desegregation is a racial problem. It's raw racial prejudice, and there's no other name for it."[114] In June 1970 Leonard wrote to the Cabinet Committee on Desegregation predicting that the 1970–1971 school year would find 97 percent of African American children attending school in desegregated school systems.[115] He did not predict how many would be in desegregated schools, though.

The administration navigated the impending desegregation with some difficulty. The DOJ and HEW said they would send perhaps the largest federal force "ever dispatched to the South for civil rights reasons."[116] Then Mitchell said the information about the number of officials who would be dispatched was "premature."[117] A few days later, when asked about the size of the force, Nixon replied,

> Now as far as the number of Federal officials that should be sent to the South, let me emphasize that that will be based on whether those Southern districts or States that have this problem of desegregation ask for the help of either Justice Department or HEW experts. We are not going to have a forced policy in this area. Our policy is one of cooperation, rather than coercion. And we believe that is the best way to handle this very difficult problem in the Southern States.[118]

When school opened in the fall of 1970, the percent of African American students in one-race schools in the Deep South had dropped to 39.4 percent from the 78.8 percent in 1968.[119]

The Mondale Committee, in the meantime, held far-ranging hearings on equal educational opportunity, beginning in the spring of 1970 and continuing through 1971. Witnesses testified about educational theory, education finance, the state of education in the nation, and about school desegregation. Witnesses on school desegregation included social scientists, civil rights activists, and HEW and DOJ officials. Southern senators pressed the government witnesses on the disparity between the government's treatment of Southern and Northern school systems. Former attorney general Ramsey Clark and Mondale both opined that the distinction between de facto and de jure segregation was bad policy. Civil rights activists, Clark, former assistant attorney general Stephen J. Pollak, and Senators Mondale and Jacob Javits (R-New York) criticized the administration for the 1969 delay in desegregation, the emphasis on court rather than HEW enforcement, and expressed skepticism about plans for 1970.[120] Pollak listed three prerequisites for a successful enforcement program: "a statement of a clear standard; communication of the will to see that the standard is met; and prompt action to deal with violations." He concluded that by those standards, the administration record failed. Pollak pointed out that, with 439 school districts under court order in DOJ cases and twenty-seven lawyers in the Education Section of the CRD, each lawyer would be responsible for seventeen school cases, too large a caseload for effective enforcement.[121]

Leonard took a group of career CRD attorneys to Capitol Hill, where he testified "that those districts which have an official policy of segregation to iron out, will, for practical purposes, be desegregated this coming fall term." Leonard noted that the week before, the department had filed "multi-district and state-agency suits against school systems in the states of Mississippi, Florida, Arkansas, and South Carolina," following the course set in *Lee* and the Georgia statewide suit.[122] He acknowledged that African American children might meet some forms of discrimination in the desegregated schools, but said, "We will have eliminated a traditional dual system" and would now need to monitor and follow up on in-school discrimination. Mitchell noted that five hundred school systems would be desegregating for the first time.[123] Roy Reed of the *New York Times* reported that "neither segregationists nor integrationists are pleased by the Justice Department's mass law suits against the last hold-out segregated school districts." The so-called integrationists noted that Southern Republicans were reassuring segregationists that the administration's statements should not alarm them.

H. R. Haldeman, Nixon's chief of staff, complained that Ehrlichman and Elliot Richardson, Finch's successor at HEW, "want to do more than we really have to do." Reporting on a dinner on the presidential yacht with Harlow, Ehrlichman, Finch, Schultz, and Ed Morgan "supposedly regarding Southern schools," Haldeman said, "Did meet with above plus Mitchell earlier to go over Southern policy again. Keeps ramming it home."[124] A lawyer for the NAACP LDF was not happy about the new statewide suits, because the "Government is integrating schools, but it is not eliminating discrimination."[125] Still, Gary Orfield, the leading scholar of the government's school desegregation enforcement, generally critical, conceded that when school opened in 1970, "many of the last resisting systems of the southern black belt had desegregated. For a time, the DOJ was again playing its traditional role."[126]

After the Supreme Court's decision in *Green* the court in *Lee* had necessarily turned to more individualized examination of each school system, to completely eradicate the dual school system.[127] The DOJ and HEW worked closely together, with HEW experts drafting plans showing how to maximize desegregation in the school district and the department presenting the plans to the court.[128] The result was that, while some one-race schools remained, the schools of Alabama became among the most racially integrated in the country. By 1970 36.5 percent of African American students in Alabama public schools attended majority white schools, up from 8.6 percent two years earlier. Nationwide 33 percent attended majority white schools.[129] As the Alabama State Advisory Committee to the United States Commission on Civil Rights reported in 1977, "The desegregation of schools and public accommodations—crisis areas of the early days—are usually 'givens' today." That same year the commission reported "that desegregation actions taken over the last 10 years were effective in achieving sweeping reductions in the isolation of racial and ethnic minorities within numerous school districts."[130]

Nixon's opposition to crosstown busing had little impact on the *Lee* school systems, which were in rural counties and small cities. Nixon may have found it politically expedient to become a punching bag for civil rights activists, but the government vigorously enforced the *Lee* orders. The desegregation orders brought a flurry of related issues with them–compliance and second-generation discrimination. The Johnson administration had taken positions on some issues, but not on others. Just as Alabama's efforts to prevent equitable access to the franchise for Black citizens did not end with court orders in voting rights cases, entry of the *Lee* orders did not bring an end to the state's efforts to frustrate school desegregation. For example, in Alabama, as elsewhere, some predominantly white cities sought to secede from desegregating school systems to escape desegregation orders. Early in the Nixon administration, the small town of Guntersville, in Marshall County, formed its own school system. Jerris Leonard told the court that the new school system "should inherit the obligation of the Marshall County Board of Education to cease operating the Lakeview School as an all-Negro school."[131] The DOJ consistently took the same position in later cases. For example, George Wallace, elected governor again in 1971 and gearing up to run for president against Nixon, came to Calhoun County to support the secession of Oxford City. When the DOJ opposed the secession, Wallace charged that the attorney general had violated Nixon's antibusing policy. The department pressed on and prevailed in the Court of Appeals.[132]

Toward the end of President Johnson's administration Judge Johnson had requested that Assistant Attorney General Pollak have DOJ staff analyze reports regarding desegregation of trade schools and junior colleges. Pollak responded that the analysis reflected that "no meaningful progress toward desegregation of these institutions has been made in the past year." Ninety-nine percent of white students attended white institutions, and 66 percent of African Americans attended African American institutions. Only token faculty desegregation had taken place. Pollak followed up with a letter to the state superintendent's lawyers suggesting further steps to desegregate the trade schools and junior colleges and asking for a commitment to do so. It was this letter that led the Nixon administration in April 1969 to seek court enforcement of the order to desegregate those higher education institutions.[133] Unlike the elementary and secondary education cases, the courts had never explained how to desegregate higher education; they had simply required nondiscrimination in student admissions. Alabama's system of trade schools and junior colleges, however, included building and maintaining racially dual institutions throughout the state. Mobile and Birmingham each had one white and one Black trade school and one white and one Black junior college. Gadsden, Montgomery, and Tuscaloosa each had one white and one Black trade school.

The expansion of the trade schools and junior colleges was one of the signal accomplishments of Wallace's governorship, and some of these schools had been built and assigned their racial designation after the court had ordered Wallace and Superintendent Meadows to promote school desegregation. The trade schools and junior colleges differed from elementary and secondary school systems in several respects. Not only did they serve older students—their students had chosen to attend them rather than (or in addition to) taking a full-time job, joining the military, or going to a university. Unlike Alabama's public universities, the trade schools and junior colleges were open-admissions institutions serving commuters from defined geographic areas. In response to a court order to submit desegregation plans, the Alabama defendants proposed to continue most dual attendance areas, left faculties largely segregated, maintained program duplication, and continued separate transportation areas based on race. The district court had, in a case about four-year universities, said it was "reluctant at this time to go much beyond preventing discriminatory admissions."[134]

The DOJ could have simply proposed that open admissions without regard to race would suffice. Instead, it followed the logic of cases that, in other circumstances, had required Southern officials to overcome the effects of their past discrimination. The department submitted desegregation plans that HEW had devised, adopting some desegregation techniques used in elementary and secondary school systems and suggesting additional techniques based on the nature of postsecondary education. For example, the government proposed eliminating overlapping attendance zones; thus, students in the Mobile area would receive bus transportation to junior college based on where they lived, rather than based on the race for which the college had been designed. And the state would be required to provide new curricula in the Black junior college, to attract white attendees.

The trial court adopted many of the government's suggestions, but the court of appeals expressed concern.[135] It noted that desegregation law principles that apply to elementary and secondary education "have not been applied generally to institutions of higher learning in the same manner" and expressed "some reluctance to require school attendance zones for college level institutions."[136] This led the parties to agree to a consent decree requiring the defendants to study other options for desegregation. The court of appeals sent the case to the district court in Mobile, rather than returning it to the three-judge court in Montgomery.[137]

The *Lee* case lingered. The Alabama legislature continued to attempt to thwart desegregation legislatively. Second-generation issues of in-school discrimination, discrimination by athletic leagues, and discrimination against Black faculty and staff generated more litigation. Eventually the individual school systems were joined as defendants and in March 1970 their cases were sent to the judicial district where they were located.

The statewide order in *Lee* did not cover school districts already under court order, including the largest districts—Birmingham and its environs, and Mobile, Montgomery, and Huntsville. The statewide order did, however, apply to many "small rural districts . . . where resistance to desegregation has often been the most determined and violent." In the end, those districts proved easier to desegregate, because their structure was so simple.[138] The order applied as well to smaller cities, such as Tuscaloosa, Anniston, Selma, and Gadsden, where the structure was more complex but resistance was still strong. Five years after the decree was entered, civil rights groups could report that "the crude recalcitrance of the past seems to be waning," but that resegregation was a growing problem.[139]

Although the statewide desegregation order had outlined detailed requirements for desegregation of elementary and secondary schools, the order relating to trade schools and junior colleges was brief and general. The state board and department of education were ordered not to deny admission to these schools based on race; they were to eliminate dual attendance zones based on race; and to desegregate faculty. The order's impact was minimal, and only later would the district court impose requirements with teeth.

ANNISTON

In 1961 the small industrial city of Anniston in east central Alabama was the site of violent mob attacks on Freedom Riders, culminating in an attempt to burn them alive in their Greyhound bus and to beat to death riders on a Trailways bus. In 1963, when the Anniston public library decided to allow African Americans to have library cards and use the facility, a white mob attacked and severely beat two African American ministers as they attempted to ascend the library steps. Although African Americans asked the Anniston Board of Education to desegregate as early as fall 1954, they did not follow up with a lawsuit when the board ignored the request.[140] In the summer of 1964, though, the board agreed with local African American leaders to desegregate the following year.

Anniston was one of the ninety-nine school systems placed under the *Lee* umbrella, though, and indeed, what happened next became an integral part of the record in that case, demonstrating how local systems were held hostage by the Wallace administration. Anniston adopted a freedom of choice plan and sent to HEW a statement of compliance with Title VI. As the superintendent explained in his deposition in *Lee*, he asked HEW to accept board minutes in lieu of the required HEW form, "due to the existence in our state of certain factors which may infringe on our ability to carry forward an orderly program if adverse publicity to our School System develops during the political campaigns."[141] Like other school systems in Alabama, Anniston officials had been summoned to meet with Wallace three times when Wallace urged defiance of the guidelines. The Anniston board's lawyer told the superintendent that this "would certainly be the best way out of the pressure pot."[142] The board, African American civil rights groups, the *Anniston Star*, the biracial Human Relations Council, the mayor, and influential businessmen all supported the desegregation plan. Nonetheless, when school opened in September 1965 only sixty-eight of a possible thirty-two hundred African American students attended a formerly all-white school in Anniston. African American parents in the city expressed fear, based on television and newspaper accounts of "trouble in connection with school desegregation elsewhere."[143] So it was hardly surprising that so few African Americans volunteered to integrate white Anniston schools.[144]

The following year, Anniston reassigned seven teachers to schools of the other race, and 239 African American students enrolled in white schools, though no whites attended Black schools.[145] By 1968, with Anniston one of the districts the state superintendent of education was required to bring into compliance, the three-judge court ordered that forty-seven teachers be assigned across racial lines. In 1969 the court added the Anniston school system as a defendant. In 1970, while Nixon was drafting his statement on school desegregation, the court held a hearing on how to meet *Green*'s requirement that it "fashion steps which promise realistically to convert promptly to a system without a 'white' school and a 'Negro' school, but just schools." The private plaintiffs and the United States objected to the school district's proposal for completing student desegregation. The proceedings revealed a three-way schism in the positions of the school district, the government, and the private plaintiffs. The school district essentially proposed a neighborhood school plan. HEW proposed a combination of school closings and pairings. A typical pairing of two K–6 schools, one Black and the other white, would place all K–3 students from both schools in one school and all students in grades 4–6 in the other. The private plaintiffs objected that the HEW plan would fail "to disestablish racially identifiable elementary schools," and they proposed additional school pairings. The local African American community had objected to a proposal to close the Black high school. The private plaintiffs' lawyers might have felt obligated to represent the wishes of the local Black community; the government lawyers would have shown deference to local desires but would have ultimately represented the broader public interest, as they understood the law, the facts, and policies.

The three-judge court rejected both the Nixon DOJ's plea that it adopt the HEW plan and the private plaintiffs' plea for additional desegregation. Instead, it relied on what it believed was a pragmatic approach, based on its superior understanding of the local situation. Judge Johnson summed up the court's approach: "The members of this court have been dealing with the Anniston School System for several years now, we are very thoroughly familiar with the racial patterns and the effects of these lines."[146] The court approved the school district's student assignment plan on March 17 and 23 but disapproved the closing of the Black high school. It also ordered that faculties be racially balanced. Nixon issued his statement the following day.

Although one might have thought that Nixon's statement dovetailed with the court's decision, the week after reading the statement I found myself working on a memorandum explaining to the solicitor general why the government should appeal. He agreed, and the United States joined the private plaintiffs in appealing. The Court of Appeals, however, upheld the lower court plan as giving "the maximum possible desegregation that is feasible." The court praised the judges below for their "nearly six years . . . conscientious effort to desegregate Alabama's public schools."[147]

Having approved a plan to finally desegregate the Anniston schools, the three-judge court now transferred the Anniston case to the jurisdiction of the United States District Court for the Northern District of Alabama in Birmingham. Unlike Judges Rives and Johnson in Montgomery, the federal judges in Birmingham were at best reluctant enforcers of federal nondiscrimination requirements. Plaintiffs had successfully appealed adverse school desegregation rulings from the Northern District of Alabama in separate cases from Birmingham, Bessemer, Fairfield, and Jefferson County.

When schools opened in the fall of 1970, the Anniston school district failed to comply with the faculty desegregation ratios required by the three-judge court or enforce the school zone boundaries. The school district's lawyer, in response to a letter from Leonard pointing out these failures, listed good faith efforts of the district, while not disputing that desegregation of faculty and students fell short. He described the district's efforts "directed at trying to ensure the survival of quality education in Anniston" and noted that the departure of some white teachers had led to "a surplus of black teachers." Instead of offering to correct deficiencies, the lawyer promised that the district would "do its best to implement any instructions it may get from the Court concerning the information furnished." When DOJ lawyer Paul Hancock met with Dr. George Layton, the school superintendent, Layton disagreed with Hancock's reading of the court order and—well aware that the school system would find a sympathetic ear from Northern District judges—suggested that "the best solution would be for us to file a motion and thus the court would interpret the order."[148]

Faced with the brush-offs from the school district, the Education Section proposed to Leonard that the division file a motion that not only sought enforcement of the three-judge court's order but also sought a new desegregation plan, since the projected level of desegregation under that order had not been reached.[149] Leonard approved the motion, which was filed in March 1971. The motion pointed out that five traditionally Black schools continued to have enrollments over 90 percent African American and majority African American faculties, while nine other schools continued to have predominantly white student enrollments and faculties. It alleged that "the disproportionate number of Negro teachers and staff members assigned to the [Black] schools indicates that they are schools intended for Negro students." The motion also alleged that the student assignment plan would leave the five schools identifiable as intended for African American students and that reasonable methods were available to "provide all students with an opportunity to receive a substantially desegregated education."[150]

Paul Hancock shared a colorful memory of the hearing:

> I remember you [Brian Landsberg] lecturing me that I would not win the case before Judge [Clarence] Allgood and that my focus should be on developing a record for appeal. Mea culpa, but I did not think you were correct. I was very confident in a victory. The evidence was strong. Judge Allgood seemed to like me as we talked about football in our pre-hearing meetings; he was a huge Auburn fan and I boasted of the Big 10 and Notre Dame. Although I was a young and inexperienced lawyer, he told [United States Attorney] Wayman Sherrer that he liked the way I argued with witnesses (which you probably did not). (I was trying to emulate the aggressive approach of the great LDF lawyer Avon Williams who worked on many of our cases in Memphis.)

> You came to Birmingham to nurse me through the hearing. At a break during the day, Judge Allgood asked me to approach the bench. You, Wayman and [Assistant U.S. Attorney] Audrey Gaston attempted to join me, but Judge Allgood said "I only want to talk to Mr. Hancock." You and others on our team appeared to be frightened for what I might encounter. When I reached the bench Judge Allgood said almost these precise words: "Mr. Hancock, did you know that Auburn has a 'nigra' on its football team this year. Things seem to be going well and the fans cheer when he scores a touchdown." I responded that I was aware of that.
>
> I returned to the counsel table and slumped into my chair. You, Wayman and Audrey rushed to me, asking what the judge said. I was devastated and could only say: "You're right, we are going to lose." I will never forget that event.[151]

Judge Allgood, while he did order the defendants to propose a more effective desegregation plan, dragged the proceedings out for eighteen months and then approved the school district's proposal to essentially continue the challenged plan, largely because he shared the district's fear of white flight "based in part on [his] experience in other cases."[152]

By the time of Allgood's ruling, the Supreme Court had rebuffed the Nixon administration again, this time in a desegregation case from a large metropolitan school district, including Charlotte, North Carolina, and its surrounding county. The DOJ had filed a rambling amicus brief in the case, called *Swann v. Mecklenburg County Board of Education*, signed only by the solicitor general and Leonard. No career lawyer in the Office of the Solicitor General or the CRD would sign. The lower court plan proposed to desegregate the entire Charlotte-Mecklenburg school system by assigning children to formerly one-race schools throughout the city and county even though that would require some children to ride a bus across town. The school board attacked the plan as imposing busing to achieve a racial balance. The government's brief agreed that the school district's proposed desegregation failed to achieve a "unitary" school system. However the brief, apparently attempting to hew to Nixon's policy statement and disavow the "busing" plan, offered this question-begging locution: "If the decision of the district court was based on an understanding that racial balance is a constitutional requirement, it cannot be supported." The brief concluded that "it would be appropriate for this Court to enunciate the standards which are applicable to cases of this sort and to remand the case . . . for further proceedings in the light of those standards."[153] While adopting some of the language of the government brief, the Supreme Court did enunciate standards. It upheld the lower court plan, noting that "in a system with a history of segregation, the need for remedial criteria of sufficient specificity to assure a school authority's compliance with its constitutional duty warrants a presumption against schools that are substantially disproportionate in their racial composition."[154]

I recall being summoned, on June 1, 1971, to Attorney General Mitchell's inner office on the fifth floor, along with Frank Dunbaugh, my boss, and David L. Norman, who would shortly become assistant attorney general when Leonard resigned to take another job in the administration. Mitchell wanted us to explain the significance of the *Swann* decision. We showed the taciturn attorney general a map of a large Southern urban school system and told him that compliance with *Swann* would require extensive crosstown busing. He puffed on his pipe and thanked us for the report. The Nixon strategy of quickly finishing up the job of desegregating the schools had not anticipated that the court would tighten the standards for desegregation. *Swann* led to a new round of litigation, this time against urban school systems with some remaining one-race schools.

Based on *Swann*, Norman asked the solicitor general to approve an appeal from Judge Allgood's order in the Anniston school case. Within a week Norman and I were summoned to meet with Representative Bill Nichols, D-Alabama and a strong Wallace supporter; the Anniston school superintendent; the board's chairman and lawyer; and the United States attorney. We spent an hour discussing the appeal. The school district representatives reiterated their fear of white flight, noting that white enrollment had declined by four hundred in one year. Norman pointed out that Anniston High School was a brand new, very fine facility attended by most whites and a few African Americans, while Cobb High School was virtually all Black. The school district representatives expressed some willingness to unitize the high school grades, but not elementary schools. We agreed to seek an extension of time for filing a brief in the court of appeals, in order to pursue settlement negotiations, and two days of negotiation led to agreement on a new plan that would completely desegregate the secondary schools and further desegregate the elementary schools, though leaving two of the latter all-Black. A month after Richard Nixon was reelected, the court of appeals vacated Allgood's order and sent the case back to him to consider the new plan.[155]

In the wake of his reelection Nixon ordered all presidential appointees to submit their resignations. He selectively accepted resignations of those officials whom he wished to replace, including Assistant Attorney General for Civil Rights David Norman and Solicitor General Erwin Griswold. He nominated as Norman's successor J. Stanley Pottinger. Robert Bork succeeded Griswold. Pottinger had served as the head of HEW's Office for Civil Rights after Leon Panetta's departure, and the DOJ had worked with him extensively on school desegregation cases. Although Nixon had twice chosen him to replace civil rights officials whose enforcement of the law had displeased the president, division attorneys who had gotten to know him believed that Pottinger's experience at HEW had prepared him well for his new job. The DOJ's treatment of Anniston gave an early indication that they would not be disappointed. In a letter signed J. Stanley Pottinger by Paul F. Hancock the department told the Anniston system that the school board must present the agreed upon plan to the district court for approval and that no further delay of desegregation could be allowed.[156]

The Anniston appeal had led to a schism between the department and the private plaintiffs, now represented by U. W. Clemon and Norman Chachkin. Clemon was an African American lawyer in Birmingham (later appointed to the federal district court in Birmingham by President Carter) and Chachkin worked for the LDF in New York. The private plaintiffs had not joined the United States' 1971 motion for supplemental relief. Of course, the original plaintiffs in *Lee* were not from Anniston and had, in any event, long since graduated from school. However, given the peculiar procedural posture of the case, it was assumed that their lawyers could continue to represent African American students in Alabama school systems covered by the *Lee* orders. When the school district and DOJ agreed on the desegregation plan, the private plaintiffs reentered the case and objected that the new plan would leave some schools racially segregated. Judge Allgood, though, approved the plan with some minor changes. Now the private plaintiffs filed an appeal.[157]

The private plaintiffs had a point. The case law entitled African American students to complete desegregation of all schools "at once." The government filed a brief pointing out that the three-judge court's approval of a less effective plan had been affirmed on appeal and that the new plan approved by Judge Allgood would increase desegregation and would require further consideration of methods to desegregate the two remaining all-Black elementary schools for 1974–1975. The approved plan would lead to immediate substantial desegregation in 1973–1974, while "it is probable that the appellate process and proceedings on remand would not have been completed in time for implementation of a plan of desegregation any earlier than the commencement of the 1973–74 school year, if that soon."[158] However, as the private plaintiffs pointed out the DOJ had failed "entirely in its brief to state that the district court's approval of the instant plan excluding pairing was legally correct."[159]

The department had traded a possible win on appeal for a sure approval of a compromise plan. But was it legitimate to bargain away the rights of the students in the two remaining all-Black elementary schools? The private plaintiffs' brief skewered the United States for failing to address the issues in the 1973 appeal. They observed that "the government seeks to pose as some sort of impartial expert desirous of aiding the Court, rather than as a litigant with a position to defend."[160] And they argued that department's belief that its appeal might not be successful "is certainly not a basis upon which the legal sufficiency of the district court's order may properly rest."[161] The court of appeals, though, thought that Judge Allgood had "exercised reasonable discretion under the circumstances," and affirmed. It did note that the school board had committed to "continue to study means of desegregating" the two all-Black elementary schools.[162]

The private plaintiffs filed papers asking the full court of appeals to review the decision of the three-judge appellate panel, which, they argued, at best "approved a delay of yet another year in completing the process of desegregation in Anniston" in violation of the Supreme Court's ruling in *Alexander* that further delay was not permissible. The DOJ's response remarkably acknowledged that rehearing en banc might be proper.[163] Three of Nixon's assistant attorneys general—Leonard, Norman, and Pottinger—had now agreed that Anniston schools should be completely desegregated. The court of appeals, however, declined to rehear the case, so the desegregation plan approved by the trial court remained in place for the moment. The following year the parties agreed to a plan to desegregate the remaining Black elementary schools.[164] In twelve years Anniston had gone from being the site of the notorious attack on Freedom Riders to a city whose schools were desegregated.

Conclusion

> But these men are your brothers, your lost younger brothers, and if the word "integration" means anything, this is what it means, that we with love shall force our brothers to see themselves as they are, to cease fleeing from reality and begin to change it, for this is your home, my friend. Do not be driven from it. Great men have done great things here and will again and we can make America what America must become.
>
> —*James Baldwin, "A Letter to My Nephew,"* Progressive, *December 1, 1962*

The revolution by law had reached its peak. A central feature of Alabama's racial caste system, its regime of official racial separation and subordination in the public schools had been overthrown by a unique coalition of civil rights activists and, as George Wallace called them, pointy-headed federal bureaucrats. Racial discrimination in education did not end but did diminish and was driven underground in the form of white flight to private schools and declining state support for public education. Yet George Wallace's pledge of segregation forever stands forever discredited, and Alabama's schools are less segregated than the schools of most other states. Sixty-five years after *Brown v. Board of Education*, almost a third of Alabama's African American students in public schools attended majority white schools while only 8 percent of California's African American students did.[1] These statistics present an incomplete picture, but a roughly accurate idea of the extent of change and of desegregation.

Lee offers lessons that can help answer questions about the future of equal education in the United States. Unequal education is a pillar of the racial caste system, and the federal government must not remain silent when states discriminate racially in providing educational opportunity. The caste system undermines democracy. Each branch has the responsibility to challenge racially discriminatory deprivations of equal education. It is not realistic to leave enforcement of the equal protection clause of the Fourteenth Amendment to private parties alone. In this battle of African American parents against the State of Alabama, "the U.S. government fully participated and was a significant part of the legal team," as Fred Gray put it.[2] In *Lee* the federal government contributed superior force when the state attempted to obstruct desegregation. It contributed experience, a large litigation team, the expertise of the Office of Education, and an established relationship with the court. It helped develop the legal principles that defined desegregation and that allowed statewide desegregation cases.

The role of the DOJ evolved with experience. When President Truman supported filing an amicus brief in *Brown* he could not have foreseen the extent to which the federal government would become involved in desegregation. *Brown* gave enforcement responsibility to the federal courts, and interference with desegregation orders enmeshed the DOJ in backing up the courts, as well as leading to federal military protection of the desegregation process. It became apparent that the latter would drag on interminably if the federal government did not intervene. And so, the DOJ and, later, HEW undertook a full-bore offensive on the racially dual school systems in the South. This led to the need to refine the definition of what desegregation meant. Definition of standards for desegregation led to so-called second-generation issues and government participation in resolving them. The next step, beyond the purview of this book, saw the Supreme Court declare the job completed, even though a final victory had not been achieved. The question is whether experience will bring the federal government to revisit racial equality in public education.

The framers created three independent branches of government, as Federalist 51 explains, "to control the abuses of government." In the case of school desegregation, however, the existence of three branches served not to constrain government from acting but to facilitate action even without full and simultaneous support of all three. Each branch played a role in the revolution, commenced by President Truman and the Supreme Court in the *Brown* case, in a ratchet process that discouraged reversing course. Successive administrations each left an imprint shaping how the racial caste system was to end. The federal role grew. President Truman and his Committee on Civil Rights sparked the federal involvement in eliminating the racial caste system, including laws requiring racially segregated schools. President Eisenhower, even as he harbored doubts, enlisted the DOJ and the Army to enforce federal court orders to desegregate. His support for civil rights legislation led to the creation of the CRD and the Commission on Civil Rights. The DOJ was drawn into school desegregation cases even before 1964, when Congress authorized the attorney general to challenge segregation. Under the Kennedy and Johnson administrations, the CRD built on the understanding of the racial caste system it had acquired when combatting voter discrimination. A leading study of desegregation litigation concludes, “What the courts had done before 1964 affected what the executive branch was able to do administratively and . . . such administrative action in turn affected subsequent litigation.”[3]

No branch of the federal government could single-handedly desegregate the schools of the Deep South. The Supreme Court could pronounce that the Constitution prohibited state-imposed racial segregation of the public schools, and some school systems would voluntarily comply. But the courts needed the help of the executive branch to enforce *Brown* in the Deep South. Conversely, without authorization from the courts or the Congress, the executive branch could not bring about desegregation. Together, though, the judicial and executive branches were able to desegregate the schools with only minimal, grudging help from a Congress in which Southern members held disproportionate power. Even after the Southern stranglehold had loosened, Congress continued to punt the responsibility to develop standards for desegregation to the executive and the courts. Presidents Johnson and Nixon gave personal attention to the issue.

Was *Lee* itself revolutionary? The revolution is not complete. While *Lee* helped overturn the official racial caste system, the system had become so entrenched in American society that vestiges endure in culture, if not law. As Isabel Wilkerson says, “The caste system in America is four hundred years old and will not be dismantled by a single law or any one person, no matter how powerful.”[4] The ratchet principle did not guarantee continued progress but promised that there would be no retrogression in the law. The Supreme Court, sometimes with encouragement from the DOJ, has limited the ability of school systems to combat the racial isolation that persists in many schools.[5] While retaining the formal principle that former racially dual school systems must erase the effects of past discrimination, the practical effect of Supreme Court rulings has been resegregation in some school systems. As we gain deeper understanding of the deep-rooted origins of the racial caste system in the United States, the ratchet principle can protect the path for dismantling it and completing the ongoing revolution.

Yale Law Professor Bruce Ackerman’s constitutional history, *The Civil Rights Revolution*, laments, “the sun is setting on the civil rights revolution.”[6] However, African American voices continue to seek equal educational opportunity. James Baldwin wrote “A Letter to My Nephew” a little over a month before Fred Gray filed *Lee v. Macon County Board of Education*. Baldwin’s words in the epigraph to this chapter recognize that white Americans must embrace the reality that their future depends on creating a just community. If whites recognize what African Americans and other racial minorities already know, they will press the federal government once again to support those voices. The DOJ can play an important role if its lawyers follow the path laid in bringing desegregation to the South. This means developing facts, developing an understanding of the local community and of the positions of civil rights groups, refining legal doctrine, and shaping remedies to fit. It means challenging state policies that cause racial disparities in discipline, curriculum, and school finance, tilt in favor of private schools, and any other state actions that undermine the objectives of *Lee.*

School desegregation was necessary but not sufficient to assure equal educational opportunity and dismantle the racial caste system. Official separation policies ended when the three branches of government treated the desegregation of the schools of the South as a high priority. Desegregation began with the executive and judicial branches. The path to equal education will resume when a branch of government again adopts it as a high priority. The *Lee* case shows that progress through government action is possible.

EPILOGUE

In 1968 Anthony Lee sent a letter to MaryLee Campbell, the lead paralegal on the government trial team in *Lee v. Macon County Board of Education.* He wrote that he was "eternally grateful for the diligence you have shown in your work on the Lee v. Macon case." He said that although he was "just one of the plaintiffs in the case," he looks "upon that case as the most significant achievement that I have ever had the joy of participating in." The accompanying photo of Lee was inscribed, "Diligence for the just cause defeats all foes."[7] Lee had attended Auburn University after high school, the first African American to begin as a freshman and graduate from Auburn. When he wrote the letter he was a first-year law student at Rutgers but was drafted because the Tuskegee draft board denied him a deferment. He served in Vietnam as a legal clerk, in Alabama as a parole officer, and in California as a trade show installer. When he retired he returned to his childhood home in Tuskegee.[8]

His lawyer was not so satisfied. Fred Gray, age eighty-nine in 2020, told the *New York Times,* "The same problems we tried to resolve, they have not been solved. I think that what the Constitution requires, we're still a long way away from solving the problems we need to have solved." He added, "I thought the white power structure, once they saw what black Americans were capable of, that they could perform equally . . . . it would change their hearts, but I don't think the hearts and minds of many people have changed."[9] Still, although the public schools of Macon County remained almost all Black, Alabama's schools, like those of Louisiana, Mississippi, Georgia, and other Deep South states, had a higher level of desegregation than New York or California. And in the third decade of the third millennium, if, in the words above the Department of Justice doorway, justice "resides in the hearts and souls of the citizens," a growing recognition of the need to dismantle the last vestiges of our racial past may provide the impetus to complete the revolution.

Notes

ABBREVIATIONS USED IN THE NOTES

BMPP, JFKL	Burke Marshall Personal Papers, John F. Kennedy Presidential Library
DDEL	Dwight D. Eisenhower Presidential Library
FDRL	Franklin D. Roosevelt Presidential Library
FMJP, LOC	Frank M. Johnson Papers, Library of Congress
HSTL	Harry S. Truman Presidential Library
JDP, PUL	John Doar Papers, Princeton University Library
LOC	Library of Congress
LBJL	Lyndon B. Johnson Presidential Library
LGP, RNL	Leonard Garment Papers, Richard Nixon Presidential Library
NARA	National Archives and Records Administration

PREFACE

1. Suzy Platt, *Respectfully Quoted: A Dictionary of Quotations* (New York: Barnes & Noble, 1993), 184. Attributed to Plato but reported as unverified.

2. Owen Fiss, *Injunctions* (Mineola, NY: Foundation Press, 1974); Larry W. Yackle, *Reform and Regret: The Story of Federal Judicial Involvement in the Alabama Prison System Story* (New York: Oxford University Press, 1989); Joseph Bagley, *The Politics of White Rights: Race, Justice, and Integrating Alabama's Schools* (Athens: University of Georgia Press, 2018).

INTRODUCTION

1. The title of this book is based on a never completed project of Burke Marshall (by then a professor at Yale Law School), Renata Adler (novelist and essayist), and Owen Fiss (professor at Yale Law School, who had worked as a special assistant to Assistant Attorney General for Civil Rights John Doar) to publish photographs and text memorializing the civil rights movement. Owen Fiss, *Pillars of Justice: Lawyers and the Liberal Tradition* (Cambridge, MA: Harvard University Press, 2017), 74.

2. Erica Frankenberg et al., *Harming Our Common Future: America's Segregated Schools 65 Years after Brown*, May 10, 2019, the UCLA Civil Rights Project, Center for Education and Civil Rights, https://escholarship.org/uc/item/23j1b9nv.

3. E.g., J. Harvie Wilkinson III, *From Brown to Bakke: The Supreme Court and School Integration, 1954–1978* (New York: Oxford University Press, 1979); Richard Kluger, *Simple Justice* (New York: Vintage Books, 2004); Stephen L. Wasby, *Race Relations Litigation in*

an Age of Complexity (Charlottesville: University of Virginia Press, 1995); Jack Greenberg, *Crusaders in the Courts* (New York: Basic Books, 1994); Michael J. Klarman, *From Jim Crow to Civil Rights: The Supreme Court and the Struggle for Racial Equality* (New York: Oxford University Press, 2004); Fred D. Gray, *Bus Ride to Justice: Changing the System by the System: The Life and Works of Fred Gray, Preacher, Attorney, Politician*, rev. ed. (Montgomery, AL.: New South Books, 2013). See also Jack Peltason, *Fifty-Eight Lonely Men: Southern Federal Judges and School Desegregation* (Urbana: University of Illinois Press, 1971). Two leading books on the federal government's role are Gary Orfield, *The Reconstruction of Southern Education: The Schools and the 1964 Civil Rights Act* (New York: Wiley-Interscience, 1969) and Stephen C. Halpern, *The Limits of the Law: The Ironic Legacy of Title VI of the 1964 Civil Rights Act* (Baltimore: Johns Hopkins University Press, 1995). For a description of the litigation by both the NAACP Legal Defense Fund and the federal government, see Stephen L. Wasby, Anthony A. D'Amato, and Rosemary Metrailer, *Desegregation from Brown to Alexander: An Exploration of Supreme Court Strategies* (Carbondale: Southern Illinois University Press, 1977), 210.

4. See Brian K. Landsberg, "Enforcing Desegregation: A Case Study of Federal District Court Power and Social Change in Macon County Alabama," *Law & Society Review* 48, no. 4 (2014): 867.

5. Michael J. Klarman, *From Jim Crow to Civil Rights: The Supreme Court and the Struggle for Racial Equality* (New York: Oxford University Press, 2004).

6. Bruce Ackerman, *We the People Volume 3: The Civil Rights Revolution* (Cambridge, MA: Belknap, 2014), 255–256.

7. Gary Orfield, *Must We Bus? Segregated Schools and National Policy* (Washington, DC: Brookings Institution, 1978), 288–289.

8. Derrick Bell, *Race, Racism and American Law*, 2nd ed. (Boston: Little, Brown, 1984), 437–438, 444.

9. Pete Johnson, speech at the 50th Anniversary of Desegregation in Tuskegee, Tuskegee 1963 Symposium, sponsored by Auburn University and Tuskegee Human and Civil Rights Multicultural Center, Tuskegee, Alabama, August 23, 2013. The team's decision harkened back to a Northern swim team's dissolution rather than have an African American teammate, many years earlier. In 1937 the Germantown High School in Philadelphia, Pennsylvania, dissolved its swim team rather than allow William Coleman, an African American student, to participate. William T. Coleman and Donald Bliss, *Counsel for the Situation: Shaping the Law to Realize America's Promise* (Washington, DC: Brookings Institution Press 2010), 7–8. Coleman went on to a distinguished career as Supreme Court clerk, lawyer, and President Gerald Ford's secretary of transportation, only the second African American to serve in the cabinet.

10. Governor George C. Wallace, Inaugural Address, January 14, 1963, Montgomery, Alabama, Alabama Department of Archives & History.

11. George C. Wallace, Executive Order Number 9, September 2, 1963, Alabama Department of Archives and History, Montgomery, Alabama.

12. Willie Wyatt, interview with Joseph Bagley, January 4, 2012, Stone Mountain, Georgia.

13. "Judges," *Time*, May 12, 1967.

14. See in re Wallace, 170 F. Supp. 63 (M.D. Ala. 1959); US Commission on Civil Rights, *Report of the United States Commission on Civil Rights 1959* (Washington, DC: US Government Printing Office, 1959), 70–88, available at https://www.crmvet.org/docs/ccr_rights_us_6100.pdf.

15. See Jack Bass, *Unlikely Heroes* (Tuscaloosa: University of Alabama Press, 1981); idem., *Taming the Storm: The Life and Times of Judge Frank M. Johnson and the South's Fight over Civil Rights* (New York: Doubleday, 1993).

16. Milliken v. Bradley, 418 U.S. 717 (1974).

CHAPTER 1. THE RATCHET PRINCIPLE

1. See Milton Korman's oral argument for the defendant Washington, DC, school board in Bolling v. Sharpe in *Brown v. Board: The Landmark Oral Argument before the Supreme Court*, ed. Leon Friedman (New York: New Press, 2004), 128–133. See also Joy Milligan, "Subsidizing Segregation," *Virginia Law Review* 104, no. 5 (2018): 847, 864–869 at nn. 57–83; Second Morrill Act, ch. 841, 26 Stat. 417, § 1 (1890).

2. Risa L. Goluboff, *The Lost Promise of Civil Rights* (Cambridge, MA: Harvard University Press, 2007), 127.

3. Franklin D. Roosevelt, State of the Union Address, January 11, 1944.

4. Jill Priluck, "The Second Bill of Rights," *Lapham's Quarterly*, June 11, 2018, https://www.laphamsquarterly.org/roundtable/second-bill-rights.

5. Richard Kluger, *Simple Justice: The History of Brown v. Board of Education and Black America's Struggle for Equality* (New York: Knopf, 2004), 50.

6. Jonathan F. Mitchell, "Textualism and the Fourteenth Amendment," *Stanford Law Review* 69, no. 6 (2017): 1237, 1302. (. . . "decades-long refusal by Congress or the states to enforce the Fifteenth Amendment or Section 2 of the Fourteenth Amendment").

7. Plessy v. Ferguson, 163 U.S. 537 (1896).

8. Nikole Hannah-Jones, "The 1619 Project," *New York Times Magazine*, August 18, 2019.

9. Elena Kagan, "Presidential Administration," *Harvard Law Review* 114, no. 8 (2001): 2245, 2246.

10. Earl M. Maltz, "The Civil Rights Act and the Civil Rights Cases: Congress, Court, and Constitution," *Florida Law Review* 64 (1992): 606, 615–617.

11. Clark Clifford to Harry S. Truman, "Memorandum for the President," November 19, 1947, HSTL, https://www.trumanlibrary.gov/public/1948Campaign_CliffordMemo.pdf.

12. Letter from Harry S. Truman to Ernest W. Roberts, August 18, 1948, Teaching American History, Ashbrook Center, Ashland University, https://teachingamericanhistory.org/library/document/letter-to-ernest-w-roberts/.

13. "Whole Nation Moved to Action on Ga. Lynching," *Hartford Chronicle*, August 3, 1946; Richard Gergel, *Unexampled Courage: The Blinding of Sgt. Isaac Woodard and the*

Awakening of President Harry S. Truman and Judge J. Waties Waring (New York: Sarah Crichton Books, 2019); "Dixie Justice Prevails—Louisiana Lynchers Go Free," *San Antonio Register*, March 7, 1947.

14. *To Secure These Rights: The Report of the President's Commission on Civil Rights*, 1947, vii, HSTL, https://www.trumanlibrary.org/civilrights/srights2.htm#62.

15. Harry S. Truman, State of the Union Address, January 6, 1947.

16. Harry S. Truman, Address before the NAACP, June 29, 1947.

17. *To Secure These Rights*, 65.

18. Harry S. Truman, "Memorandum of Disapproval," November 2, 1951, reproduced in *Civil Rights, the White House, and the Justice Department, 1945–1968*, ed. Michal Belknap, vol. 7 (New York: Garland, 1991), 9.

19. Joy Milligan, "Subsidizing Segregation," *Virginia Law Review* 104, no. 5 (September 2018): 865, 866, 880n136.

20. Truman, Special Message to Congress on Civil Rights, February 2, 1948, HSTL, https://www.trumanlibrary.gov/library/public-papers/20/special-message-congress-civil-rights.

21. Kluger, *Simple Justice*, 251.

22. Brief of the United States as Amicus Curiae at 4–5, Shelley v. Kraemer, 334 U.S. 1 (1948), 1947 WL 44159.

23. Shelley v. Kraemer, 334 U.S. 1, 20–21 (1948).

24. Brief for the United States at 10–11, Henderson v. United States, 339 U.S. 816 (1950), 1949 WL 50329.

25. Sweatt v. Painter, 339 U.S. 629, 634–635 (1950); McLaurin v. Oklahoma State Regents, 339 U.S. 637 (1950).

26. Brief of the United States as Amicus Curiae at 2, 6, Brown v. Board of Education, 347 U.S. 483 (1954), 1952 WL 82045.

27. David A. Nichols, *A Matter of Justice: Eisenhower and the Beginning of the Civil Rights Revolution* (New York: Simon & Schuster, 2007), 6; Peter G. Boyle, *Eisenhower* (London: Routledge, 2014), 31, 12, 20.

28. Nichols, *A Matter of Justice*, 40–45.

29. Allen Shivers to Dwight D. Eisenhower, July 16, 1953, Official Files, Box 731, File 142A-4(1), DDEL, reprinted in Belknap, *Civil Rights*, 7:17.

30. Herbert Brownell, *Advising Ike: The Memoirs of Attorney General Herbert Brownell* (Lawrence: University Press of Kansas, 1993), 195.

31. Leon Friedman, ed., *Argument: The Oral Argument before the Supreme Court in Brown v. Board of Education of Topeka, 1952–55* (New York: Chelsea House, 1983), 250.

32. Brown v. Board of Education, 347 U.S. 483 (1954).

33. Bolling v. Sharpe, 347 U.S. 497 (1954).

34. Dwight D. Eisenhower, news conference, May 19, 1954.

35. Earl Warren, *The Memoirs of Earl Warren* (Garden City, NY: Doubleday, 1977), 289.

36. Friedman, *Argument*, 413, 435. A lawyer for the Clarendon County, South Carolina, school board told the court, "I do not think that we will send—the white people of the district will send their children to the Negro schools."

37. Friedman, *Argument*, 369, 457.

38. Friedman, *Argument*, 503–505.

39. Brown v. Board of Education of Topeka, 349 U.S. 294 (1955).

40. Dwight D. Eisenhower, State of the Union Message, January 10, 1957.

41. J. W. Peltason, *Fifty-Eight Lonely Men: Southern Federal Judges and School Desegregation* (New York: Harcourt Brace & World, 1961), 4.

42. Herbert Brownell, "Civil Rights in the 1950s," *Tulane Law Review* 69, no. 3 (1995): 781, 790; Herbert Brownell to Chairman and Members of the Anderson County Board of Education, Clinton, Tennessee, December 4, 1956, reproduced in Belknap, 7:90–91.

43. E.g., Letter from President Eisenhower to Billie Graham, March 22, 1956, DDEL; "The President's News Conference of June 19, 1957," in *The Public Papers of the Presidents of the United States Dwight D. Eisenhower 1957* (Washington, DC: Federal Register, 1957), 475. ("It was time for moderation and the development of a plan that everybody of good will could support").

44. Notes on the legal principles, n.d., Hagerty Papers, B 6 (1), EL, cited in Nichols, 175, 317–318.

45. Legislative History of Civil Rights Act of 1957, prepared in Civil Rights Division, and Notes of Legislative Leaders Meeting, July 16, 1957, reproduced in *Civil Rights, the White House, and the Justice Department, 1945–1968*, ed. Michal Belknap, vol. 12 (New York: Garland Publishing, 1991), 51, 82, 257, 263–264.

46. US Congress, Senate, *Civil Rights—1957: Hearings before the Subcommittee on Constitutional Rights of the Committee on the Judiciary*, 85th Congress, 1st. sess., February 14, 15, 16, 18, 19, 20, 21, 26, 27, 28, March 1, 4, and 5, 1957, 7–9.

47. US Congress, House of Representatives, Minority Report on H.R. 6127, 1957, 85th Cong., 1st. sess., H. Rep. no. 291, 46.

48. Bernard Schwartz, ed., *Statutory History of the United States: Civil Rights Part II* (New York: Chelsea House, 1970), 928.

49. Schwartz, *Statutory History of the United States*, 930.

50. Gilbert C. Fite and Richard B. Russell Jr., *Senator from Georgia* (Chapel Hill: University of North Carolina Press, 1991), 337.

51. Robert B. McKay, "With All Deliberate Speed": A Study of School Desegregation," *New York University Law Review* 31 (1956): 991, 1075–1078.

52. "President Backs Court U.S. Order," *New York Times*, September 10, 1957.

53. Dwight D. Eisenhower, the President's Press Conference, July 17, 1957.

54. David Halberstam, *The Fifties* (New York: Open Road Media, 2012), 170.

55. September 9, 1957, District Court Order by Ronald N. Davis, US district court judge, quoted in Faubus v. United States, 254 F.2d 797 (8th Cir. 1958).

56. Roy Reed, *Faubus: The Life and Times of an American Prodigal* (Fayetteville: University of Arkansas Press, 1997), 170; "Foes of Integration Blocked in Arkansas," *New York Times*, November 2, 1955; Herbert Brownell to Chairman and Members of the Anderson County Board of Education, Clinton, Tennessee, Dec. 4, 1956, reproduced in Belknap, *Civil Rights*, 7:90–91.

57. Herbert Brownell to the President (November 7, 1957), 13–14, reproduced in Belknap, 7:145, 157–158, citing Universal Oil Co. v. Root Refining Co., 328 U.S. 575 (1946).

58. Peltason, *Fifty-Eight Lonely Men*, 170–173.

59. Peltason, 177, quoting 2 Race Rel. L. Reporter 929, 930 (1957).

60. Press release, September 24, 1957, Kevin McCann Collection of Press and Radio Conferences and Press Releases, Box 20.

61. Halberstam, *The Fifties*, 171.

62. J. Lee Rankin to Sherman Adams, October 28, 1957, DDEL, https://www.eisenhowerlibrary.gov/sites/default/files/research/online-documents/civil-rights-little-rock/1957-10-28-rankin-to-sherman.pdf; "Schools under Court Order to Desegregate and Complying with Order," DDEL, https://www.eisenhowerlibrary.gov/sites/default/files/research/online-documents/civil-rights-little-rock/attachment-court-order-plan-for-school.pdf; Evans v. Buchanan, 152 F. Supp. 886 (D. Del. 1957).

63. Cooper v. Aaron, 358 U.S. 1 (1958).

64. Unattributed document, August 9, 1960, Box 107, JDP, PUL; "Legislation Providing for Action by Attorney General to Effect School Desegregation," Box 107, JDP, PUL, citing a February 2, 1959, memorandum from Mr. Greene to Mr. White.

65. See Liva Baker, *The Second Battle of New Orleans: The Hundred-Year Struggle to Integrate the Schools* (New York: HarperCollins, 1996), 361–362. The role of amicus curiae dates back at least to the 1700s; Samuel Krislov, "The Amicus Curiae Brief: From Friendship to Advocacy," *Yale Law Journal* 72, no. 4 (1963): 694.

66. Faubus v. United States, 254 F.2d 797 (1958) ("The public interest in the administration of justice should be represented in these proceedings.").

67. US Commission on Civil Rights, *Education 1961 U.S. Commission on Civil Rights Report*, book 2 (1961), 181; US Commission on Civil Rights, *Civil Rights '63: 1963 Report of the United States Commission on Civil Rights* (Washington, DC: US Government Printing Office, 1963), 69, available at https://www.crmvet.org/docs/ccr_63_civil_rights.pdf.

68. From July 1, 1958, to June 30, 1959, the CRD brought three voting rights cases and one case to enforce a Civil Rights Commission subpoena. Many of its cases, however, were at best tangential to civil rights. Office of the Attorney General, *Annual Report of the Attorney General of the United States for the Fiscal Year Ended June 30, 1959* (1959), 180–197.

69. Office of the Attorney General, *Annual Report*, 185, 193; In re George C. Wallace, 170 F.Supp. 63 (MD Ala. 1959).

70. Owen Fiss, "A Guided Conversation with John Doar by Owen Fiss," *McGeorge Law Review* 44 (2013): 293, 294.

71. Owen Fiss, *Pillars of Justice: Lawyers and the Liberal Tradition* (Cambridge, MA: Harvard University Press, 2017), 62.

72. John Doar, *Twelve Years of Civil Rights Legislation, 1957–1968: Laws Both Fundamental and Astounding*, undated manuscript, 7.

73. Dorothy Shelton Landsberg, "A Remembrance of John Doar," eulogy, January 24, 2015, Princeton, New Jersey.

74. Taylor Branch, *Parting the Waters: America in the King Years, 1954–1963* (New York: Simon & Schuster, 1989), 374.

75. "JFK and the Blue Bomb," JFKL, posted July 27, 2016, https://jfklibrary.tumblr.com/post/148052724156/jfk-and-the-blue-bomb; Branch, *Parting the Waters*, 362, 366, 374–375; James H. Meriwether, "Worth a Lot of Negro Votes: Black Voters, Africa and the 1960 Presidential Campaign," *Journal of American History* 95, no. 3 (2008): 737–738.

76. John F. Kennedy, *Profiles in Courage* (New York: Pocket Books, 1957), 136.

77. Kennedy, *Profiles in Courage*, 139, 140.

78. Carl M. Brauer, *John F. Kennedy and the Second Reconstruction* (New York: Columbia University Press, 1977), 64. Eastland and Smith were segregationist leaders in the Senate and House of Representatives.

79. John F. Kennedy, Inaugural Address, January 20, 1961.

80. John F. Kennedy, State of the Union Address, January 30, 1961.

81. See Victor S. Navasky, *Kennedy Justice* (New York: Atheneum, 1971), 98.

82. A conversation with John Doar by Smith McKeithen and Emma McKeithen Jennings, August 11, 2014, 6; Eric Williamson, "Unseating Segregation for a Night," *University of Virginia Lawyer*, Spring 2018, https://www.law.virginia.edu/uvalawyer/article/unseating-segregation-night. As a law student at the University of Virginia, just a few years earlier, Kennedy had invited Ralph Bunche to speak, over vehement opposition from university authorities. Bunche refused to speak to a segregated audience, and the audience for this speech was integrated.

83. Robert F. Kennedy, Law Day Address at the University of Georgia Law School, Athens, Georgia, May 6, 1961.

84. "Equality Rights Improve Life for South, JFK Aide Says," *Montgomery Advertiser*, June 28, 1961.

85. Burke Marshall, Oral History Transcript, interview with T. H. Baker, October 28, 1968, LBJL, 14, https://discoverlbj.org/item/oh-marshallb-19681028-1-74-215.

86. Branch, 388; e.g., Burke Marshall, interview with Blackside for *Eyes on the Prize: America's Civil Rights Years (1954–1965)*, November 4, 1985, Film and Media Archive, Henry Hampton Collection, Washington University Libraries; Fiss, "A Guided Conversation," 293, 294.

87. John Kirby interview transcript, interview with his son, John Kirby, author archive, 32.

88. Fiss, "A Guided Conversation," 293, 295–296.

89. Fiss, *Pillars of Justice*, 66; see John Doar, *Burke Marshall's Memorial*, Yale Law Journal 113, no. 4 (2004): 791.

90. Fiss, *Pillars of Justice*, 67.

91. Robert H. Jackson, "The Federal Prosecutor," *Journal of the American Judicial Society* 24 (1940): 18, 20, https://www.roberthjackson.org/speech-and-writing/the-federal-prosecutor/.

92. Fiss, *Pillars of Justice*, 75.

93. FBI Report, File no. 161–201, re John Michael Andrew Doar, January 7, 1965, quoting Vernol R. Jansen Jr.

94. "FBI File on John Doar," January 13, 1965, https://archive.org/stream/foia _Committee_For_Public_Justice-HQ-EBF-8/Committee_For_Public_Justice-HQ-EBF-8 _djvu.txt.

95. John Doar, interview with S. A. Andretta, FBI Report on John Doar, December 31, 1963, sent on January 6, 1965.

96. US Congress, Senate, Subcommittee on Constitutional Rights, Committee on the Judiciary, Nomination of John Doar, February 25, 1965, 89th Cong., 1st Sess., 8.

97. "Prosecutor for Rights John Michael Doar," *New York Times*, December 4, 1965.

98. Doar, interview with Andretta.

99. See Brian K. Landsberg, *Enforcing Civil Rights: Race Discrimination and the Department of Justice* (Lawrence: University Press of Kansas, 1997), 78.

100. US Congress, Senate, Committee on the Judiciary, Nomination of Burke Marshall, 87th Cong., 1st Sess., March 2, 1961.

101. Bush v. Orleans Parish School Board, 191 F. Supp. 871, 876 (E.D. La. 1961).

102. Bush v. Orleans Parish School Board at 877, n. 12.

103. Bush v. Orleans Parish School Board at 878.

104. United States v. Barnett, 330 F.2d 369, 371 (1963).

105. Baker, *Second Battle of New Orleans*, 395; Branch, 665–669.

106. Transcript of conversation between Attorney General Robert F. Kennedy and Governor Wallace, Montgomery, Alabama, April 25, 1963, 5, reproduced in Belknap, 7:473.

107. US President, "Unlawful Obstructions of Justice and Combinations in the State of Alabama," Proclamation no. 3542 of June 11, 1963. Compare US President, "Obstruction of Justice in the State of Arkansas," Proclamation no. 3204, September 23, 1957.

108. See Elizabeth Jacoway, *Turn Away Thy Son: Little Rock, the Crisis That Shocked the Nation* (New York: Simon & Schuster, 2007), 62; see also the desegregation and resegregation of the University of Alabama in 1956, following mob violence; Diane McWhorter, *Carry Me Home: Birmingham, Alabama, the Climactic Battle of the Civil Rights Revolution* (New York: Simon & Schuster, 2001), 99; Branch, 181; Letter from J. Edgar Hoover to Maxwell M. Rabb, secretary to the cabinet, "Racial Tension and Civil Rights," March 1, 1956, sent March 9, 1956, DDEL, 9.

109. Burke Marshall, "Burke Marshall Oral History Interview," interview with Anthony Lewis, Washington, DC, June 13, 1964, JFKL, 66.

110. Burke Marshall to Byron White, "Incidents Requiring Intervention of Deputy United States Marshals," July 14, 1961, reproduced in Belknap, 7:188–189.

111. Marshall, "Burke Marshall Oral History Interview," 43.

112. Department of Justice, Progress in the Field of Civil Rights: A Summary, January 20 to November 20, 1961, 003426, Box 92, JDP, PUL.

113. Remarks by Assistant Attorney General Burke Marshall at the 14th Annual Conference, National Civil Liberties Clearing House, March 29, 1962, Box 13, BMPP, JFKL.

114. Burke Marshall to Democratic National Committee, May 21, 1962, Box 013, BMPP, JFKL, 3.

115. See generally Gary Orfield, *The Reconstruction of Southern Education: The Schools and the 1964 Civil Rights Act* (New York: Wiley-Interscience, 1969), 27–32, characterizing

the decision to bring lawsuits instead of taking administrative enforcement action as "the tactic of avoiding controversial policy decision by leaving them to the courts."

116. Burke Marshall, Statement before the House of Representatives, Ad Hoc Subcommittee on Integration in Federally Assisted Education of the Committee on Education and Labor, April 16, 1962.

117. Burke Marshall to Attorney General, August 22, 1962, February 20, 1961, Box 36, Folder Schools General I, JDP, PUL.

118. U.S. v. County School Board of Prince George County, 221 F. Supp. 93 (E.D. Va. 1963); Monday Reports to Attorney General, January 3, 1963, and January 18, 1963, Box 016, BMPP, JFKL.

119. "School Desegregation," *Congressional Quarterly*, August 1, 1962, 4–6.

120. Doar, interview with Blackside for *Eyes on the Prize.*

121. Burke Marshall to Reverend Power McLeod, October 29, 1962, Series 1.01, BMPP, JFKL; Burke Marshall, "Burke Marshall Oral History Interview," 67.

122. Goss v. Board of Education, 373 U.S. 683 (1963).

123. Brief of United States as Amicus Curiae, Goss v. Bd. of Educ. 373 U.S. 683 (1963) 1963 WL 105481.

124. Burke Marshall, *Federalism and Civil Rights* (New York: Columbia University Press: 1964), 77.

125. Burke Marshall, "Memorandum for the Attorney General, re: Huntsville, Alabama, School Situation," July 31, 1962, reproduced in Belknap, 7:191–192.

126. United States v. City of Jackson, Mississippi, 318 F.2d 1 (5th Cir. 1963); United States of America v. Madison County Board of Education, 219 F. Supp. 60 (N.D. Ala. 1963), aff'd 326 F.2d 237 (5th Cir. 1964).

127. Burke Marshall to Leslie W. Dunbar, February 26, 1963, in Belknap, 7:460–462; Nicholas Katzenbach, "Nicholas Katzenbach, Oral History Interview," interview with Anthony Lewis, November 16, 1964, Washington, DC, JFKL, JFK #1, 19; Martin Luther King Jr., "Give Us the Ballot," address delivered at the Prayer Pilgrimage for Freedom, May 17, 1957, in *The Papers of Martin Luther King, Jr.* (Berkeley: University of California Press, 2000), 208, 210; Burke Marshall to Staige D. Blackford, September 25, 1963, reel 007, School Desegregation, United States Department of Justice FOIA Files Online.

128. See Milligan, 905.

129. See Brooks Hayes, "Memorandum for the President," November 30, 1962, Belknap, 7:452; Bob Duke, "Keep Away, Wallace Tells Pro-Segregation Zealots," *Montgomery Advertiser*, June 1, 1963; Jack Bass, *Taming the Storm: The Life and times of Judge Frank M. Johnson and the South's Fight over Civil Rights* (New York: Doubleday, 1993), 207.

130. William P. Mitchell, TCA announcement, June 17, 1963, Box 7, Folder 9, Tuskegee Civic Association Files, Tuskegee University Archives.

131. John W. Macy to Robert F. Kennedy, June 6, 1963, Box 017, BMPP, JFKL; Kennedy's thank you note two weeks later simply said he would "read it with interest at the first opportunity." Kennedy to Macy, June 19, 1963, JFKL.

132. Burke Marshall, speech at Howard University Law School, approximately 1962, Box 013, BMPP, JFKL, 3.

133. Compare Jack Greenberg, *Crusaders in the Courts* (New York: Basic Books, 1994), 287, with Larry Yackle, "A Worthy Champion for Fourteenth Amendment Rights: The United States in Parens Patriae," *Northwestern University Law Review* 92 (1997): 111, 130. But see Seth Davis, "Implied Public Rights of Action," *Columbia Law Review* 114, no. 1 (2014): 1.

CHAPTER 2. MACON COUNTY AND ALABAMA'S RACIAL CASTE SYSTEM

1. Stephen L. Wasby, *Race Relations Litigation in an Age of Complexity* (Charlottesville: University Press of Virginia, 1995), 61–62; see Brian K. Landsberg, *Enforcing Civil Rights: Race Discrimination and the Department of Justice* (Lawrence: University Press of Kansas, 1997), 8, 27.

2. Charles Spurgeon Johnson, *Shadow of the Plantation* (Chicago: University of Chicago Press, 1934), 129, as quoted in Gunnar Myrdal, *An American Dilemma* (New York: Harper & Brothers, 1944), 894.

3. Alabama Constitution, sec. 256.

4. See Manuel Roig-Franzia, "Alabama Vote Opens Old Racial Wounds, School Segregation Remains a State Law as Amendment is Defeated," *Washington Post*, November 28, 2004.

5. Isabel Wilkerson, "America's Enduring Caste System," *New York Times Magazine*, July 5, 2020.

6. Wayne Flynt, *Alabama in the Twentieth Century* (Tuscaloosa: University of Alabama Press, 2004), 319.

7. Mab Segrest, interview with Andy Hornsby, March 15 [unspecified year], Oral History for the David Mathews Center for Civic Life, Auburn University.

8. See Brian K. Landsberg, *Free at Last to Vote: The Alabama Origins of the 1965 Voting Rights Act* (Lawrence: University Press of Kansas, 2007), 51.

9. "Classified Population of the States and Territories by County on the First Day of June 1860, State of Alabama," accessed November 30, 2021, https://www2.census.gov/library/publications/decennial/1860/population/1860a-04.pdf#.

10. Landsberg, *Free at Last*, 10.

11. Robert J. Norrell, *Reaping the Whirlwind* (New York: Alfred A. Knopf, 1985), 3–4, 13.

12. Norrell, *Reaping the Whirlwind*, 23.

13. Risa L. Goluboff, *The Lost Promise of Civil Rights* (Cambridge, MA: Harvard University Press, 2007), 79–80.

14. See photo in *Southern Courier*, May 4–5, 1968; Fred D. Gray, *Bus Ride to Justice: Changing the System by the System: The Life and Works of Fred Gray, Preacher, Attorney, Politician*, rev. ed. (Montgomery: New South Books, 2013), 294–302. This episode was dramatized on television, in *Miss Evers' Boys* in 1997; Anne Kendrick Walker, *Tuskegee and the Black Belt: A Portrait of a Race* (Richmond: Dietz Press, 1944), 74.

15. Tuskegee Normal and Industrial Institute became Tuskegee University in 1985. See "History of Tuskegee University," Tuskegee University, accessed May 6, 2021, https://www.tuskegee.edu/about-us/history-and-mission; Flynt, *Alabama in the Twentieth Century*, 336.

16. Booker T. Washington, *Up from Slavery* (Garden City, NY: Doubleday, 1922), 106.

17. Lyman Abbott in Washington, *Up from Slavery*, xxiii–xxi.

18. See Washington, 108; Norrell, 17, 22; Giles v. Harris, 189 U.S. 475 (1903); Richard H. Pildes, "Democracy, Anti-Democracy, and the Canon," *Constitutional Commentary* 17, no. 2 (2000): 295, 305.

19. Washington, 113, 115, 122, 123.

20. Norrell, 20.

21. Virginia Van Der Veer Hamilton, *Alabama: A Bicentennial History* (New York: Norton, 1984), 96.

22. Norrell, 25, 27, 47.

23. Johnson, *Shadow of the Plantation*, 208.

24. Founder's Day Address of Governor Chauncey Sparks, April 4, 1943, Tuskegee Institute, reproduced in Walker, *Tuskegee and the Black Belt*, xv, xvii.

25. Sparks address in Walker, *Tuskegee and the Black Belt*, xv.

26. "Gerrymandering: New Use for an Old Device: Many Eyes Focused on What Is Believed a Court-Proof Plan," January 13, 1958, unknown newspaper; Norrell, 80.

27. Norrell, 80.

28. Southern Education Report, December 1966 at 22, quoting book review by Bob Smith in the Charlotte news, of Reed Saratt, *The Ordeal of Segregation* (New York: Harper & Row, 1966); Gomillion v. Lightfoot, 364 U.S. 339 (1960). Engelhardt said "desegregating the schools will lead to rape! Damn niggers stink; they're unwashed; they have no morals; they're just animals." Quotation from J. W. Peltason, *Fifty-Eight Lonely Men: Southern Federal Judges and School Desegregation* (New York: Harcourt, Brace & World, 1961), 38, citing William Peters, *The Southern Temper* (New York: Doubleday, 1959), 208.

29. Senate Joint Resolution, Alabama Act no. 894, September 21, 1953.

30. Charles M. Cooper, "Segregation in Public Schools," Alabama Legislative Reference Service, November 26, 1952; idem., "The School Segregation Problem," Alabama Legislative Reference Service, January 9, 1954.

31. Jeff Roche, *Restructured Resistance: The Sibley Commission and the Politics of Desegregation in Georgia* (Athens: University of Georgia Press, 2010), 34.

32. John Temple Graves [the younger], "This Afternoon," *Birmingham Post*, April 29, 1946.

33. See Ian Haney López, *Dog Whistle Politics: How Coded Racial Appeals Have Reinvented Racism & Wrecked the Middle Class* (New York: Oxford University Press, 2014), 16.

34. Quoting John Temple Graves [the elder]. "He Defends Lynch Law," *New York Times*, August 12, 1903.

35. See Genesis 9:21–25.

36. Alabama Legislature, Senate, Report of Alabama Interim Legislative Committee on Segregation in the Public Schools, Regular Session, 1955, 2.

37. Alabama Constitution, sec. 102, Miscegenation Laws.

38. See U.S. v. Jefferson County Board of Education, 372 F.2d 836, 872–73 (5th Cir. 1966), 380 F.2d 385 (5th Cir. 1967) (en banc), cert. denied, 389 U.S. 840 (1967).

39. Reinhold Niebuhr, *Moral Man and Immoral Society: A Study of Ethics and Politics* (Louisville: Muriwai Books, 2017), 10.

40. W. T. Hayes to Frank M. Johnson, September 28, 1963, Box 160, Folder 6, FMJP, LOC.

41. Annie Laney to Frank M. Johnson, February 11, 1964, Box 160, Folder 8, FMJP, LOC.

42. Anonymous to Frank M. Johnson, August 8, 1964, Box 159, Folder 3, FMJP, LOC.

43. Gene Howard, *Patterson for Alabama: The Life and Career of John Patterson* (Tuscaloosa: University of Alabama Press, 2008), 99–100.

44. John Hayman, *Bitter Harvest: Richmond Flowers and the Civil Rights Revolution* (Montgomery: Black Belt Press, 1996), 117.

45. Elizabeth Jacoway, *Turn Away Thy Son: Little Rock, the Crisis That Shocked the Nation* (Fayetteville: University of Arkansas Press, 2007), 62

46. Shuttlesworth v. Birmingham Board of Education, 162 F. Supp. 372, 381 (N.D. Ala. 1958), aff'd, 358 U.S. 101 (1958).

47. Anders Walker, *The Ghost of Jim Crow: How Southern Moderates Used Brown v. Board of Education to Stall Civil Right* (New York: Oxford University Press, 2009), 13.

48. Jack Bass, *Taming the Storm: The Life and Times of Judge Frank M. Johnson Jr. and the South's Fight over Civil Rights* (New York: Doubleday, 1993), 214. For discussion of white "moderate" leaders' use of pupil placement laws to minimize desegregation in Mississippi, Florida, and North Carolina, see Walker, *Ghost of Jim Crow*, 13.

49. Thurgood Marshall, "General Discussion—Third Session," *Journal of Negro Education*, 3 (1952) at 335, quoted in Jack Greenberg, *Crusaders in the Courts: Legal Battles of the Civil Rights Movement* (New York: Twelve Tables Press, 2004), 114.

50. US Commission on Civil Rights, *Federal Enforcement of School Desegregation*, September 11, 1969, 27, available at https://www.google.com/books/edition/Federal_Enforcement_of_School_Desegregat/lzowFBAWzFoC?hl=en&gbpv=1&printsec=frontcover.

51. Shuttlesworth v. Birmingham Bd. of Educ., 358 U.S. 101 (1958), aff'd mem. 162 F.Supp. 372 (ND Ala. 1958).

52. Briggs v. Elliott, 132 F.Supp. 776 (E.D.S.C. 1955).

53. The Inaugural Address of Governor George C. Wallace, January 14, 1963, Montgomery, Alabama.

54. Walker, *Portrait of a Race*, 5; Tuskegee Civic Association, *Trends in Selected Aspects of Public Education for Negroes in Macon County, Alabama 1938–39, 1943–44, 1948–49* (Tuskegee: Tuskegee Institute 1950), 6–8.

55. Jessie Parkhurst Guzman, *Crusade for Civic Democracy* (New York: Vantage, 1984), 4–5.

56. *The Report of the Education Commission of Alabama to the State Teachers Association*, March 23, 1939, Box C-197, Folder 5, NAACP Papers, LOC.

57. News release, "Segregation Condemned by Alabama Conference," November 2, 1950, Box A542, NAACP Papers, LOC.

58. "Achieving Our Goals of First-Class Citizenship," Walter White, Alabama, 1946–50, Box A542, Folder Speakers, NAACP Papers, LOC.

59. Excerpt from Remarks by Walter White, Annual Meeting, Alabama State Conference of Branches, November 10, 1951, Box A542, NAACP Papers, LOC.

60. Norrell, 31, 37, 38.

61. Bass, *Taming the Storm*, 340.

62. Fox Butterfield, *All God's Children: The Bosket Family and the American Tradition of Violence* (New York: Avon, 1995), 55; Norrell, 34–35.

63. Norrell, 35, 37, 38–39, 41.

64. Guzman, *Crusade for Civic Democracy*, 11, quoting a speech by Gomillion.

65. Guzman, 11.

66. Guzman, 102.

67. NAACP v. Alabama, 357 U.S. 449 (1958); Marshall-Jackson, July 31, 1950, and Jackson-Marshall, August 8, 1950, Box B135, Folder 8, NAACP Papers, LOC.

68. Joseph A. Berry, M.D., "The Chaff which the Wind Driveth Away," Annual Report, December 1951, Box A563, Folder 7, NAACP Papers, LOC, 10.

69. "You Pay for What You Get," *NAACP News* 2, no. 2 (November 13, 1955), Box A563, Folder 8, NAACP Papers, LOC.

70. Norrell, 37, 44.

71. Tolly R. Broady, "Will Two Good White Men Vouch for You?" November 1941, reprinted in *Reporting Civil Rights: Part One: American Journalism 1941–1963*, 11–14; Norrell, 44, 45.

72. Mitchell v. Wright, 62 F. Supp. 580, 582–584 (D. Ala., 1945); Mitchell v. Wright, 154 F.2d 924, 927 (5th Cir.1946); Mitchell v. Wright, 329 U.S. 733 (1946); Norrell, 63, 68.; Williams v. Wright, 29 So. 2d 295, 297 (1947); Mitchell v. Wright, 69 F. Supp. 698, 702 (M.D. Ala. 1947); "Denied Voting Privilege: Tuskegeeans File Appeal," *Pittsburgh Courier*, August 11, 1945.

73. Norrell, 69, 71, 90, 122.

74. Norrell, 74–76.

75. Political Yardstick, 1954, March 27, 1954, Box A543, Folder 1, NAACP Papers, LOC.

76. Conference of Alabama State Coordinating Committee for Registration and Voting, "What the Negro in Alabama Wants," May 30, 1954, Box A543, Folder 1, NAACP Papers, LOC.

77. Norrell, 85.

78. Ed Cony, "Negroes Boycott Town to Fight Gerrymander Voiding Their Votes," *Wall Street Journal*, November 5, 1957; 8th Anniversary Celebration, Crusade for Citizenship, "Significant Events in the Crusade for Civic Democracy in Macon County," 1965, 1; Norrell, 97.

79. Gomillion v. Lightfoot, 364 U.S. 339, 347–348 (1960).

80. "City Officials Sworn in at Historic Event," *Tuskegee News*, October 8, 1964.

81. US Commission on Civil Rights, *Report of the United States Commission on Civil*

Rights 1959 (Washington, DC: US Government Printing Office, 1959), 69, https://www.crmvet.org/docs/ccr_rights_us_6100.pdf.

82. United States v. Alabama, 362 U.S. 602 (1960); United States v. Alabama, 192 F. Supp. 677, 679–680 (M.D. Ala. 1961).

83. United States v. Alabama, 192 F. Supp. 677 (M.D. Ala. 1961); Decree, United States v. Alabama, Civil Action no. 479-E (M.D. Ala. 1961).

84. United States v. Alabama, 192 F. Supp. 677 (M.D. 1961), Civil Action no. 479-E.

85. US Congress, Senate, Committee on the Judiciary, *Civil Rights Division 1964 Status Report Hearings on S. 1564,* 89th Congress, 1st. sess., March–April 1965, 1175, 1185.

CHAPTER 3. THE SCHOOL DESEGREGATION CASE BEGINS

1. Robert J. Norrell, *Reaping the Whirlwind* (New York: Alfred A. Knopf, 1985), 136; Jessie Parkhurst Guzman, *Crusade for Civic Democracy* (New York: Vantage, 1984), 150; Dan Cobb, "Macon Negroes Demand Equal School Rights," *Birmingham News,* February 10, 1951; "Thirty-Two Negroes Ask School Desegregation in Macon County," *Birmingham World,* July 22, 1955.

2. C. A. Pruitt to D. I. Beasley, July 20, 1955 [taking Beasley's request of July 14 under advisement]; C. A. Pruitt to D. I. Beasley, September 29, 1955 [request "is being studied" by the Board]; W.C. Patton to Burke Marshall, October 31, 1955; Undated document, "Alabama," Box A226, Folder 4, Group II, NAACP Papers, LOC.

3. Guzman, *Crusade for Civic Democracy,* 150–151.

4. Della D. Sullins, speech to Tuskegee Civic Association, October 6, 1959, printed in *Women and the Civil Rights Movement, 1954–1965,* ed. Davis W. Houck and David E. Dixon (Jackson: University Press of Mississippi, 2009), 114.

5. Lee v. Macon County, 221 F. Supp. 297, 298 (M.D. Ala. 1963).

6. Appendix B, Trial Brief of the United States, Lee v. Macon County Board of Education, Civil Action no. 604-E, 77.

7. Appendices A–D in Support of the Brief of the United States, Lee v. Macon County Board of Education, Civil Action no. 604-E, C-9.

8. Appendices A–D in Support of the Brief of the United States, Lee v. Macon County Board of Education, Civil Action no. 604-E, C-20.

9. Robert K. Carr, *Federal Protection of Civil Rights: Quest for a Sword* (Ithaca: Cornell University Press, 1947), 138.

10. U.S. v. Madison County Bd. of Educ., 219 F.Supp. 60, 61 (N.D. Ala. 1963), aff'd. 326 F.2d 237 (5th Cir. 1964), cert. den. 379 U.S. 929 (1964).

11. US Congress, House of Representatives, Committee on the Judiciary, Rept. 914, Part 2, Additional Views of Mr. McCulloch, 88th Cong., 1st sess., December 2, 1943, 22.

12. US Congress, House of Representatives, Committee on the Judiciary, Rept. 914, Part 2, Additional Views of Mr. McCulloch, 88th Cong., 1st sess., December 2, 1943, 19.

All districts in Mississippi and South Carolina also remained segregated. Except for Atlanta and New Orleans, all districts in Georgia and Louisiana were also segregated.

13. Tuskegee Civic Association, 8th Anniversary Celebration: Crusade for Citizenship, June 29, 1965.

14. Tuskegee Civic Association, *Annual Report*, December 9, 1962, Report of the Public Education Committee, Box 113, JDP, PUL.

15. Letter from C. G. Gomillion to Fred Gray, January 7, 1963, Box 7, Folder 3, TCA Files, Tuskegee Archives.

16. Letters to I. V. Billis and others (including the Lees) and to Mr. and Mrs. Nelson Boggan and others; C. G. Gomillion to Fred Gray, January 7, 1963, Box 7, Folder 3, TCA Files, Tuskegee Archives.

17. Tuskegee Civic Association, Cover of Program for the 6th Anniversary Celebration, Crusade for Citizenship, June 25, 1963.

18. J. W. Peltason, *Fifty-Eight Lonely Men: Southern Federal Judges and School Desegregation* (New York: Harcourt, Brace & World, 1961), 12–13.

19. Jack Bass, *Taming the Storm: The Life and Times of Judge Frank M. Johnson Jr. and the South's Fight over Civil Rights* (New York: Doubleday, 1993), 21.

20. John Doar to Burke Marshall, School Desegregation, March 19, 1961, Box 36, Folder School Desegregation I, JDP, PUL.

21. Richard T. Rives to Elbert P. Tuttle, January 30, 1963. Chief Judge Tuttle promptly responded that prior cases had held that a three-judge court was not required. Elbert P. Tuttle to Richard T. Rives, February 4, 1963, Box 21, Folder 1, FMJP, LOC.

22. Burke Marshall, "Memorandum for the Attorney General," Monday Report, February 11, 1963, Box 001, BMPP, JFKL.

23. Taylor v. Board of Education of City School District of City of New Rochelle, 191 F. Supp. 181 (S.D.N.Y. 1961); Taylor v. Board of Education, 294 F.2d 36 (2d Cir. 1961); Goss v. Board of Education, 373 U.S. 683 (1963).

24. Frank M. Johnson Jr., "The Role of the Federal Courts in Institutional Litigation," *Alabama Law Review* 32 (1981): 271, 274.

25. Owen M. Fiss, "The Fate of an Idea Whose Time Has Come: Antidiscrimination Law in the Second Decade after Brown v. Board of Education," *University of Chicago Law Review* 41, no. 4 (1974): 742, 754.

26. United States v. Miami, 614 F.2d 1322, 1332 (5th Cir. 1980), aff'd. 664 F.2d 435 (5th Cir. 1981) (en banc).

27. Anthony Lewis, *Make No Law: The Sullivan Case and the First Amendment* (New York: Random House, 1991), 27.

28. Fred D. Gray, *Bus Ride to Justice: Changing the System by the System: The Life and Works of Fred Gray, Preacher, Attorney, Politician*, rev. ed. (Montgomery: New South Books, 2013), 15.

29. Testimony of Austin Meadows, Transcript of November 30, 1966, Hearing, 22; Alabama Code, Title 52, Section 40(1) [state funding out-of-state graduate school for Black students excluded from white graduate school where there was no in-state school for Blacks].

30. Letters from Frank M. Johnson to John Doar, August 11, 1966, March 23, 1967, July 8, 1966, and July 10, 1967, FMJP, LOC.

31. Brian K. Landsberg, "The Kennedy Justice Department's Enforcement of Civil Rights: A View from the Trenches," in *John F. Kennedy History, Memory, Legacy: An Interdisciplinary Inquiry*, ed. John Delane Williams, Robert G. Waite, and Gregory S. Gordon (Grand Forks: University of North Dakota, 2010), 194, 209.

32. The Inaugural Address of Governor George C. Wallace, January 14, 1963, Montgomery, Alabama, Alabama Department of Archives & History.

33. "What They Say, Gov. Wallace Reaffirms Intent to Keep Segregation," *Southern School News*, February 1963, 10.

34. Craig Gilbert, "An American Hero," *Milwaukee Journal Sentinel*, August 9, 2009.

35. Bass, *Taming the Storm*, 232.

36. James P. Turner, *Selma and the Liuzzo Murder Trials: The First Modern Civil Rights Convictions* (Ann Arbor: University of Michigan Press, 2018), 88.

37. John F. Kennedy, Radio and Television Report to the American People on Civil Rights, June 11, 1963.

38. Order Adding the United States as a Party, Lee v. Macon County Board of Education, July 16, 1963.

39. Burke Marshall to the Director of the Federal Bureau of Investigation, August 19, 1963, Civil Rights Division FOIA Files Online, DOJ.

40. Bass, 232; Rock Island C.R.R. v. United States, 254 U.S. 141, 143 (1920) (Oliver Wendell Holmes Jr. stated, "Men must turn square corners when they deal with the Government").

41. E. J. Dionne Jr., "Political Hacks v. Bureaucrats: Can't Public Servants Get Some Respect?", Brookings Institution, March 1, 2001, https://www.brookings.edu/articles/political-hacks-v-bureaucrats-cant-public-servants-get-some-respect/.

42. St. John Barrett to John Doar, August 21, 1963, Civil Rights Division FOIA Files Online, DOJ.

43. John Hayman, *Bitter Harvest: Richmond Flowers and the Civil Rights Revolution* (Montgomery: Black Belt Press, 1996), 188.

44. Bob Labaree, "It Doesn't Seem Difficult," *Southern Courier*, August 3–4, 1968.

45. Gray describes the US lawyers as "a significant part of the legal team." Gray, *Bus Ride to Justice*, 209.

46. Lee v. Macon County Board of Education, 221 F. Supp. 297 (M.D. Ala. 1963).

47. Tentative Findings and Conclusions, Lee v. Macon County Board of Education, Civil Action no. 604-E (M.D. Ala. 1963).

48. Taylor Branch, *Parting the Waters: America in the King Years, 1954–1963* (New York: Simon & Schuster, 1989), 872.

49. Including Dorothy Shelton, later my wife.

50. Ramsey Clark to Burke Marshall, August 21 and 28, 1963, Box 021, BMPP, JFKL.

51. John Doar to Burke Marshall, Placement of Lawyers for Opening of Schools, August 26, 1963, Box 021, BMPP, JFKL.

52. John Doar to Burke Marshall, Report on Status of School Desegregation—Macon County, Alabama, August 26, 1963, Box 021, BMPP, JFKL Burke Marshall Collection.

53. Doar to Marshall, Report on Status of School Desegregation.

54. "School Board Gets Rush of Applications from Negroes," *Tuskegee News*, August 15, 1963.

55. Mac Harris, "Integration Shift Wins Macon Okay," *Montgomery Advertiser*, August 30, 1963.

56. Willie Wyatt, interview with Joseph Bagley, Stone Mountain, Georgia, January 4, 2012.

57. Letter from Susie Sanders to John Doar, Correspondence, Schools, October 26, 1964, Box 38, Southeastern Section, JDP, PUL.

58. See Robert Heinrich, "Montgomery: The Civil Rights Movement and its Legacies" (PhD diss., Brandeis University, 2008), 267.

59. Norrell, *Reaping the Whirlwind*, 140–141; U.S. v. Wallace, 222 F. Supp. 2d 485, 496 (M.D. Ala. 1963).

60. Willie Wyatt, interview with Maggie Martin, "Remembering 1963," January 13, 2014, Alabama Public Radio.

61. Anthony Lee, interview with Maggie Martin, "Remembering 1963," January 13, 2014, Alabama Public Radio.

62. Rebecca Wadsworth Sickles, interview with Maggie Martin, "Former Students Look Back 50 Years After Integration of Tuskegee High School," September 1, 2013, Alabama Public Radio. A novel about the summer of 1963 in Tuskegee (called Beulah in the novel) describes "a man in a gray suit and a French-cuffed shirt" approaching a state trooper in the middle of the street, announcing that he was John Doar from the DOJ and demanding to speak with Al Lingo, head of the Alabama state troopers. Janice Ward Parrish, *The Sweet Shade of a Chinaberry Tree* (Amherst: Hard Shell Word Factory, 2005), 161.

63. Executive Order no. 9, September 2, 1963, George C. Wallace, Governor of Alabama.

64. Flowers later ran unsuccessfully for governor against Lurleen Wallace. He was supported by several Black groups and by Martin Luther King Jr.; Jeff Frederick, *Stand Up for Alabama: Governor George Wallace* (Tuscaloosa: University of Alabama Press, 2007), 174.

65. "Local Group Launches Campaign to Set Up Private Schools with State Aid Grants," *Tuskegee News*, September 5, 1963.

66. Undated document, "Alabama," Box A226, Folder 4, NAACP Papers.

67. He made the proclamation in a television speech, quoted in United States v. Barnett, 330 F.2d 369, 373 (5th Cir. 1963).

68. United States v. Wallace, 222 F.Supp. 485, 487 (M.D. Ala. 1963); Joseph Bagley, *The Politics of White Rights: Race, Justice, and Integrating Alabama's Schools* (Athens: University of Georgia Press, 2018), 65.

69. Willie Wyatt, interview with Joseph Bagley, Stone Mountain, Georgia, January

4, 2012; Affidavit of John Martin, September 9, 1963, Attached to Complaint in United States v. Wallace, 222 F. Supp. 485 (M.D. Ala. 1963) (Civ. A. no. 1976-N).

70. Bass, *Taming the Storm*, 209.

71. Bass, 209.

72. Brown v. Plata, 563 U.S. 493, 500 (2011).

73. Richard Rives to Frank M. Johnson, September 21, 1963.

74. Temporary Restraining Order, September 9, 1963, reported in 8 Race. Rel. L. Rep 803, 916 (1963); Governor George Wallace, Executive Order 13, reported in 8 Race. Rel. L. Rep 803, 913 (1963); President John F. Kennedy, Proclamation 3554, Obstructions of Justice in the State of Alabama, September 10, 1963; President John F. Kennedy, Executive Order 11118, Providing Assistance for Removal of Unlawful Obstructions of Justice in the State of Alabama, September 10, 1963; Executive Order reported in 8 Race. Rel. L. Rep. 803, 919 (1963).

75. Defendant's Memorandum Brief in Opposition to Motion for a Preliminary Injunction, United States v. Wallace, September 24, 1963. The United States filed a Memorandum of Points and Authorities in Support of Motion for Preliminary Injunction, citing cases that supported the court's jurisdiction and the authority of the DOJ to bring the suit.

76. Transcript, hearing of September 24, 1963, 75.

77. Transcript, hearing of September 24, 1963, 76.

78. Joseph Bagley, *The Politics of White Rights: Race, Justice, and Integrating Alabama's Schools* (Athens: University of Georgia Press 2018), 73–74.

79. United States v. Wallace, 222 F.Supp. 485, 488 (M.D. Ala. 1963) (Civ. A. no. 1976-N). This ruling adopts verbatim the language of paragraph 32 of the complaint.

80. Judy Smith, 50th Anniversary of Desegregation in Tuskegee, Tuskegee 1963 Symposium, Tuskegee Human and Civil Rights Multicultural Center, August 24, 2013. She was student body president in 1963.

81. Pete Johnson, 50th Anniversary of Desegregation in Tuskegee, Tuskegee 1963 Symposium.

82. Sickles, "Former Students Look Back."

83. Bagley, *Politics of White Rights*, 70.

CHAPTER 4. NEW YEAR, NEW SCHOOLS, NEW LAW

1. Tuskegee Civic Association, *Annual Report, Report of the President*, December 8, 1963. C. G. Gomillion, the TCA President, also thanked "those few white citizens who encouraged, and urged, their fellow citizens to accept the decision of the Federal Court and keep their children in school. Theirs was not an easy task." Box 113, JDP, PUL.

2. St. John Barrett to John Doar, Tuskegee, Alabama School Desegregation, October 28, 1963, Box 57, Alabama Schools, General, JDP, PUL.

3. Goss v. Board of Education, 373 U.S. 683 (1963).

4. "Fala Takes Charge of White House Parley; Educators Drop Rural Schools to Cheer Dog," *New York Times*, October 6, 1944.

5. "Alabama," *New York Times*, June 1, 1955. The following year he cryptically told the *Times* that gaps remain "not due to discrimination but to economics." Peter Kihss, "States Resisting, Alabama," *New York Times*, March 13, 1956.

6. Peter Kihss, "Negro Co-Ed Is Suspended to Curb Alabama Clashes," *New York Times*, February 7, 1956.

7. Burke Marshall to William Moyers, February 4, 1963, File HU 2–5, Box 50, LBJL.

8. Willie Wyatt, interview by Joe Bagley, January 4, 2012, Stone Mountain, Georgia. See generally Bagley, *The Politics of White Rights* (Athens: University of Georgia Press, 2018), 82. An Associated Press photo marked "Daily News," February 5, 1964, shows law enforcement watching while a nonuniformed person kicks Merritt while he is lying on the grass. Governor Wallace later lamented this treatment of a newsperson: "This sort of thing must not be allowed to happen." See Claude Sitton, "Six Negroes Barred at Alabama School," *New York Times*, February 6, 1964.

9. Answer, United States v. Rea, served February 25, 1964, DOJ file 144–100–2-1, Box 1, Section 1, NARA.

10. United States v. Rea, 231 F. Supp. 772 (M.D. Ala. 1964).

11. Burke Marshall to Director, FBI, March 13, 1964. DOJ File 144–100–2-1, Box 1, Section 1, NARA; Barrett File, May 4, 1964, and May 18, 1964, Section 2, NARA.

12. Carol Nelson, "Auburn Integration 'Firsts' Share Their Stories as Part of Commemoration, King Week Events," Auburn University, http://ocm.auburn.edu/newsroom/featured_story/integration_luncheon.html#.YOTe5R11Ci4, last updated January 24, 2014.

13. Jonathan Sutin to Investigation File, February 13, 1964, DOJ File 144–100–2-1, Box 1, Section 1, NARA.

14. Fred D. Gray, *Bus Ride to Justice: Changing the System by the System: The Life and Works of Fred Gray, Preacher, Attorney, Politician*, rev. ed. (Montgomery: New South Books, 2013), 206–207.

15. Gray, *Bus Ride to Justice*, 207.

16. Austin Meadows to Robert F. Kennedy, March 4, 1964, Box 21, Folder 4, FMJP, LOC.

17. St. John Barrett to Burke Marshall, February 17, 1964, DOJ file 144–100–2-1, Box 1, Section 1, NARA (describing positions he would take at the hearing on February 21); Motion of Richmond M. Flowers, as Attorney General of the State of Alabama, served February 18, 1964, DOJ File 144-100-2-1, Box 1, Section 1, NARA.

18. Answer of Defendant Alabama State Board of Education at 6, Lee v. Macon County Board of Education, Civil Action no. 604-E, filed February 20, 1964.

19. Motion of Defendants State Board of Education and Individual Members to Dissolve and Modify Temporary Restraining Order Discharge Defendants and to Dismiss, Lee v. Macon County Board of Education, Civil Action no. 604-E, filed February 20, 1964.

20. Judge Frank M. Johnson's Notes on Hearing of February 21, 1964, Box 21, Folder 1, FMJP, LOC.

21. Memorandum Brief of the United States in Support of Plaintiffs' Motion for a Preliminary Injunction, March 13, 1964, DOJ File 144–100–2-1, Box 1, Section 1, NARA.

22. "Classes Ordered for Negro Pupils of Burned School," *New York Times*, April 29, 1964.

23. See Memorandum Opinion and Injunction, filed April 28, 1964; Memorandum, Box 21, Folder 2, FMJP, LOC (signed "jg"). The initials may stand for Jane Gordon, then the deputy clerk of court, who sometimes took dictation from Judge Johnson; "Classes Ordered for Negro Pupils of Burned School."

24. Lee v. Macon County Board of Education, 231 F. Supp. 743 (M.D. Ala. 1964). The court also reviewed the desegregation plan proposed by the Macon County Board of Education, approving it in part and disapproving it in part.

25. Decree, Lee v. Macon County Board of Education, 231 F. Supp. 743 (M.D. Ala. 1964).

26. Charles T. Clotfelter, *After Brown: The Rise and Retreat of School Desegregation* (Princeton: Princeton University Press, 2004), 26, links progress in school desegregation after 1964 to enforcement of the Civil Rights Act by federal bureaucrats and "a series of Supreme Court decisions" but does not argue that the court decisions were related to the Act. Others, such as Gerald Rosenberg, *The Hollow Hope: Can Courts Bring About Social Change* (Chicago: University of Chicago Press, 2008) argue that it was the act, not *Brown*, that desegregated the South.

27. Appendix C, Table VI, Trial Brief of the United States, Lee v. Macon County Board of Education, Civil Action no. 604-E (1967).

28. Robert A. Caro, *The Passage of Power: The Years of Lyndon Johnson* (New York: Vintage, 2012), 485.

29. Don Oberdorfer, "Judge Smith Moves with Deliberate Drag," *New York Times*, January 12, 1964.

30. Stephen C. Halpern, *The Limits of the Law: The Ironic Legacy of Title VI of the 1964 Civil Rights Act* (Baltimore: John Hopkins University Press, 1995), 44.

31. James Chisum, "School Aid Funds Revised Upward," *Birmingham News*, September 3, 1965. $546,105 was slated to go to Macon County schools.

32. Burke Marshall for the Attorney General, June 14, 1962, Box 107, Civil Rights—Legislation, JDP, PUL.

33. Attorney General's Press Conference, April 2, 1963: Sending Proposed Voting Rights Act of 1963, Box 008, BMPP, JFKL.

34. Nicholas Katzenbach, "Oral History Interview," interview with Anthony Lewis, November 29, 1964, Washington DC, JFKL, JFK.

35. Katzenbach, "Oral History Interview," 126.

36. Audio recording of meeting between President John F. Kennedy, Attorney General Robert Kennedy, Assistant Attorney General Burke Marshall, and Assistant Special Counsel to the President Lee C. White, and Special Counsel to the President Theodore Sorensen, May 20, 1963, Meetings: Tape 88, Civil Rights Legislation, JFKL; Legislative Possibilities, May 20, 1963, Box 30, Theodore Sorenson Collection, JFKL, reproduced in *Civil Rights, the White House, and the Justice Department, 1945–1968*, ed. Michal Belknap, vol. 13 (New York: Garland Publishing 1991), 26–27.

37. Legislative Possibilities, May 20, 1963, from Theodore Sorenson Collection, JFKL, reproduced in Belknap, *Civil Rights*, 13:26, 27.

38. John F. Kennedy, Civil Rights Address, Washington, DC, June 11, 1963.

39. US Congress, Senate, *Hearings before the Committee on the Judiciary*, 88th Cong., 1st sess., July 18, 1963, 98–99.

40. Burke Marshall at Press Conference of Attorney General Robert F. Kennedy, October 15, 1963, reproduced in Belknap, 13:67, 86.

41. Caro, *The Passage of Power*, 9.

42. Caro, 465.

43. US Congress, Senate, Committee on the Judiciary, *Civil Rights—The President's Program, 1963: Hearings before the Committee on the Judiciary on S. 1731 and S. 1750*, 88th Cong., 1st sess., July 16, 17, 18, 24, 25, 30, August 1, 8, 23, and September 11, 1963, 257, 358.

44. Senator Ellender of Louisiana, quoted in Bernard Schwartz, ed., pt. 2, *Statutory History of the United States: Civil Rights* (New York: Chelsea House, 1970), 1314.

45. Senator Olin Johnston of South Carolina stated, "Title IV of the substitute bill demonstrates the vicious approach of its authors in their attacks against the South." In Schwartz, *Statutory History*, 1399, 1408.

46. Senator Paul Douglas of Illinois, quoted in Schwartz, 1279.

47. Schwartz, 1280.

48. See also US Congress, House of Representatives, *Hearings before the Committee on Rules on H.R. 7152*, 88th Cong. 2nd sess., January 9, 14, 15, and 16, 1964, 458 ("The proposed legislation ultimately would result in total Federal control of the education processes in the United States); Barbara Whalen and Charles Whalen, *The Longest Debate: A Legislative History of the 1964 Civil Rights Act* (Washington, DC: Seven Locks Press, 1985), 141.

49. Civil Rights Act of 1964, 42 U.S.C. § 2000c(b) (1964).

50. Michael Wise, "Congress, Busing, and Federal Law," *Civil Rights Digest* 5, no. 5 (1973): 30.

51. Civil Rights Act of 1964, 42 U.S.C § 2000h-2 (1964).

52. Civil Rights Act of 1964, 42 U.S.C. § 2000c-6(a) (1964).

53. Matthew Delmont, "The Origins of "Antibusing" Politics: New York City Protests and Revision of the Civil Rights Act," Gotham Center of New York History, accessed July 17, 2019, https://www.gothamcenter.org/blog/the-origins-of-antibusing-politics-new-york-city-protests-and-revision-of-the-civil-rights-act.

54. Civil Rights Act of 1964, 42 U.S.C. § 2000c-6(a) (1964).

55. See US Commission on Civil Rights, *Federal Enforcement of School Desegregation*, September 11, 1969, 28, available at https://www.google.com/books/edition/Federal_Enforcement_of_School_Desegregat/lzowFBAWzFoC?hl=en&gbpv=1&printsec=frontcover.

56. Suggestions from David L. Norman attached to memorandum from John Doar to Section Chief of the Civil Rights Division, October 30, 1967, author achive.

57. "Elimination of Racial Discrimination," Message from the President of the United States Proposing Enactment of Legislation to Make Authority against Civil Rights

Violence Clear and Sure, May 2, 1966, 89th Congress 2nd Session, House of Representatives, Document no. 432, 3, 6.

58. Brian K. Landsberg to Stephen J. Pollak, Legislative Program, 91st Congress, undated, author archive.

59. Schwartz, 1128, 1131, 1135. Senator Hubert Humphrey of Minnesota, the Senate floor manager of the bill, defended Title VI as a simple "requirement that the local school authority refrain from racial discrimination in treatment of pupils and teachers, and authority to achieve compliance . . . by cutoff of funds or other means authorized by law."

60. Nicholas deB. Katzenbach to Senator John Sherman Cooper, April 24, 1964, in *Administrative History of the Civil Rights Division of the Department of Justice during the Johnson Administration*, ed. Michal Belknap, vol. 17 (New York: Garland Publishing, 1991) 584, 590.]

61. John Egerton, *Speak Now Against the Day: The Generation Before the Civil Rights Movement in the South* (Chapel Hill: University of Noth Carolina Press, 1994), 619.

62. 45 C.F.R. § 80.4(c).

63. Ruby Grant Martin, interview with Thomas Harri Baker, February 24, 1969, Oral History Collection, LBJL, 7.

64. Gary Orfield, *The Reconstruction of Southern Education: The Schools and the 1964 Civil Rights Act* (New York: Wiley-Interscience, 1969), 88. Quoting a letter from the North Carolina state superintendent of education to Francis Keppel in the U.S. House of Representatives Committee on the Judiciary, *Hearings, Guidelines for School Desegregation*, 89th Cong., 2d sess., 1966, 123.

65. Carl A. Auerbach to David Seeley and G.W. Foster Jr., "The Need for Standards of Public School Desegregation for Purposes of Title VI of the Civil Rights Act of 1964 and Procedures for Implementing Them," March 29, 1965, School Desegregation-General, Box 57, JDP, PUL.

66. Unsigned memorandum, April 23, 1965, on White House stationery with cover slip from Douglas Cater to Marvin Watson, April 26, 1965, Box 50, Ex HU 2–5, LBJL. See also Ruby Grant Martin interview, 7.

67. Orfield, *Reconstruction of Southern Education*, 92.

68. Letter from Secretary Gardner, quoted by Commissioner of Education Howe; Howe Deposition Summary, 4.

69. US Commission on Civil Rights, *Survey of School Desegregation in the Southern and Border States*, 1965–66 (Washington, DC: United States Government Publishing Office, 1966), 5, available at https://www.crmvet.org/docs/ccr_sch_desegregation_south_border_6202.pdf.

70. Brown v. Board of Education, 349 U.S. 294, 300 (1955).

71. John Doar to Burke Marshall, August 14, 1964, Box 57, Alabama Schools—General, JDP, PUL.

72. Lee White to President Johnson, September 5, 1964, attaching memo from Katzenbach to President, September 4, 1964, re School Desegregation in Alabama Pursuant to Federal Court Orders, August 24, 1968, Box 51, Executive HU 2–5, LBJL.

73. FBI Memorandum, May 26, 1964, DOJ File 144–100–2-1, Box 1, Section 2, NARA;

Jonathan Sutin to Investigation File, September 4, 1964, DOJ file 144–100–2-1, Box 1, Section 3, NARA; "Football Team History Tuskegee Indians," accessed February 5, 2015, http://www.ahsfhs.org/teams2/teampage.asp?Team=Tuskegee; "Football Team History Macon Academy Knights," accessed February 5, 2015, http://www.ahsfhs.org/teams2/teampage.asp?Team=Macon%20Academy; John Doar to St. John Barrett, October 29, 1964, DOJ File 144–100–2-1, Box 1, Section 3, NARA; John Doar to St. John Barrett, February 1, 1965, DOJ File 144–100–2-1, Box 1, Section 3, NARA.

74. Carson v. Warlick, 238 F.2d 724, 728 (4th Cir. 1956), cert. den. 353 U.S. 910 (1957).

75. Shuttlesworth v. Birmingham Board of Education, 162 F. Supp. 372, 379 (N.D. Ala. 1958), aff'd. 358 U.S. 101 (1958).

76. Shuttlesworth v. Birmingham Board of Education, 162 F. Supp. 372, 382 (N.D. Ala. 1958), aff'd. 358 U.S. 101 (1958).

77. Orleans Parish School Board v. Bush, 242 F.2d 156 (5th Cir. 1957); Gibson v. Board of Public Instruction, Dade County, 272 F.2d 763 (5th Cir. 1959); Bush v. Orleans Parish School Board, 308 F.2d 491 (5th Cir. 1962); Order of August 7, 1964, Lee v. Macon County Board of Education, Civil Action no. 604-E.

78. Jonathan Sutin to Investigation File, May 5, 1965, DOJ File 144–100–2-1, Section 3, NARA; John Doar to Frank M. Johnson, May 13, 1965, responding to Frank M. Johnson's May 7, 1965 letter, which is not in the file, DOJ File 144–100–2-1, Box 1, Section 3, NARA; Jonathan Sutin to John Doar, May 26, 1965, DOJ file 144–100–2-1, Box 1, Section 3, NARA; Joe C. Wilson to Mr. & Mrs. Charlie Hughley re two children, July 29, 1965, Box 37, Folder Investigation, Schools, Southeastern, JDP, PUL; Frank Dunbaugh to John Doar, February 17, 1966, DOJ file 144–100–2-1, Box 1, Section 3, NARA.

79. James Chisum, "Plans Held Key to School 'Mix,'" *Birmingham News*, July 28, 1965.

80. James Chisum, "Not So Bad, Speaker Says; Educators Told to Face Mixing," *Birmingham News*, August 16, 1965.

81. "Dr. Letson's Helpful Counsel," *Birmingham News*, August 17, 1965.

82. James Chisum, "Slow White Student May Benefit by Mix," *Birmingham News*, August 17, 1965.

83. United States v. State of Alabama, 252 F. Supp. 95 (M.D. Ala. 1966).

CHAPTER 5. THE CASE GOES STATEWIDE

1. Plaintiff's Motion for Order to Show Cause, Lee v. Macon County Board of Education, Civil Action no. 604-E, September 22, 1966.

2. Dan Dowe, "Wallace Federal Court Rulings Encouraged Suit," *Birmingham News*, September 23, 1966; see United States v. Barnett, 346 F.2d 99 (5th Cir. 1965) (dismissing the civil and criminal contempt proceedings from 1962).

3. Order of September 30, 1966, Lee v. Macon County Board of Education, Civil Action no. 604-E.

4. Frank M. Johnson-John Doar, September 23, 1966, FMJC, LOC.

5. Owen Fiss to Brian Landsberg, January 20, 2016.

6. St. John Barrett to John Doar, August 30, 1966.

7. See Brian K. Landsberg, *Free at Last to Vote: The Alabama Origins of the 1965 Voting Rights Act* (Lawrence: University Press of Kansas, 2007), 148–149.

8. St. John Barrett, *The Drive for Equality: A Personal History of Civil Rights Enforcement, 1954–1965* (Baltimore: PublishAmerica, 2009), 23, 27, 28, 94.

9. Handwritten notes taken by Brian Landsberg on October 17, 1966, Landsberg Files.

10. Robert Moses, Thelton E. Henderson Center Symposium, UC Berkeley Law, September 21, 2007.

11. Complaint of the Plaintiffs, NAACP v. Wallace, Civil Action no. 2457-N (M.D. Ala. 1966) (filed September 12, 1966); Stephen L. Wasby, *Race Relations Litigation in an Age of Complexity* (Charlottesville: University Press of Virginia, 1995), 316–329; Jack Greenberg, *Crusaders in the Courts* (New York: Basic Books, 1994), 478–486; Complaint of the United States, NAACP v. Wallace, Civil Action no. 2457-N (M.D. Ala. 1966) (the United States intervened on November 22, 1966).

12. Order, NAACP v. Wallace, Civil Action no. 2457-N (M.D. Ala. 1966) (issued November 23, 1966).

13. Complaint of the United States, NAACP v. Wallace, Civil Action no. 2457-N (M.D. Ala. 1966), 5 (the United States intervened on November 22, 1966).

14. Howe Deposition Summary, 15.

15. United States v. Cartwright, 230 F. Supp. 873 (M.D. Ala. 1964); United States v. Hines, 9 Race Rel.L.Rep. 1332 (N.D. Ala. 1964). And in its case attacking the validity of the Alabama poll tax, the CRD argued that lack of educational opportunity led to inability to pay the poll tax. In doing so, it relied in part on my deposition of Dr. Gomillion. See United States v. Alabama, 252 F. Supp. 95 (M.D. Ala. 1966).

16. The defendants also conducted depositions of the US commissioner of education and a civil rights specialist in the United States Office of Education.

17. Trial Brief of the United States, Appendix C, Table I, Lee v. Macon County Board of Education, Civil Action no. 604-E (1967).

18. Jimmie Breslin, *How the Good Guys Finally Won* (New York: Viking Press 1975), 111–112.

19. Horace Mann Bond, *Negro Education in Alabama: A Study in Cotton and Steel* (Washington, DC: Associated Publishers, 1939); Charles Quaintance to Frank Dunbaugh, Education Records of the State That Show Racial Discrimination, Box 37, Folder May 1966–October 1966 Investigation-Schools-Southeastern, III, JDP, PUL.

20. Lee v. Macon County Board of Education, 267 F. Supp. 458, 471 (M.D. Ala 1967).

21. Deposition of Superintendent Woodrow W. Elliot, Lee v. Macon County Board of Education, Civil Action no. 604-E, 8. In a press conference in September Governor Wallace had threatened to use his "police power" to prevent teacher desegregation. William O. Bryant, "Makes Threat to Use State Police Power," *Birmingham News*, September 10, 1966.

22. Trial Brief of the United States, Appendix C, Table 1, Government Exhibit 156, Lee v. Macon County Board of Education, Civil Action no. 604-E (1967), 83.

23. Trial Brief of the United States, Appendix C, Table 1, Government Exhibit 139, Lee v. Macon County Board of Education, Civil Action no. 604-E (1967), 85.

24. Government Exhibit 137, Lee v. Macon County Board of Education, Civil Action no. 604-E (1967); Trial Brief of the United States, Appendix C, Tables I and II, Lee v. Macon County Board of Education, Civil Action no. 604-E (1967).; Testimony of Dr. George Layton, November 30, 1966. Compare Government Exhibit 127 in this hearing with P1, Exhibit 3 in the 1964 hearing. See Botts Deposition, 243; Lee v. Macon County Board of Education, 267 F. Supp. 458, 473 (M.D. Ala. 1967).

25. Deposition of Ramsey, Lee v. Macon County Board of Education, Civil Action no. 604-E (1967) 15; Deposition of J. C. Blair, Lee v. Macon County Board of Education, Civil Action no. 604-E (1967), 45.

26. Trial Brief of the United States, Lee v. Macon County Board of Education, Civil Action no. 604-E (1967), 111–112.

27. Senate Joint Resolution, Alabama Act no. 894, September 21, 1953.

28. See House Joint Resolution, Alabama Act no. 42, February 2, 1956; Trial Brief of the United States, Appendix C, Table I, Lee v. Macon County Board of Education, Civil Action no. 604-E (1967), 120, 124; Lee v. Macon County Board of Education, 267 F. Supp. 458, 469 (M.D. Ala. 1967).

29. Lee v. Macon County, 231 F. Supp. 743, 756 (M.D. Ala. 1964).

30. Transcript, Lee v. Macon County, Civil Action no. 604-E (November 30, 1966), 78.

31. Transcript, Lee v. Macon County, Civil Action no. 604-E (November 30, 1966), 114.

32. Lee v. Macon County, 267 F. Supp. 458, 469 (M.D. Ala. 1967).

33. Trial Brief of the United States, Lee v. Macon County, Civil Action no. 604-E (1967), 120.

34. Speech Prepared for Delivery by George C. Wallace Governor of Alabama before the Legislature of Alabama in Special Session Assembled, July 26, 1966, 12.

35. Brown v. Board of Education, 349 U.S. 294, 301 (1955).

36. Landsberg Meeting Notes with John Doar, August 24, 1966; Frank Dunbaugh to John Doar, August 17, 1966, 6.

37. Trial Brief of the United States, Lee v. Macon County, Civil Action no. 604-E (1967), 117.

38. Trial Brief of the United States, Lee v. Macon County, Civil Action no. 604-E (1967), 124.

39. Trial Brief of the United States, Lee v. Macon County, Civil Action no. 604-E (1967), 124–126.

40. For example, the government had asked the court to enjoin the defendants from discriminating on the basis of race; the court limited the injunction to discrimination relating to the public schools. The government asked the court to order all future school construction to "further the eradication of the vestiges of the dual system and the elimination of the effects of segregation;" the court changed the phrase to "further the disestablishment of state enforced or encouraged public school segregation and eliminate

the effects of past state enforced or encouraged racial discrimination in the State's public school system." Annotated Draft Decree, Box 19, Folder 7, FMJP, LOC, 2–3.

41. Annotated Draft Decree, Box 19, Folder 7, FMJP, LOC, paragraph IV, 6–8.

42. J. Harvie Wilkinson III, *From Brown to Bakke: The Supreme Court and School Integration, 1954–1978* (New York: Oxford University Press, 1979), 111.

43. United States v. Jefferson County Board of Education, 372 F.2d 836 (1966), aff'd. en banc, 380 F.2d 385 (1987).

44. Civil Rights Act of 1964, 42 U.S.C. 2000d-1 (1964).

45. Civil Rights Act of 1964, 42 U.S.C. 2000d-3 (1964).

46. Civil Rights Act of 1964, sec. 702 (1964).

47. Civil Rights Act of 1964, 42 U.S.C. 2000c(b) (1964).

48. Civil Rights Act of 1964, 42 U.S.C. 2000c-6 (1964).

49. Undated Memorandum, Brian Landsberg to Trial File, Oral Argument, Lee v. Macon County Board of Education and NAACP v. Wallace, February 3, 1967.

50. Greenberg, *Crusaders in the Courts*, 342.

51. These quotes are from my notes of the oral argument and probably include some paraphrasing. Author archives.

52. Briggs v. Elliott, 132 F. Supp. 776, 777 (E.D.S.C. 1955).

53. Mr. Norman to John Doar, Freedom of Choice, February 25, 1967.

54. George Harmon, "History-Making Court to Sit Here," *Jacksonville Journal*, March 9, 1967.

55. Thatcher Walt, "Old Integration Arguments Renewed," *Jacksonville Journal*, March 10, 1967.

56. "Courts Asked to Help HEW on School Integration: Guidelines Aired by U.S. Panel Here," *Florida Times-Union*, March 11, 1967.

57. Transcript of Oral Argument, March 10, 1967, before en banc United States Court of Appeals for the Fifth Circuit, United States v. Jefferson County Board of Education, 247–248.

58. Transcript of Oral Argument, March 10, 1967, before en banc United States Court of Appeals for the Fifth Circuit, United States v. Jefferson County, 248.

59. Transcript of Oral Argument, March 10, 1967, before en banc United States Court of Appeals for the Fifth Circuit, United States v. Jefferson County, 249–250.

60. Transcript of Oral Argument, March 10, 1967, before en banc United States Court of Appeals for the Fifth Circuit, United States v. Jefferson County, 255.

61. Owen Fiss, *Pillars of Justice: Lawyers and the Liberal Tradition* (Cambridge, MA: Harvard University Press, 2017), 55.

62. Transcript of Oral Argument, March 10, 1967, before en banc United States Court of Appeals for the Fifth Circuit, United States v. Jefferson County, 258–259.

63. Transcript of Oral Argument, March 10, 1967, before en banc United States Court of Appeals for the Fifth Circuit, United States v. Jefferson County, 262.

64. Transcript of Oral Argument, March 10, 1967, before en banc United States Court of Appeals for the Fifth Circuit, United States v. Jefferson County, 276.

65. United States v. Jefferson County, 380 F.2d 385, 389 (5th Cir. 1967) (en banc).

66. F. Peter Libassi to the Honorable Douglass Cater, School Desegregation Policies, November 16, 1966, Box 58, School Desegregation Guidelines, Correspondence, JDP, PUL.

67. Harold Howe II to L. H. Fountain of North Carolina, December 19, 1966, in US Congress, House of Representatives, Committee on the Judiciary, *Guidelines for School Desegregation, Hearings before the Special Subcommittee on Civil Rights of the Committee on the Judiciary*, 89th Cong., 2d sess., December 14, 15, and 16, 1966, 205.

68. David S. Seeley through Harold Howe II to F. Peter Libassi, Presidential Approval of Guidelines, January 25, 1967, Box 57, School Desegregation-General, JDP, PUL.

69. St. John Barrett to John Doar, Presidential Approval of Guidelines, February 9, 1967, and Owen Fiss to John Doar, February 9, 1967. Both sources are in Box 57, Presidential Approval of School Desegregation Guidelines, JDP, PUL.

70. See Nathaniel E. Gozansky, Kenneth Gignilliat, and William Horwitz, "School Desegregation in the Fifth Circuit," *Houston Law Review* 5 (1968): 946, 959, 965 (1968); Lurleen Wallace and Ernest Stone were elected in November 1966. Today, the state superintendent is appointed by the state board of education, but in 1966 that office was elective. See Deposition of Austin R. Meadows, November 30, 1966, Lee v. Macon County, Civil Action no. 604-E 109.

71. Lee v. Macon County, 267 F. Supp. 458, 465 (1967).

72. Lee v. Macon County, 267 F. Supp. 458, 478, 480–491 (M.D. Ala. 1967).

73. NAACP v. Wallace, 269 F. Supp. 346, 351 (1967).

74. Jack Bass, *Taming the Storm: The Life and Times of Judge Frank M. Johnson Jr. and the South's Fight over Civil Rights* (New York: Doubleday, 1993), 229.

75. Lee v. Macon County, 267 F. Supp. 458, 474 (M.D. Ala. 1967).

76. "State Studies Desegregation for Schools," *Alabama Journal*, March 23, 1967.

77. Randolph Pendelton, "Court Orders Full School Integration," *Birmingham Post-Herald*, March 23, 1967.

78. "The Inevitable Decision," *Alabama Journal*, March 23, 1967.

79. "An Alabama First: All Federal Schools," *Montgomery Advertiser*, March 23, 1967.

80. "The Courts, HEW, and Southern School Desegregation," *Yale Law Journal* 77, no. 2 (1967): 321, 365, n. 146.

81. See Evans v. Buchanan, 207 F. Supp. 820 (1962).

CHAPTER 6. AFTERMATH

1. Address by Governor Lurleen Wallace, Joint Session, Alabama Legislature, March 30, 1967, Box 21, Folder 5, FMJP, LOC.

2. See Governor Lurleen Wallace's speech on March 30, 1967, concerning the decree of this Court of March 22, 1967, which does not appear to have any basis in fact, Box 21, Folder 6, FMJP, LOC; Al Fox, "Lurleen Polished, Emotional in Speech," *Birmingham News*, March 3, 1967. See also Johnson-Rives and Grooms, April 4, 1967 (referring to "several gross misrepresentations made during that speech as to what we ordered and decreed"); Janean

Mann, "Judge Notes Errors in Governor's Speech," *Birmingham Post-Herald*, April 1, 1967 (quoting Judge Grooms's point by point refutation of Wallace's charges).

3. Dan Dowe, "Escape Hatch Left Open?" *Birmingham News*, March 31, 1967.

4. "Another Axe-Grinding," *Birmingham News*, March 31, 1967.

5. "Grab Your Hats—Here We Go Again," *Montgomery Advertiser*, April 2, 1967.

6. Don F. Wasson, "Brewer Sees Chaos under Court Decree," *Montgomery Advertiser*, April 13, 1967.

7. Edward J. Lepoma, "Four Governors Vow to Take Schools Fight to Congress," *Birmingham Post-Herald*, April 18, 1967; "12 Governors Asked to Conference Here," *Alabama Journal*, April 13, 1967; Randolph Pendleton, "8 Governors Snub Summit Bid," *Birmingham Post-Herald*, April 14, 1967; "The 'Summit' Fizzles," *Alabama Journal*, April 15, 1967.

8. Wallace v. United States, 389 U.S. 215 (1967). See Application for Stay, filed in District Court on April 10, 1967.

9. Dan Dowe, "School Boards, Judges Join to Defy Governor," *Birmingham News*, April 16, 1967.

10. Report of State Superintendent of Education in accordance with decree of March 22, 1967; see Joseph Bagley, *The Politics of White Rights: Race, Justice, and Integrating Alabama's Schools* (Athens: University of Georgia Press, 2018), 118; Landsberg Meeting Notes, April 19, 1967, Landsberg Files; Report of the United States on Desegregation Plans Submitted Pursuant to the Court's Decree of March 22, 1967, served on April 20, 1967.

11. Order, Lee v. Macon County, 267 F. Supp. 458, 465 (M.D. Ala. 1967). The four districts were Autauga County, Cullman County, Bibb County, and Pickens County; Report of the United States on Amended Desegregation Plans Submitted Pursuant to the Court's Decree of March 22, 1967 and Court's Order of April 24, 1967; Docket, Order Adding Parties Defendant and Order to Show Cause, Lee v. Macon County, Civil Actio no. 604-E (on May 26, 1967, adding these school systems: Marengo County, Linden City, and Thomasville from the Southern District and Jasper City and Marion County from the Northern District of Alabama); Lee v. Macon County, July 28, 1967. Only Bibb County remained noncompliant.

12. See U.S. Department of Health, Education, and Welfare, Revised Statement of Policies for School Desegregation Plans under Title VI of the Civil Rights Act of 1964 (March 1966). §181.49, Assignment According to Choice, which gave the option for a school system to give preference to minority student's choices and notify all students of their assignments; §181.46, Letters to Parents, Notices, and Choice Forms; §181.17(a) Official Support for Desegregation Plan required official support for the desegregation plan; §181.16, Attendance Outside School System of Residence was a provision relating to arrangements for attendance outside the school system of residence. See also 45 C.F.R. § 80.4(c).

13. Phyllis Theroux Title VI Task Force Meeting Notes, June 15, 1965.

14. David Rubin Presentation on Title VI Questions, June 15, 1965.

15. Memorandum from Ruben Ortenberg, attorney with the Southeastern Section to Steven J. Pollak, first assistant Civil Rights Division, June 1965, 1.

16. Memorandum from Ortenberg to Pollak.

17. US Congress, Senate, Paul Rilling Statement before the U.S. Senate Select Committee on Equal Educational Opportunity, June 15, 1970, 987.

18. Gary Orfield, *The Reconstruction of Southern Education: The Schools and the 1964 Civil Rights Act* (New York: Wiley-Interscience, 1969), 55–57.

19. Orfield, *Reconstruction of Southern Education*, 321.

20. Orfield, 334.

21. US Commission on Civil Rights, *Federal Civil Rights Enforcement Effort* (Washington, DC: US Government Printing Office, 1970), 976, available at https://static.ewg.org/reports/2021/BlackFarmerDiscriminationTimeline/cr12en2.pdf.

22. Commission on Civil Rights, *Federal Civil Rights Enforcement Effort*, 976.

23. F. Peter Libassi, Special Assistant to the Secretary for Civil Rights to Douglass Cater, Joseph A. Califano, and John Doar, April 6, 1967, HU 2–5, LBJL.

24. James Chisum, "State Faces Mounting Pressures on Mixing," *Birmingham News*, April 11, 1967; idem., "Pupil Can't Choose Teacher, Says USOE Official," *Birmingham News*, April 12, 1967.

25. Excerpt from Barrett's argument on April 15, 1967, Box 21, Folder 8, FMJP, LOC. The court apparently had the court reporter transcribe this one excerpt.

26. 45 C.F.R. §80.4(c)(1) (1967).

27. Reuben Ortenberg to St. John Barrett, May 2, 1967, author archive.

28. Landsberg Meeting Notes, April 27, 1967, attended by Derrick Bell, Richard Fairley, Goldia Dargan, Ann Lassiter, Chet Relyer, Ruby Martin of HEW and Alexander Ross, Walt Gorman, Reuben Ortenberg, and Ken Frankland. Leon Panetta describes Martin as "a strong, black woman lawyer, born in Arkansas, who never forgot" that "the black children who had been getting the short end of the stick for years" came first. Leon Panetta and Peter Gall, *Bring Us Together: The Nixon Team and the Civil Rights Retreat* (Philadelphia: Lippincott, 1971), 53.

29. NAACP v. Wallace, 269 F. Supp. 346, 352 (1967).

30. Alexander Ross to Frank Dunbaugh, Status of Alabama School Litigation, June 28, 1967; "Chambers, Lanett City School Boards Approve Rights Plan: 30-Day Period Given Students to Make Choice," *Valley Times-News*, March 30, 1966; Letter from J. T. Greene, superintendent, Lanett City School District to Harold B. Williams, James R. Dunn, Ernest Stone, and Judge Frank M. Johnson, June 30, 1967.

31. James Dunn to the Lee v. Macon case file, July 14, 1967.

32. Derrick Bell to John Doar, July 14, 1967.

33. Merle W. Loper to Investigation File, July 12, 1967; James Dunn to Area File, Lee v. Macon County Board of Education, July 12, 1967.

34. Bagley, *The Politics of White Rights*, 129.

35. Lee v. Macon County, 270 F. Supp. 859, 866 (M.D. Ala. 1967).

36. J. T. Greene to Frank M. Johnson, Harold B. Williams, James Dunn, and Ernest Stone, June 30, 1967; DOJ Memorandum on Lanett, undated, Landsberg Files.

37. Alanson W. Willcox to John Doar, August 18, 1967, DOJ File 144–100–2–1, Container 337, NARA.

38. John Doar to David L. Norman, August 21, 1967, DOJ File 144–100–2–1, Container 337, NARA.

39. Brian Landsberg to David L. Norman, August 22, 1967, DOJ File 144–100–2–1, Container 337, NARA.

40. David L. Norman to John Doar, Undated Memorandum, DOJ file 144–100–2–1, Container 337, NARA.

41. Stephen C. Halpern, *On the Limits of the Law: The Ironic Legacy of Title VI of the 1964 Civil Rights Act* (Baltimore: Johns Hopkins University Press, 1995), 72.

42. Brian Landsberg to Frank Dunbaugh, attorney for the Southern Section, Office of Planning and Coordination, October 25, 1967, 1.

43. E.g., Cullman County School District, Order of May 18, 1967, 12 Race Rel. L. Rep. 615, 743–744 (1967); Bibb County School District, Marion County School District, Thomasville City School District, Orders of May 18 and June 14, 1967, 12 Race Rel. L. Rep. 615, 743–748 (1967); Henry County School District, Order of October 30, 1967, 12 Race Rel. L. Rep. 615, 1844 (1968).

44. Frank Dunbaugh to John Doar, School Openings in Alabama, August 21, 1967, Box 57, School Openings in Alabama 1967–68 School Year, JDP, PUL.

45. John M. Rosenberg to Brian K. Landsberg, Legal Actions against Interference with School Desegregation, August 22, 1967, Box 57, School Openings in Alabama 1967–68 School Year, JDP, PUL; Letter from Daniel M. Pochoda to Brian K. Landsberg, Legal Actions against Interference with School Desegregation, September 1, 1967, 11.

46. Frank M. Johnson to John Doar, August 18, 1967, Box 57, Alabama School Openings 1967–68, JDP, PUL.

47. John Doar, "Memorandum for the File," August 22, 1967.

48. See e.g., "Wallace's New Stunt Will Flop, as He Knows," *Montgomery Advertiser*, August 24, 1967, which noted that the "painful compliance" with court orders to desegregate faculty "will be thrown into utter confusion at the last minute. . . . Such confusion, which the former Governor feeds on, will add dangerous excitement and turmoil to an already delicate situation—accomplishing nothing in the end but more trouble, more suits, new defeats."

49. Decision and Decree on Act no. 266, 12 Race Rel. L. Rep. 1765, 1837, 1839 (1968).

50. Frank Dunbaugh to John Doar, "Anticipated Developments in School Desegregation in the Southeastern Section," September 15, 1967, Box 37, Folder November 1966, Investigation, School Desegregation, Southeastern Section IV, JDP, PUL.

51. See Order of October 12, 1967, 12 Race Rel. L. Rep. 1765, 1840 (1967) for Cherokee County, Chilton County, Dallas County, Limestone County, and Washington County School Districts.

52. Memorandum from Walter Gorman to Frank Dunbaugh, Attorney for the Southern Section, January 29, 1968 (the August 2, 1967, decree required Dr. Stone to report itemized inequalities in the school districts and plans toward eliminating inequalities); Frank Allen to Frank M. Dunbaugh, Lee v. Macon—Enforcement of Decree through State Superintendent's Office. The memorandum states, "the first [Dr. Stone] heard about [the noncompliance letter] was when an irate county superintendent came into

his office with the letter." Also Frank Allen, Conference with HEW Officials on Enforcement, February 8, 1968.

53. Motion of Alabama State Teachers Association to intervene, September 2, 1967; Order of September 20, 1967; Fred D. Gray, *Bus Ride to Justice: Changing the System by the System: The Life and Works of Fred Gray, Preacher, Attorney, Politician*, rev. ed. (Montgomery: New South Books, 2013), 221.

54. Lee v. Macon County Board of Education, 283 F. Supp. 194 (M.D. Ala. 1968).

55. See U.S. Motion filed February 20, 1968, Lee v. Macon County Board of Education, Civil Action no. 604-E; Order, March 11, 1968, Lee v. Macon County Board of Education, Civil Action no. 604-E; Decision of April 1, 1968, Lee v. Macon County, 283 F. Supp. 194, 197, 198 (M.D. Ala 1968); St. John Barrett (who had moved to HEW as deputy general counsel) to Peter Goldschmidt in HEW's Office of General Counsel, Civil Rights Division, Briefing Session for Alabama Survey Teams, October 16, 1967, referring to planned October 23 briefing session; Brian Landsberg to Frank Dunbaugh, Lee v. Macon County Enforcement, October 25, 1967.

56. Brian Landsberg to David Norman, October 31, 1967.

57. Owen Fiss to David Norman and Brian Landsberg, October 19, 1967.

58. The Supreme Court affirmed Lee v. Macon County and denied cert in the Jefferson County case. However, it granted cert in Green v. County School Board.

59. Frank M. Johnson to Stephen J. Pollak, January 17, 1968, author archive.

60. Stephen J. Pollak to Frank M. Johnson, February 17, 1968, author archive.

61. Stephen J. Pollak to Ernest Stone, March 14, 1968, author archive.

62. Estelle Fine, "Five Days of Talk about Discrimination," *Southern Courier*, May 18–19, 1968.

63. Testimony of Mr. & Mrs. Bernard Shambrey, Tr., Hearing before the U.S. Commission on Civil Rights, Montgomery, Ala., April 27–May 2, 1968, 39, quoted in US Commission on Civil Rights, *Federal Enforcement of School Desegregation*, September 11, 1969, 22, available at https://www.google.com/books/edition/Federal_Enforcement_of_School_Desegregat/lzowFBAWzFoC?hl=en&gbpv=1&printsec=frontcover.

64. The Crenshaw County incident is detailed by Judge Johnson in United States v. Crenshaw County Unit of United Klans of America, 290 F. Supp. 181, 183–84 (M.D. Ala. 1968) (Johnson notes "this Court's considerable experience with freedom of choice"); US Commission on Civil Rights, *Federal Enforcement of School Desegregation*, 24.

65. Lawrence Ross to Monroe County School File, September 7, 1966, Box 37, folder Investigation, Schools, Southeastern, III, JDP, PUL.

66. Shuttlesworth v. Birmingham Bd. of Educ., 358 U.S. 101 (1958), aff'g mem. 162 F.Supp. 372 (N.D. Ala. 1958); Report of United States Commission on Civil Rights for 1959, 324.

67. John Doar to Owen Fiss, September 9, 1967, author archive.

68. Frank Schwelb to Stephen Pollak, January 13, 1968; Frank Schwelb to Stephen Pollak, January 17, 1968, author archive.

69. Civil Rights Division Final Draft of Brief in Green v. County School Board, et. al., February 7, 1968, author archive.

70. Assistant Attorney General Stephen J. Pollak, Memorandum for the Solicitor General, February 23, 1968, in *Administrative History of the Civil Rights Division of the Department of Justice during the Johnson Administration, Civil Rights, the White House, and the Justice Department, 1945–1968*, ed. Michal R. Belknap, vol. 17 (New York: Garland, 1991), 10–12.

71. Memorandum for the United States as Amicus Curiae, Green v. County School Board, et. al. (OT 1967, nos. 695, 740 and 805).

72. Petitioner's Brief, Green v. County School Board of Kent County (OT 1967, no. 695), 35.

73. Claiborne argument in *Landmark Briefs and Arguments of the Supreme Court of the United States: Constitutional Law*, ed. Philip B. Kurland and Gerhard Casper, vol. 66 (Washington, DC: University Publications of America, 1975), 288.

74. Oral argument of Russell Rice, Sr. in Monroe v. Board of Commissioners, no. 740 OT 1967, April 3, 1968, in Kurland and Casper, *Landmark Briefs and Arguments*, 66:250.

75. Brief of Defendants, Raney v. Board of Education, no. 805, OT 1967, 18.

76. Argument of Robert V. Light in Raney, in Kurland and Casper, 277 (if we assigned white students to the Black school, "we know from experience that the white students will not continue to attend those schools"). See also the brief of the defendants in Green, in Kurland and Casper, at 146–147n26.

77. Claiborne argument in Kurland and Casper, 286–287.

78. Report of the National Advisory Commission on Civil Disorders.

79. Green v. County School Board, 391 U.S. 430, 438, 442 (1968).

80. Anonymous, Steven Pollak Files, 1968.

81. Hugh Davis Graham, *The Civil Rights Era* (New York: Oxford University Press, 1990), 373. Graham cites to J. Harvey Wilkinson III, *From Brown to Bakke* (New York: Oxford University Press, 1979), 112.

82. Gordon E. Harvey, *A Question of Justice: New South Governors and Education, 1968–1976* (Tuscaloosa: University of Alabama Press, 2002), 45–46.

83. Quoted in Harvey, *A Question of Justice*, 21.

84. Bagley, 179.

85. Harvey, 23.

86. Mary Ellen Gale, State to Defend Choice Plans, *Southern Courier*, June 15–16, 1968, 1.

87. Motion of Plaintiffs, June 7, 1968; Motion of United States, July 15, 1968.

88. Board minutes of June 12, 1968, quoted in Jeff Frederick, *Stand Up for Alabama: Governor George Wallace* (Tuscaloosa: University of Alabama Press, 2007), 244.

89. Deposition of J. R. Pittard, June 26, 1968, 19.

90. Harvey, 23.

91. Dan Dowe, "Boycott Not Violation, Brewer Says," *Birmingham News*, September 25, 1969.

92. Motion for Court to Relinquish Jurisdiction, Lee v. Macon County, Civil Action 70–251-S (for Talladega County School System filed on November 4, 1983); see Order of

May 9, 1969 (the court had ordered the school system to place 30 percent of its African American students in formerly all-white schools by fall 1969).

93. James M. Fallows, "145 Steps Suggested to Integrate Schools," *Southern Courier*, August 31–September 1, 1968.

94. Letter from Stephen Pollak to Miss Marylee Campbell, October 7, 1968.

95. Quoted in Harvey, 22; Harris v. Crenshaw County Board of Education, 259 F. Supp. 167 (M.D. Ala. 1966).

96. Montgomery County Board of Education v. Carr, 400 F.2d 1 (5th Cir. 1968) (modifying faculty desegregation order). The modification was reversed in United States v. Montgomery County Board of Education, 393 U.S. 1116 (1969).

97. Montgomery County Bd. of Educ. v. Carr, 402 F. 2d. 782, 785 (5th Cir. 1969). Chief Judge Brown, dissenting from denial of en banc rehearing.

98. Carr v. Montgomery County Board of Education, 289 F. Supp. 647 (M.D. Ala. 1968), aff'd. as modified, 400 F.2d 1 (5th Cir. 1968), modifications reversed, 292 U.S. 1116 (1969). The order was issued before the Supreme Court's decision in Green.

99. Jack Bass, *Taming the Storm: The Life and Times of Judge Frank M. Johnson and the South's Fight over Civil Rights* (New York: Doubleday, 1993), 265.

100. Lee v. Macon County, 292 F. Supp. 363, 368 (M.D. Ala. 1968).

101. Decree, Lee v. Macon County, Civil Action no. 604-E, August 28, 1968.

102. Lee v. Macon County, 292 F. Supp. 363 (MD Ala. 1968).

103. Harvey, 24, 27, 29.

104. HEW News Release, June 18, 1971, attaching statistical comparisons, by state, of desegregation in 1968–1969 and 1970–1971 school years.

105. Order of October 14, 1968, Lee v. Macon County, Civil Action no. 604-E.

106. Order of October 23, 1968, Lee v. Macon County.

107. Stephen J. Pollak to Frank Dunbaugh, Lee v. Macon, October 19, 1968, DOJ Files, NARA.

108. Frank Allen to Stephen J. Pollak, November 26, 1968, DOJ Files, NARA.

109. "Legends in the Law: A Conversation with Stephen J. Pollak," *Washington Lawyer*, December–January 2000.

CHAPTER 7. "WATCH WHAT WE DO"

1. John Ehrlichman, *Witness to Power: The Nixon Years* (New York: Simon & Schuster, 1982), 222.

2. See Ian Haney López, *Dog Whistle Politics: How Coded Racial Appeals Have Reinvented Racism & Wrecked the Middle Class* (New York: Oxford University Press, 2014), 23–24.

3. Robert B. Semple Jr., "Nixon Scores U.S. Method Of Enforcing Integration; Nixon Scores Federal Method for Spurring School Integration," *New York Times*, September 13, 1968, quoted in Gary Orfield, *The Reconstruction of Southern Education: The Schools and the 1964 Civil Rights Act* (New York: Wiley-Interscience, 1969), 345–346.

4. Briefing given to Nixon on Columbia School Fight, Columbia State, August 9, 1968, quoted in Leon E. Panetta and Peter Gall, *Bring Us Together: The Nixon Team and the Civil Rights Retreat* (New York: J. B. Lippincott, 1971), 6.

5. Robert Ellsworth interview transcription, January 30, 2008, RNL, 57.

6. See, e.g., Gary Orfield, *Must We Bus? Segregated Schools and National Policy* (Washington, DC: Brookings Institution, 1978), 243.

7. Alexander v. Holmes County Board of Education, 396 U.S. 19 (1969).

8. Swann v. Charlotte-Mecklenburg Bd. of Educ., 402 U.S. 1 (1971).

9. Jack Greenberg interview with the Southern Oral History Program for the Civil Rights History Project, September 18, 2011, LOC, 12.

10. Memorandum from Lamar Alexander to Bryce Harlow, "Key Biscayne, a New School Desegregation Policy," undated, RNL; Memorandum from Patrick J. Buchanan to the President, February 12, 1970, attaching "a middle re-write of a speech I have been working for the Vice President for Atlanta, February 21st." Box 12, Bryce Harlow Series V, RNL.

11. George P. Schultz, "How a Republican Desegregated the South's Schools," *New York Times*, January 8, 2003; William L. Taylor, "The Justice Department and Race Relations," *Integrated Education*, May–June 1974.

12. Memorandum from the President to John Ehrlichman, copy for Bob Haldeman—no distribution beyond those two, January 28, 1972.

13. Gary Orfield, "Turning Back to Segregation," in *Dismantling Desegregation: The Quiet Reversal of Brown v. Board of Education*, by Orfield and Susan E. Eaton (New York: The New Press, 1996), 9.

14. Orfield, *Must We Bus?*, 291, 334.

15. Rosemary C. Salamone, *Equal Education Under Law* (New York: St. Martin's, 1986), 66.

16. James T. Patterson, *Brown v. Board of Education: A Civil Rights Milestone and Its Troubled Legacy* (New York: Oxford University Press 2001), 155.

17. Bruce Ackerman, *We the People: The Civil Rights Revolution*, vol. 3 (Cambridge, MA: Belknap, 2014), 251–252.

18. Dean J. Kotlowski, *Nixon's Civil Rights: Politics, Principle, and Policy* (Cambridge, MA: Harvard University Press, 2009), 16.

19. Gareth Davies, "Richard Nixon and the Desegregation of Southern Schools," *Journal of Policy History* 19, no. 4 (2007): 367, 368.

20. Evan Thomas, *Being Nixon* (New York: Random House, 2016), xiv.

21. Memorandum from the President to John Ehrlichman, January 28, 1972.

22. Orfield, *Must We Bus?*, 288–289.

23. Leonard Garment interview transcription, April 6, 2007, RNL, 20.

24. US Commission on Civil Rights, "Annual Review, School Desegregation," *Civil Rights Digest* 4, no. 4 (1971): 4, 7.

25. Panetta and Gall, *Bring Us Together*, 4.

26. Panetta and Gall, 62.

27. Stephen C. Halpern, *On the Limits of the Law: The Ironic Legacy of Title VI of the 1964 Civil Rights Act* (Baltimore: Johns Hopkins University Press, 1995), 86.

28. Richard Harris, *Justice: The Crisis of Law, Order, and Freedom in America* (New York: E. P. Dutton, 1970), 193.

29. Harris, *Justice*, 193, quoting deputy assistant attorney general Nathan Lewin.

30. Thomas, *Being Nixon*, 261.

31. See generally US Congress, Senate, Department of Justice Nominations, *Hearing before the Committee on the Judiciary*, 91st Cong., 1st sess., Jan. 29, 1969, 44–49.

32. Davies, "Richard Nixon and the Desegregation of Southern Schools," 367, 369.

33. John D. Skrentny, "Zigs and Zags: Richard Nixon and the New Politics of Race," in *Winning While Losing: Civil Rights, the Conservative Movement and the Presidency from Nixon to Obama*, ed. Kenneth Osgood and Derrick E. White (Gainesville: University Press of Florida 2014), 27

34. Hugh Davis Graham, *The Civil Rights Era: Origins and Development of National Policy 1960–1972* (New York: Oxford University Press, 1990), 382.

35. Quoted in James Boyd, "Nixon's Southern Strategy: 'It's All in the Charts,'" *New York Times*, May 17, 1970.

36. Richard Nixon, the President's News Conference, February 6, 1969.

37. Harris, 193, quoting deputy assistant attorney general Nathan Lewin.

38. Jerris Leonard to Frank M. Johnson, March 5, 1969, and March 6, 1969. DOJ Files, NARA. The court, however, granted the Russellville request for delay, based on the school board's assurance on March 16, 1969, that it would operate a unitary system in 1970 even if the new building was not completed. The order was filed on December 20, 1969, and the Nixon administration's first filing in Lee came in April 1969, when it moved for more desegregation of Alabama's trade schools and junior colleges.

39. In addition to Guntersville and Russellville, see motions of Shelby County Board of Education (January 13, 1969 and February 15, 1969), Escambia County School Board (February 12, 1969), Thomasville City Board of Education (February 15, 1969), Coosa County School Board (February 18, 1969), Tuscaloosa City Board of Education (February 22, 1969), Autauga County School Board (February 24, 1969), Auburn City Board of Education (February 25, 1969), Marion City Board of Education (February 26, 1969), Decatur City Board of Education (February 26, 1969), Selma City Board of Education (February 26, 1969), Tallapoosa County Board of Education (February 27, 1969), Sylacauga City Board of Education (February 27, 1969).

40. Motion of the United States for Further Relief in Connection with Trade Schools and Junior Colleges, April 30, 1969.

41. Order of August 6, 1969, Lee v. Macon County, Civil Action no. 604-E.

42. See Southern Regional Council, "The Federal Retreat in School Desegregation," December 1969, 8. The statement is reproduced in US Commission on Civil Rights, *Federal Enforcement of School Desegregation*, September 11, 1969, Appendix C, 8, available at https://www.google.com/books/edition/Federal_Enforcement_of_School_Desegregat/lzowFBAWzFoC?hl=en&gbpv=1&printsec=frontcover.

43. Allan Wolk, *The Presidency and Black Civil Rights: Eisenhower to Nixon* (Rutherford, NJ: Fairleigh Dickinson University Press, 1971), 151.

44. Thomas, 257.

45. Lamar Alexander to Bryce Harlow, "Key Biscayne, a New School Desegregation Policy," undated, RNL.

46. United States v. State of Georgia, Civil Action no. 12972 (N.D. Ga.). Two years earlier John Doar had proposed calling on the Georgia state superintendent of education to "begin steps at the state level to abolish the dual system similar to the steps required of the Alabama state officials in the Lee case" and Attorney General Ramsey Clark had endorsed Doar's proposal. Memorandum for John Doar, June 3, 1967, returned with the notation "This seems right, John." Box 36, JDP, PUL. However, many Georgia school systems remained out of compliance.

47. Harris, 198–199.

48. John M. Mitchell, Address to the American Bar Association, August 13, 1969.

49. Brief for Plaintiff-Appellant, United States v. Hinds County School Bd., 417 F.2d 852 (5th Cir. 1969), 5; Panetta and Gall, 253–256, quoting letter from Robert Finch to judges of the Fifth Circuit, August 19, 1969.

50. Adams v. Mathews, 403 F.2d 181 (5th Cir. 1968).

51. Jack Rosenthal, "School Desegregation: In Washington: Slowdown by the Administration," *New York Times*, August 31, 1969.

52. Richard Nixon, The President's News Conference, September 26, 1969.

53. See Gary J. Greenberg, "Revolt at Justice," *Washington Monthly*, December 1969, 32.

54. Jack Rosenthal, "School Desegregation: In Washington: Slowdown by the Administration," *New York Times*, August 31, 1969.

55. Fred P. Graham, "Nixon Aide Warns Quick Integration Can't Be Enforced," *New York Times*, September 30, 1969.

56. "Retreat from the Law," *New York Times*, October 1, 1969.

57. Transcript of Oral Argument, October 23, 1969, Alexander v. Holmes County Board of Education, 396 U.S. 19 (1969).

58. Alexander v. Holmes County Board of Education, 396 U.S. 19 (1969).

59. Richard Nixon, The President's News Conference, December 8, 1969; Bob Woodward and Scott Armstrong, *The Brethren* (New York: Simon & Schuster, 1979), 56. Nixon was reportedly "content," because the end of further delay "was the Court's fault, not his."

60. Southern Regional Council, "The Federal Retreat in School Desegregation," 70.

61. Memorandum from the Department of Justice, Civil Rights Division, Memorandum no. 69–4, Reorganization of Civil Rights Division, September 24, 1969; James P. Turner, *Selma and the Liuzzo Murder Trials: The First Modern Civil Rights Convictions* (Ann Arbor: University of Michigan Press 2017), xv. The division had seen frequent reorganizations in the prior ten years. In 1969 I was deputy chief of the Central Section, which had been created as part of an effort to shift more resources to civil rights enforcement in the North.

62. US Congress, Senate, Senate Select Committee on Equal Educational Opportunity, July 7, 1970, 1619.

63. Stephen E. Ambrose, *Nixon: The Triumph of a Politician, 1962–1972* (New York: Simon & Schuster, 1987), 407.

64. US Commission on Civil Rights, *Federal Civil Rights Enforcement Effort* (Washington, DC: US Government Printing Office, 1970), 972, 975, available at https://static.ewg.org/reports/2021/BlackFarmerDiscriminationTimeline/cr12en2.pdf; US Congress, Senate, Jerris Leonard Statement before the U.S. Senate Select Committee on Equal Educational Opportunity, July 13, 1970, 1797. The total number of CRD staff was 274. The Education Section was allocated 17 percent of the total, with twenty-eight lawyers and six paralegals.

65. The subheading for this section is taken from John Herbers, "School Integration Entering Critical Stage," *New York Times*, June 21, 1970.

66. US Congress, Senate, Paul Rilling Statement before the U.S. Senate Select Committee on Equal Educational Opportunity, June 15, 1970, 978.

67. US Congress, Senate, Julian Bond Statement before the U.S. Senate Select Committee on Equal Educational Opportunity, June 15, 1970, 932.

68. US Congress, Senate, Jerris Leonard Statement before the U.S. Senate Select Committee on Equal Educational Opportunity, July 13, 1970, 1804.

69. Richard M. Nixon, Statement about Desegregation of Elementary and Secondary Schools, March 24, 1970.

70. US Commission on Civil Rights, *Federal Civil Rights Enforcement Effort*, 672.

71. US Congress, Senate, Jerris Leonard, 1803.

72. Lamar Alexander to Bryce Harlow, "Key Biscane, a New School Desegregation Policy," 4.

73. The quotes are from 1970 *Annual Report of the Attorney General of the United States*, 84. The description of the marching orders is based on my recollection of the event.

74. Regional Conference of United States Attorneys on Law Enforcement, Atlanta, Georgia, December 9, 1969, Box 66, LGP, RNL.

75. Email from Frank M. Dunbaugh to Brian Landsberg and others, February 14, 2020.

76. Leonard Garment interview transcription, April 6, 2007, RNL, 20.

77. Peter Kihss, "'Benign Neglect' on Race Is Proposed by Moynihan," *New York Times*, March 1, 1970, 1.

78. Thomas, 257.

79. Leonard Garment to Jim Keogh, September 25, 1969, Box 1, LGP, RNL; US Commission on Civil Rights, *Federal Civil Rights Enforcement Effort*, 1012, refers to Garment as the chief civil rights official on the White House staff.

80. William E. Timmons to Edward J. Derwinski, November 19, 1969, Box 67, LGP, RNL.

81. Leonard Garment to the Vice President, "Bussing and Student Assignment—Background for Your Face the Nation Appearance," January 31, 1970, LGP, RNL.

82. Memorandum from Patrick Buchanan to the President attaching draft speech for Vice President, February 12, 1970. Nixon speechwriter William Safire quotes part of Buchanan's memo, William Safire, *Before the Fall: An Inside View of the Pre-Watergate White House* (New York: Doubleday, 1975), 233.

83. Pat Buchanan, Draft 3, February 12, 1970, quoted in Davies, 367, 376.

84. H. R. Haldeman, *The Haldeman Diaries: Inside the Nixon White House* (New York: G. P. Putnam's Sons, 1994), 126.

85. Safire, *Before the Fall*, 234–241.

86. Lamar Alexander to Bryce Harlow, "Key Biscayne, a New School Desegregation Policy." The Civil Rights Commission took the position that "statewide court orders are not an effective means of desegregating schools," because they insulate school districts from administrative [i.e., HEW] oversight. US Commission on Civil Rights, *Federal Enforcement of School Desegregation*, 58.

87. John Ehrlichman, Memorandum for the President, Education in the South, January 26, 1970, Box 64, LGP, RNL.

88. Frank Dunbaugh to Leonard Garment, February 27, 1970, Box 63, LGP, RNL.

89. Bickel explained his proposal in two articles in the February 7 and March 14 issues of the *New Republic*, reproduced in Alexander M. Bickel, "Desegregation: Where Do We Go from Here?" *Phi Delta Kappan* 51 (1970): 518.

90. Bruce Rabb to Leonard Garment, March 4, 1970, Revised Draft of School Desegregation Statute, March 5, 1970, Box 63, LGP, RNL.

91. Leonard Garment to John Ehrlichman, A Constitutional Amendment on School Desegregation, March 7, 1970, LGP, RNL; Leonard Garment to Bill Timmons, "The 'Bickel Bill,'" March 12, 1970, Box 2, LGP, RNL.

92. Panetta and Gall, 295.

93. See Briefing Agenda, Cabinet Level Group on Desegregation, February 7, 1970; Introduction by George Schultz, Secretary of Labor, Box 64, LGP, RNL.

94. Leonard Garment Interview Transcription, April 6, 2007, RNL, 21. For example, Secretary of Labor George Schultz presided over the February 7, 1970, meeting, attended by Attorney General Mitchell, Secretary of HEW Robert Finch, presidential advisor John Ehrlichman, White House aides Rumsfeld, Harlow, Dent, Morgan, and Garment, as well as Assistant Attorney General Jerris Leonard, HEW Office of Civil Rights Director Leon Panetta, and several staff members. See Bradley H. Patterson, Jr., Note to the Guard, February 6, 1970, and Briefing Agenda, Cabinet Level Group on Desegregation, February 7, 1970, Box 64, LGP, RNL.

95. Email from Frank M. Dunbaugh to Brian Landsberg and others, February 14, 2020.

96. Bryce Harlow to Staff Secretary, February 19, 1970, RNL.

97. Email from Frank M. Dunbaugh, October 12, 2018.

98. Bradley H. Patterson, Jr., interview with Terry W. Good, Room 182, Old Executive Office Building, September 10, 1974. Patterson was Garment's executive assistant.

99. US Commission on Civil Rights, *Federal Civil Rights Enforcement Effort*, 1012, n. 223, quoting the *Washington Post, Potomac Magazine*, June 7, 1970, and an interview with Robert J. Brown, Special Assistant to the President, April 9, 1970.

100. Haldeman, *Haldeman Diaries*, 126.

101. Richard Nixon, "Statement about Desegregation of Elementary and Secondary

Schools," March 24, 1970; Swann v. Charlotte-Mecklenburg Bd. of Educ., 402 U.S. 1 (1971).

102. John Herbers, "President Draws the Line on Integration," *New York Times*, March 29, 1970.

103. Panetta and Gall, 369; Paul M. Rilling, "Desegregation: The South Is Different," *New Republic*, May 16, 1970, 17–18, quoted in Orfield, *Must We Bus?*, 288.

104. Tom Wicker, "In the Nation: This Way to the Egress," *New York Times*, March 26, 1970.

105. Robert B. Semple, Jr., "Nixon Under Pressure: A Cautious and Shrewd Performance," *New York Times*, March 29, 1970.

106. Conrad cartoon, reproduced in Bickel, "Desegregation: Where Do We Go from Here?," 518, 519.

107. Gerald P. Choppin to Jerris Leonard, Weakly Report, April 1, 1970, 6.

108. Jerris Leonard to John Ehrlichman, Execution of Directions from the President per his Statement on Elementary and Secondary School Desegregation of March 24, 1970, March 31, 1970, Leonard Garment files, Box 64, LGP, RNL.

109. Davies, 367, 381.

110. US Commission on Civil Rights, *Federal Civil Rights Enforcement Effort*, 976, n. 143, quoting letter from Jerris Leonard to Howard A. Glickstein, Aug. 25, 1970.

111. See email from Frank M. Dunbaugh to Thomas Chleboski, December 4, 2018.

112. Charles Rabb, "Education Report/HEW, Justice Lawyers Draft Plans to Implement Supreme Court's Busing Decision," *National Journal*, June 19, 1971, 1305, 1306. The article described the Nixon administration's initial response to the Supreme Court's decision in Swann v. Charlotte-Mecklenburg Board of Education, 402 U.S. 1 (1971), but this kind of collaboration preceded Swann.

113. Attorney General of the United States, 1970 Annual Report, 84; Hearings, Senate Select Committee on Equal Educational Opportunity, August 6, 1970, 1752.

114. "The Mixmasters," *Time Magazine*, July 6, 1970. Mardian later was convicted of conspiracy to obstruct justice, as part of the Watergate scandal.

115. Jerris Leonard to Cabinet Committee on Desegregation, June 4, 1970.

116. Jack Rosenthal, "100 Federal Aides to Assume Role in Desegregation," *New York Times*, July 17, 1970. See also Ken W. Clauson, "U.S. Will Send 100 to South to Enforce Desegregation," *Washington Post*, July 17, 1970, quoting Attorney General John Mitchell, "Without fervor, without passion, we will enforce the law."

117. A. D. Horne, "Finch Answers Thurmond Blast," *Washington Post*, July 20, 1970.

118. Richard Nixon, The President's News Conference, July 30, 1970.

119. US Commission on Civil Rights, "Annual Review, School Desegregation," *Civil Rights Digest* 4, no. 4 (1971): 7.

120. US Congress, Senate, *Hearings in the Senate Select Committee on Equal Educational Opportunity*, August 11, 1970, 1825. Clark spoke of the need in DOJ and HEW for "adequate budgets and personnel to enforce the law." US Congress, Senate, *Hearings in the Senate Select Committee on Equal Educational Opportunity*, July 7, 1970, 1617.

121. US Congress, Senate, *Hearings in the Senate Select Committee on Equal Educational Opportunity*, August 11, 1970, 1832.

122. US Congress, Senate, *Hearings in the Select Committee on Equal Educational Opportunity*, July 13, 1970, 1688.

123. US Congress, Senate, *Hearings in the Senate Select Committee on Equal Educational Opportunity*, July 13 and August 13, 1970, 1679, 1895.

124. H. R. Haldeman Diaries Collection, August 13, 1970, NARA.

125. Roy Reed, "Both Sides in South Mistrust Nixon Actions on School Integration," *New York Times*, July 16, 1970.

126. Orfield, *Must We Bus?*, 328.

127. There were white "sit-ins" in fall 1970. See Joseph Bagley, *Politics of White Rights* (Athens: University of Georgia Press), 183. See Pleasant Grove discussion in Stout v. Jefferson County Board of Education, 466 F.2d 1213 (5th Cir. 1972) (citing Wright v. Emporia, 442 F.2d. 570 (4th Cir. 1971) and United States v. Scotland Neck 442 F.2d 575 (4th Cir. 1971)).

128. The Nixon administration set up Citizens' Advisory Committees, including in Alabama. See Bagley, *Politics of White Rights*, 182.

129. HEW News Release, June 18, 1971. In 1980, 44.3 percent of Black students attended predominantly white schools, above the national rate of 37.1 percent. Gary Orfield, *Public School Desegregation in the United States, 1968–1980* (Washington, DC: Joint Center For Political Studies, 1983), 6. By 1988, the percentage of Blacks in virtually all-minority schools in the Deep South had fallen to 24 percent, from 77.8 percent twenty years earlier. See table 8 in Gary Orfield and Chung-Mei Lee, "Brown at 50: King's Dream or Plessy's Nightmare?," Harvard University Civil Rights Project, January 2004, 18, 20. While Orfield and Lee state that the federal government stopped actively enforcing desegregation after 1970, they document continued rise in school desegregation from 1970 to 1988. That increase resulted from federal enforcement, not from voluntary action by Southern school boards.

130. US Commission on Civil Rights, *The Unfinished Business Twenty Years Later . . . , A Report Submitted by the Fifty-One State Advisory Committees* (September 1977), 6; US Commission on Civil Rights, *Reviewing a Decade of School Desegregation, 1966–1975: Report of a National Survey of School Superintendents* (1977), 3.

131. Jerris Leonard to Frank M. Johnson, Jr., March 8, 1969.

132. Lee v. Macon County, 448 F.2d 746 (5th Cir. 1971) (Calhoun County School System, Defendant-Appellee, and City of Oxford School System, Defendant-Appellee. The court upheld the appeals by NEA and United States and required that "the city cannot secede from the county where the effect–to say nothing of the purpose–of the secession has a substantial adverse effect on desegregation of the county school district."). See also United States v. Scotland Neck Board of Education, 407 U.S. 484 (1972). In a companion case, Wright v. Council of City of Emporia, 407 U.S. 451, 462 (1972), the Supreme Court cited with approval the Fifth Circuit's ruling in Lee. For Wallace's rhetoric on the case, see James T. Wooten, "Wallace to Seek Ruling on Busing," *New York Times*, August 18, 1971. See also Bagley, 202–203.

133. Stephen J. Pollak to Frank M. Johnson, November 26, 1969; Stephen J. Pollak to Goodwyn, Smith & Bowman, December 14, 1968; Motion of the United States for Further Relief in Connection with Trade Schools and Junior Colleges, April 30, 1969.

134. Alabama State Teachers Ass'n. v. Alabama Pub. School & College Authority, 289 F.Supp. 784 (M.D. Ala. 1968), aff'd. per curiam 393 U.S. 400 (1969).

135. Lee v. Macon County, 317 F. Supp. 103 (M.D. Ala. 1970).

136. Lee v. Macon County, 453 F.2d 524, 527 (5th Cir. 1971).

137. Lee v. Macon County, 468 F.2d 956 (5th Cir. 1972).

138. The Alabama Council on Human Relations, American Friends Service Committee, Delta Ministry of the National Council of Churches, NAACP Legal Defense and Education Fund, Inc., Southern Regional Council, and Washington Research Project, *It's Not Over in the South: School Desegregation in Forty-Three Southern Cities Eighteen Years after Brown* (Atlanta: Southern Education Foundation and Urban Coalition, May 1972), i.

139. Alabama Council on Human Relations et al., *It's Not Over in the South*, iii, 4.

140. Taylor Branch, *Parting the Waters: America in the King Years*, 1954–1963 (New York: Simon & Schuster, 1989), 417–419; Patterson Toby Graham, *A Right to Read: Segregation and Civil Rights in Alabama's Public Libraries, 1900–1965* (Tuscaloosa: University of Alabama Press, 2002), 91–98.

141. Testimony of Revis Hall, quoted in Trial Brief of the United States (1967), 23.

142. Kimbrough Deposition, U.S. Exhibit 4.

143. US Commission on Civil Rights, *Survey of School Desegregation in the Southern and Border States, 1965–66*, 31–32, 35, available at https://www.crmvet.org/docs/ccr_sch_desegregation_south_border_6202.pdf.

144. US Commission on Civil Rights, *Survey of School Desegregation in the Southern and Border States*, 1965–66, 35. See generally Bagley, 98.

145. Trial Brief of the United States, 121; Revis Hall Deposition Summary. Hall noted that by December, 216 Negro students were enrolled in white schools.

146. Quoted in Lee v. Macon County, 429 F.2d 1218, 1222 (5th Cir. 1970).

147. Lee v. Macon County, 429 F.2d 1218 (5th Cir. 1970).

148. Paul Hancock to File, Anniston City School System, February 9, 1971.

149. Brian Landsberg to Jerris Leonard, Motion for Supplemental Relief, Anniston City School System, Lee v. Macon County, Civil Action no. 70251-S (N.D. Ala.).

150. United States' Motion for Supplemental Relief, Lee et al v. Macon County Board of Education, no. 7–251-S (N.D. Ala.) (filed March 3, 1971).

151. Email from Paul Hancock to Brian Landsberg, October 9, 2018.

152. Order of August 15, 1972, Lee et al v. Macon County, Civil Action no. 7–251-S (N.D. Ala.).

153. Brief of the United States at 29, 31, Swann v. Charlotte Mecklenburg Board of Education (1970), 1970 WL 122661.

154. Swann v. Charlotte Mecklenburg Board of Education, 402 U.S. 1, 26 (1971).

155. Memorandum from David L. Norman to the Solicitor General, Appealing Lee v. Macon County Board of Education (Anniston City School System) (N.D. Ala.), August

31, 1972; Brian Landsberg to Trial File, Anniston Schools, September 8, 1972; see Lee v. Macon County Board of Education, 483 F.2d 244, at n. 2 (5th Cir. 1973).

156. Letter from J. Stanley Pottinger by Paul F. Hancock to Walter J. Merrill, 12 February 12, 1973.

157. Lee v. Macon County, 483 F.2d 244 (5th Cir. 1973).

158. U.S. Brief on Plaintiffs' Request for Rehearing en banc, 4, 6.

159. Brief of Private Plaintiffs, 6.

160. Brief of Private Plaintiffs, 5.

161. Brief of Private Plaintiffs, 8.

162. Lee v. Macon County , 483 F.2d 244, 245–46 (5th Cir. 1973).

163. "In light of the possible ambiguity in the panel decision, a rehearing could be granted for the purpose of affirming the decision and to clarify the effect of the panel's affirmance and to make clear that there is no conflict with previous decisions of this Court. The case could then be remanded with specific directions for the district court to receive plans and hold hearings on desegregation of the two schools concerned under such timetable as this Court deems appropriate." U.S. Brief on Plaintiffs' Request for Rehearing en banc, 7.

164. Lee v. Macon County, 491 F.2d 1272 (5th Cir. 1974); Letter from J. Stanley Pottinger by J. Gerald Hebert to Walter J. Merrill, July 24, 1975.

CONCLUSION

1. See Joseph Bagley, *The Politics of White Rights: Race, Justice, and Integrating Alabama's Schools* (Athens: University of Georgia Press, 2018); Erica Frankenberg et al., *Harming Our Common Future: America's Segregated Schools 65 Years after Brown*, May 10, 2019, UCLA Civil Rights Project, Center for Education and Civil Rights, https://escholarship.org/uc/item/23j1b9nv, 39, 40.

2. Fred D. Gray, *Bus Ride to Justice: Changing the System by the System: The Life and Works of Fred Gray, Preacher, Attorney, Politician*, rev. ed. (Montgomery: New South Books, 2013), 209.

3. Stephen Wasby, Anthony D'Amato, and Rosemary Metrailer, *Desegregation from Brown to Alexander* (Carbondale: Southern Illinois University Press, 1977), 210.

4. Isabel Wilkerson, *Caste: The Origins of Our Discontents* (New York: Random House, 2020), 380.

5. Parents Involved in Community Schools v. Seattle School Dist. no. 1, 551 U.S. 701 (2007).

6. Bruce Ackerman, *The Civil Rights Revolution* (Cambridge, MA: Belknap, 2014), 1.

7. Anthony Lee to MaryLee Campbell, October 3, 1968.

8. Interview of Anthony Lee by Marian Royston and Mark Wilson, September 16, 2011.

9. Ellen Barry, "They Made History in the 1960s and See It on the March Again," *New York Times*, June 19, 2020.

Bibliographic Essay

To paraphrase Robert Caro, in trying to recreate the world of the Civil Rights Division's school desegregation litigation, a basic source is of course the written materials of the litigation. See Robert A. Caro, *Master of the Senate* (New York: Alfred A. Knopf, 2002), 1051. This book relies principally on primary sources: federal court files, government documents, and interviews. Some of those sources are collected in published books, including a valuable multivolume collection, Michal R. Belknap, ed., *Civil Rights, The White House, and the Justice Department, 1945–1968* (New York: Garland, 1991). See also Leon Friedman, ed., *Brown v. Board: The Landmark Oral Argument before the Supreme Court* (New York: New Press, 2004); idem., *Argument: The Oral Argument before the Supreme Court in Brown v. Board of Education of Topeka, 1952–55* (New York: Chelsea House, 1969); Philip B. Kurland and Gerhard Casper, eds., *Landmark Briefs and Arguments of the Supreme Court of the United States: Constitutional Law*, vol. 66 (Washington, DC: University Publications of America, 1975).

Most of the documents, however, are found in National Archives and Records Administration (NARA) facilities in College Park, Maryland, and East Point, Georgia, the Kennedy, Johnson, and Nixon Presidential libraries, the John Doar collection at Princeton University, the Frank M. Johnson papers and NAACP papers at the Library of Congress, the Alabama State Archives, the Tuskegee University library archives, and my personal files. The presidential libraries also contain oral history interviews of key government officials. The David Mathews Center for Civic Life, Auburn University conducted interviews of former Tuskegee students, as did Alabama Public Radio and Joseph Bagley. See also Jack Greenberg, interview with the Southern Oral History Program for the Civil Rights History Project, Library of Congress, September 18, 2011; John Doar and Burke Marshall, interviews with Blackside, Inc., for the documentary film *Eyes on the Prize: America's Civil Rights Years (1954–1965)*, Film and Media Archive, Henry Hampton Collection, Washington University Libraries, November 15, 1985. The court cases appear in the official reporters. In addition, the Race Relations Law Reporter contains otherwise unreported cases from 1956 to 1967.

For valuable background on Tuskegee and Alabama school desegregation, I relied on Booker T. Washington, *Up from Slavery* (Garden City, NY: Doubleday, 1922); Robert J. Norrell, *Reaping the Whirlwind* (New York: Alfred A. Knopf, 1985); Joseph Bagley, *The Politics of White Rights: Race, Justice, and Integrating Alabama's Schools* (Athens: University of Georgia Press, 2018); Fred D. Gray, *Bus Ride to Justice: Changing the System by the System: The Life and Works of Fred Gray, Preacher, Attorney, Politician*, rev. ed. (Montgomery, AL: New South Books, 2013).

Gary Orfield has been tracing the progress of school desegregation and evaluating government policies since the 1960s. See Gary Orfield, *The Reconstruction of Southern Education: The Schools and the 1964 Civil Rights Act* (New York: Wiley-Interscience, 1969); idem., *Must We Bus? Segregated Schools and National Policy* (Washington, DC: Brookings

Institution, 1978); Gary Orfield and Susan E. Eaton, *Dismantling Desegregation: The Quiet Reversal of Brown v. Board of Education* (New York: New Press, 1996). Stephen L. Wasby, *Race Relations Litigation in an Age of Complexity* (Charlottesville: University of Virginia Press, 1995) provides an institutional analysis of the role of the NAACP Legal Defense Fund; see also Jack Greenberg, *Crusaders in the Courts* (New York: Basic Books, 1994). For a fascinating inside view of the work of the Department of Health, Education, and Welfare at the beginning of the Nixon administration, see Leon E. Panetta and Peter Gall, *Bring Us Together: The Nixon Team and the Civil Rights Retreat* (New York: J. B. Lippincott, 1971).

For the role of the federal courts in Alabama, see Jack Bass, *Taming the Storm: The Life and Times of Judge Frank M. Johnson and the South's Fight over Civil Rights* (New York: Doubleday, 1993) and *Unlikely Heroes* (Tuscaloosa: University of Alabama Press, 1981); also J. W. Peltason, *Fifty-Eight Lonely Men: Southern Federal Judges and School Desegregation* (New York: Harcourt, Brace & World, 1961).

Much has been written about the history of school desegregation. For the period covered by this book other principal sources are Hugh Davis Graham, *The Civil Rights Era* (New York: Oxford University Press, 1990); Michael J. Klarman, *From Jim Crow to Civil Rights: The Supreme Court and the Struggle for Racial Equality* (New York: Oxford University Press, 2004); Richard Kluger, *Simple Justice: The History of Brown v. Board of Education and Black America's Struggle for Equality* (New York: Knopf, 2004); Stephen L. Wasby, Anthony A. D'Amato, and Rosemary Metrailer, *Desegregation from Brown to Alexander* (Carbondale: Southern Illinois University Press, 1977); J. Harvie Wilkinson III, *From Brown to Bakke: The Supreme Court and School Integration, 1954–1978* (New York: Oxford University Press, 1979).

For more books specifically about the work of the CRD, see Robert K. Carr, *Federal Protection of Civil Rights: Quest for a Sword* (Ithaca: Cornell University Press, 1947) [showing the need for the division]; Owen Fiss, *Pillars of Justice: Lawyers and the Liberal Tradition* (Cambridge, MA: Harvard University Press, 2017) [providing snapshots of civil rights law pioneers]; Richard Harris, *Justice: The Crisis of Law, Order, and Freedom in America* (New York: E. P. Dutton, 1970) [providing an early critique of the Nixon Justice Department]; Brian K. Landsberg, *Enforcing Civil Rights: Race Discrimination and the Department of Justice* (Lawrence: University Press of Kansas, 1997) [describing the Division and how it works]; Burke Marshall, *Federalism and Civil Rights* (New York: Columbia University Press, 1964) [discussing policies of civil rights enforcement]; Victor S. Navasky, *Kennedy Justice* (New York: Atheneum, 1971) [critiquing the Kennedy DOJ].

Newspapers extensively covered Alabama school desegregation. The local papers include the *Birmingham News*, *Birmingham Post-Herald*, *Birmingham World*, *Montgomery Advertiser*, *Alabama Journal*, and *Tuskegee News*. National papers, especially the *New York Times*, *Washington Post*, and *Wall Street Journal*, are also informative. During the 1960s, the *Southern Courier* provided independent coverage of civil rights news.

I cite many other sources, shown in the endnotes. But the work of the Civil Rights Division centered on what John Doar called "the romance of the records," and so the original documents are at the core of the book.

Index

Note: page numbers in italics refer to figures. Those followed by *b* refer to boxes. Those followed by n refer to notes, with note number.

Ackerman, Bruce, 3, 151, 186
acquittals in federal prosecutions of violence against Blacks in South, 13
Agnew, Spiro, 150, 153, 164–165, 166, 167
Alabama, Black activism against segregation in: boycotting of white businesses (1957), 54; early history of, 51–53; first Black members of Tuskegee city council, 54–55; increased economic power and, 52, 53; increasing voting power and, 53–54, 55–56
Alabama Black Belt, 41
Alabama Constitution of 1901: prohibition on interracial marriage in, 46; racial caste system in, 40, 44
Alabama Education Association, 146
Alabama legislature: anti-guidelines laws, 100, 103–104, 122; resolution declaring *Brown* invalid, 48; resistance to school desegregation, 175
Alabama School Board: addition as *Lee* defendant, 78; closing of Tuskegee High School to avoid desegregation, 78; legal missteps, and statewide expansion of *Lee*, 78, 81–82, 100, 123; ruling enjoining interference with desegregation, 83–86; support for freedom of choice plans, 143
Alabama school desegregation. *See* school desegregation in Alabama
Alabama State Teachers Association (ASTA), 135
Alexander, Lamar, 150, 156, 162, 165
Alexander v. Holmes County Board of Education (1969), 159, 162–163, 183
Allgood, Clarence, 179–180, 182, 183
amicus curiae briefs by the Department of Justice: Eisenhower administration and, 18; Kennedy administration and, 34–35; in restrictive housing covenant cases, 15–16; in school desegregation cases, 60–61; Truman administration and, 15–17, 185
"An Appeal for Law and Order and Commonsense," 63
Anniston, Alabama: school desegregation under *Lee*, 176–183, 230n163; violent resistance to civil rights activism, 176
armed forces, desegregation of: Eisenhower and, 18; Truman and, 15
Auburn University: conference on desegregation, 98; *Lee* plaintiffs at, 80, 133
Auerbach, Carl L., 94, 121

Bagley, Joseph, vii, 73
Baldwin, James, 184, 186–187
Barnett, Ross, 72–73, 100
Barrett, St. John: background of, 101; and DOJ and HEW desegregation enforcement conflicts, 130, 131; on freedom of choice laws, 139; on government role in *Lee*, 65–66; and hearing on state tuition grants for Macon Academy (1966), 101; on HEW guidelines, 121; on *Lee* enforcement, 126; and *Lee* trial, 113; and *NAACP v. Wallace*, 116–117, 118; and statewide expansion of *Lee*, 81; on white flight from desegregation, 77–78
Bass, Jack, vii, 73–74, 122
Bell, Derrick, 3, 130
Birmingham, Alabama: children's march (May 1963), media coverage of violence at, 37; civil rights demonstrations (April 1963), 49
Black, Hugo, 159
Black Belt of Alabama: Macon County as part of, 41; opposition to desegregation in, 57
Bloody Sunday, ix, 36, 62*b*, 72
Brewer, Albert, 125, 142–143, 146, 148
Brownell, Herbert, 21, 23
Brown v. Board of Education (1954): Alabama schools' refusal to comply with, 48; Court's delegation of enforcement to lower courts, 20; criticisms of, 3–4; death of Justice Vinson and, 17, 18; effect on school desegregation, 2; Eisenhower administration amicus curiae brief in, 18; eradication of Jim Crow, 1; and evolution

Brown v. Board of Education (1954), *continued*
of DOJ role in school desegregation, 185; executive branch's statutory authority to enforce, 49; and failure of school-by-school litigation, 111–113; federal implementation, Kennedy on, 63–64; hearing on relief (*Brown II*), 19–20, 49, 94–95, 111, 113–114; lack of federal enforcement mechanisms, 20–21; lack of roadmap for change in, 1; minimal effect after ten years, 37–38; Nixon administration enforcement of, 7; Nixon on, 148, 168; period of resistance to, 152; rehearing of arguments, 18; ruling in, 18–19; Southern states' resistance to implementation of, 20; and Southern strategies to delay school desegregation, 45, 47–49; Supreme Court's difficulty reaching ruling on, 17, 18; Truman administration's amicus curiae brief in, 6, 16–17

Brown v. Board of Education (Patterson), 2

Buchanan, Patrick, 150, 164–165

Buford, K. L., 54–55

Busing: Alabama officials' opposition to, 146; court order on, 7; Eisenhower's opposition to, 7; Frank M. Johnson's opposition to, 145; Nixon on, 148, 150, 168, 173; and *Swann*, 180–181

Cabinet Level Group on Desegregation, 166–167, 170–171

Campbell, MaryLee, 144, 187

Capital Citizens Council of Little Rock, 47

Carter, Asa, 50*b*, 103

Cater, Douglass, 120, 129

Chachkin, Norman, 182

Civil Rights Act of 1866, 10

Civil Rights Act of 1870, 10

Civil Rights Act of 1957: authorization of DOJ to bring suits against discriminatory election practices, 25; creation of Commission on Civil Rights, 25, 55; creation of DOJ Civil Rights Division, 25; and federal court orders, checks on power of, 22; Part III authorizing federal prosecution of state officials, 21–23, 31, 87, 88–89; passage of, 22

Civil Rights Act of 1964: blocking of, in Congress, 86; Congressional debate on, 88–90, 92; definition of desegregation, inadequacy of, 90–91; as delayed response to *Brown*, 93; development of, 87–88; fair employment provisions, 92; and federal funding of equal education, 85; as first federal legislation to enforce *Brown*, 20–21; and forced desegregation, 86; Johnson administration enforcement of, 6; Johnson's pressure to pass, 86, 89, 90; Kennedy's proposal of, 86; Kennedy's speech on, 63–64; Northern concerns about, 91; and oral arguments in *Jefferson County*, 119–120; passage of, 90; prohibition on racial balance efforts, 117–118; public accommodations provisions, 92, 93; and school desegregation, 49, 85, 91, 149, 208n26; Southern opposition to, 89–90; Title IV, 90; Title VI, 86–87, 91–93, 117, 210n59; Title VII, 117

Civil Rights Act of 1968, 89

Civil Rights Commission: approval of freedom of choice laws, 138; criticism of CRD's litigation-focused approach, 129; hearings on school desegregation in Alabama (1968), 137; on statewide desegregation orders, 226n86. *See also* Commission on Civil Rights

Civil Rights Division of the Department of Justice (CRD): and amicus curiae briefs in school desegregation cases, 60–61; Congressional authority to prosecute school desegregation cases, 20–23, 31, 33–35, 38, 185; constant criticism of, as drain on morale, 153–154; creation of, 25, 185; early focus on voting rights cases, 25; Education Section, establishment of, 150; growth and ever-expanding responsibilities of, 25; litigation-centered approach, Civil Rights Commission criticism of, 129; and radical change effected through law, 26; reorganization of (1967), 136; rise from section to division of DOJ, 14; school desegregation cases (1963), 67; strong relations with Macon County African American community, 37; transformation into law enforcement agency, 5, 25; voting rights cases (1963), 62. *See also Lee*, and Civil Rights Division of the Department of Justice

Civil Rights Division, under Kennedy: active civil rights engagement, 31–37; administration support of, 27–28; law enforcement phase, 28–29, 31–32; number of desegregation orders monitored by, 34; personnel, 28–31; suits against schools receiving federal "impact aid," 34, 36; use of amicus curiae briefs in civil rights cases, 34–35

Civil Rights Division, under Nixon: and administration support of delay in Mississippi school desegregation, 158–159, 160; concerns about policy changes, 153; enforcement plans for 1970, reviews of, 170–171; Leonard as assistant attorney general of, 154; and Nixon's statement on school desegregation, 169–170; pressure to modify school desegregation enforcement, 167; push for immediate desegregation, 150; restructuring of, 160, 224n61

Civil Rights Era, The (Graham), 142

civil rights leaders: criticism of CRD, 34; criticisms of DOJ, 153; dislike of Nixon, 150, 153

civil rights legislation: Eisenhower's proposals for, 20; during Reconstruction, 10; Truman's proposals for, 15

Civil Rights Revolution, The (Ackerman), 3, 186

Claiborne, Louis, 140, 141

Clark, Jim: and Bloody Sunday, 72; and desegregation in Selma, 85–86; and desegregation of Macon County High School, 79; special deputies sent to Tuskegee High School, 72; and suppression of African American vote, ix

Clark, Ramsey: and court ruling prioritizing court authority over HEW's, 132; on CRD dedication, 160; and CRD school desegregation efforts, 67; and NAACP lawsuit on Alabama's anti-guidelines laws, 104; and Senate hearings on equal education opportunities, 172

Clark, Tom, 12, 104

colleges. *See* desegregation of higher education

Commission on Civil Rights: Alabama State Advisory Committee, 173; creation of, 25, 185; demand to see Alabama voter records, 5, 25; establishment of, 55; function of, 25; investigation of Macon County voter suppression, 55–56; recommendations on school desegregation, 25. *See also* Civil Rights Commission

Congress: and *Brown* ruling, lack of legislation to enforce, 20–21; and civil rights legislation, barriers to passage of, 11, 12, 48, 186; and CRD authority to prosecute school desegregation cases, 20–23, 31, 33–35, 38, 185; and Reconstruction civil rights legislation, 10; and school desegregation, limited guidance on, 96; Senate hearings of equal education opportunity, 163, 171; in Truman era, opposition to civil rights legislation, 13, 15

Connor, Eugene "Bull," 37

courts, role in forcing school desegregation, 2–3

CRD. *See* Civil Rights Division of the Department of Justice; Civil Rights Division, under Kennedy; Civil Rights Division, under Nixon.

Crisis magazine, 52

Department of Health, Education, and Welfare (HEW): and DOJ, close work together after *Green*, 173; enforcement conflicts with DOJ and *Lee* court, 126–133; enforcement plans (1970), reviews of, 170–171; evolution of role in school desegregation, 185; guidelines calling for complete desegregation by 1969, 152; shaping of desegregation process, 7–8; supervision of school desegregation, impact of statewide court orders, 162; and withholding of funds from segregated schools, 33–34, 36, 87, 92–94, 100, 104, 116–118, 120–122

Department of Justice (DOJ): Black members of staff in 1960s, 103; civil rights groups' criticisms of, 153; conference on school desegregation (1969), 162–613; desegregation law and policy, development of, 7; federal judges' respect for opinions of, 61; and federal role in desegregation as issue, 1; and HEW, close work together after *Green*, 173; and HEW, enforcement conflicts with, 126–133; involvement in civil rights under Truman, 13; under Johnson and Kennedy, dismantling South's racial caste system as goal of, 39; and *Lee* enforcement, 126, 136–137; and NAACP lawsuit on Alabama's anti-guidelines laws, 104; press's criticism of, 153; and revolution by law, completion of, 187; role in *Lee*, as key, 7–8; role in school desegregation,

Department of Justice (DOJ), *continued*
evolution of, 97, 185–186; and school desegregation in Little Rock, Arkansas, 23; and statewide expansion of *Lee*, 81; suit on state tuition grants for Macon Academy (1966), 100–103, 106–111; under Roosevelt, reluctance to address civil rights, 10. *See also* amicus curiae briefs by the Department of Justice; Civil Rights Division of the Department of Justice (CRD)

Desegregation: federal learning curve in, 32–33; federal reluctance to inflame Southern resistance, 10; reaction of Southern politicians to, 32–33; Southern support for, seeming unlikeliness, ix; threats against federal judges, 46–47; white Southerners in favor of, 63. *See also* revolution by law

desegregation of higher education: CRD role in, 70; DOJ research on segregation levels, 110; *Lee* court ruling requiring, 122–123; at University of Alabama, 32, 36; at University of Mississippi, 29, 31–33, 72–73. *See also* junior colleges, desegregation of; trade schools, desegregation of

desegregation of schools. *See* school desegregation

District of Columbia schools: desegregation of, 20; segregation in, 10, 12

Doar, John: ability to work with local officials, 68, 70; Army career of, 63*b;* author's experience working with, 30; background and career, 25–26; Black leaders' trust in, 103; and court ruling prioritizing court authority over HEW, 132; on CRD role in desegregation, 70; and CRD school desegregation efforts, 67–68; and CRD suits against schools receiving federal "impact aid," 34; and CRD transition to enforcement role, 5, 25; criticisms of, 30; departure from CRD, 136; and desegregation of University of Mississippi, 29, 32; and Frank M. Johnson, relationship with, 60, 61–62, 64*b*–65*b*, 68; on freedom of choice laws, 139; good teamwork with Marshall, 29; hands-on management approach, 30–31; and hearing on state tuition grants for Macon Academy (1966), 101; and HEW, working relationship with, 129; and HEW guidelines, presidential signature on, 121; hiring at CRD, 63*b;* honors awarded to, 26; investigations in Deep South, 29; and issue of white flight from desegregation, 77; and Kennedy administration support of CRD, 28; lack of civil rights experience, 28–29; on *Lee* enforcement, 126; as Marshall's top assistant, 28, 29; notable cases handled by, 29; on racial caste system of South, 26; on relief in *Lee*, 114; and revolution by law, 26; on school desegregation, litigation as primary tool in, 129; and school desegregation in Alabama, 68, 70, 95–96, 100, 114, 120, 133–134; and school desegregation in Georgia, 224n46; speech to Tuskegee Civic Association, 37; tempering zeal with human kindness, 29–30; and *United States v. Jefferson County Board of Education* (1966), 118–120; and *United States v. Wallace* (1963), 74–75; voting rights litigation by, 106–107; and Wallace, conflict with, 65*b;* work ethic of, 30

DOJ. *See* Department of Justice

Douglas, William O., 18

DuBois, W. E. B., 43, 52

Dunbaugh, Frank: at DOJ conference in Atlanta, 163; on DOJ-HEW committee to review desegregation plans for 1970, 171; and *Lee*, enforcement of, 134, 147; and *Swann* ruling, 181; and White House pressure on desegregation, 167

Eastland, James O., 27, 31, 47, 91

economic power of Blacks in Alabama, growth of, 44

Edmund Pettus Bridge, ix, 36, 62*b*, 72

education for African Americans, white fears of consequences of, 39–40, 46

Ehrlichman, John, 148, 151, 166, 170, 173

Eisenhower, Dwight D., 17–26; ambivalence on civil rights, 18; background and career, 17–18; and *Brown v. Board of Education*, 18–19; and Civil Rights Act of 1957, 21, 22; civil rights legislation, 20; and desegregation in Washington, DC, 18; and desegregation of armed forces, 18; and Frank M. Johnson appointment to federal bench, 5; inability to back away from predecessors' civil rights initiatives (ratchet principle), 6, 18; and school desegregation, 6, 7, 21–24, 32, 33, 185

Elementary and Secondary Education Act, 86

Engelhardt, Samuel Martin, Jr., 44, 54, 72
Evans v. Buchanan (1962), 24
executive branch: and school desegregation, limited guidance on, 96; statutory authority to enforce *Brown*, 49

faculty desegregation: in Anniston, Alabama, 177; concerns of African American teachers about, 135; court orders requiring, 145, 155; delays in achieving, 134; and DOJ and HEW enforcement conflicts, 127, 131; within freedom of choice plans, 137; ordered increases in, 145; as part of school desegregation, 117, 126, 133, 212n21; resistance to, 146; and second-generation discrimination, 175; in trade schools and junior colleges, 174
Fair Housing Act of 1968, 141
Faubus, Orville, 23, 72–73
FBI, involvement in *Lee*, 65
federal interference: Wallace on, 62–63; White Southerners' resentment of, 58
federal judges, respect for DOJ views, 61
Finch, Robert, 153, 156, 173
Fiss, Owen, vii, 61, 64*b*, 121, 136
Flowers, Richmond: and desegregation of Tuskegee High School, 72; and *Lee*, 68–69, 81; on resistance to desegregation, 63; views on segregation, 66
Folsom, Jim, 53, 54, 57
Fourteenth Amendment: equal protection clause, as grounds for school desegregation, 6; as illegitimate, in segregationists' view, 74–75, 118; passage of, 10; and school desegregation, 18–19; and "separate but equal" doctrine, 11
Frankfurter, Felix, 19
Franklin, Joan, 117, 118
Freedman's Bureau, 10–11
freedom of choice desegregation plans: adequacy of, as issue, 119; Albert Brewer's support of, 142–143; Civil Rights Commission approval of, 138; CRD's pessimism about, 138; in enforcement of *Lee*, 6, 115, 120–121, 126, 127, 131, 133, 137–138, 146–147, 155–156; Frank M. Johnson's support of, 145; as issue in *United States v. Jefferson County Board of Education* (1966), 119, 120–121; judicial decisions ending, 149; Nixon and, 148, 150, 151, 154–155; Supreme Court's refusal to invalidate (1958), 138; usefulness in early school desegregation, 138–139. *See also Green v. County School Board of New Kent County, Virginia* (1968)
From Brown to Bakke (Wilkinson), 2

Garment, Leonard, 163, 164, 165, 166, 167, 170
Georgia, statewide school desegregation suit in, 156–157, 161–162, 224n46
Goluboff, Risa, 10, 42
Gomillion, Charles: background of, 52; and gerrymandering to exclude Black voters, 54; as leader for Black equality, 51–52; and *Lee*, events leading to, 59
Gomillion v. Lightfoot (1960), 54, 59, 139
Goodwyn, Joe, 105
Goss v. Board of Education (1963), 60–61, 78
government and school desegregation, 185, 186
Graham, Hugh Davis, 142
Gray, Fred: association with NAACP LDF, 66; as attorney for plaintiffs in *Lee*, 5; career of, 61*b*–62*b*; court denigration of, as Black lawyer, 61*b*; desegregation cases litigated by, 59; and desegregation in Alabama, pace of, 97–98; and desegregation of Macon County High School, 80; on federal role in school desegregation, 184–185; and *Lee*, 59, 64, 66, 78, 81, 85, 99, 100, 111–112, 118; as one of few African American lawyers in Alabama, 5; rivalry with local NAACP attorneys, 103; and Rosa Parks, 61*b*–62*b*; on unfinished work of civil rights movement, 187–188
Greenberg, Gary, 139
Greenberg, Jack, viii, 118, 149–150, 169
Green v. County School Board of New Kent County, Virginia (1968), 138–144; Buchanan on need for reversal of, 165; closer inspection of individual school systems following, 173; CRD's approval of ruling in, 142; disruptive nature of school desegregation after, 163; DOJ brief in, 138, 139; and DOJ evidence on relief, 144; ending of freedom of choice plans, 149; focus on effectiveness as criteria for desegregation plans, 140, 141; freedom of choice plans as issue in, 138–140, 141–142, 144; importance to school desegregation, 138, 141–142; integration or desegregation as issue in, 138, 140; order requiring desegregation of Black schools and white schools, 141, 152;

Green v. County School Board of New Kent County, Virginia (1968), *continued*
requirement of terminal school desegregation plan, 142; resistance in Alabama to abandonment of freedom of choice plans, 143; on white flight, 140–141
Griswold, Erwin, 159, 182
Grooms, Hobart, 40–41, 83, 105, 118

Halberstam, David, 24
Haldeman, H. R. "Bob," 151, 173
Hancock, Paul, 179, 182
Hardeman, Ben, 82–83
Harlow, Bryce, 156, 165, 173
Hayes-Tilden Compromise of 1877, 10
HEW. *See* Department of Health, Education, and Welfare
Hollow Hope, The (Rosenberg), 2
Hood, James, 63, 70
Hoover, J. Edgar, 30
Hornsby, Preston, 53, 80, 96
Hosea Williams v. George C. Wallace (1965), 62*b*
Hospital for Sick and Injured Colored World War Veterans. *See* Tuskegee veterans hospital
housing, racial discrimination in, as contributing factor in school segregation, 163–164
Howe, Harold, 104, 121, 123
Huntsville, Alabama, schools: desegregation of, 35; and federal impact aid, 36
Hurd v. Hodge (1948), 15–16

interracial marriage, 46
Interstate Commerce Act, and CRD, 35

Jackson, Robert H., 29–30
Jim Crow. *See* racial caste system of Alabama (Jim Crow); racial caste system of the South (Jim Crow)
Johnson, Charles, 44, 79, 95
Johnson, Frank M.: and Alabama poll tax case, 98–99; appointment to federal bench, 5; background of, 60, 63*b*–64*b;* and busing, opposition to, 145; and civil rights cases, pressures in, 59–60; and Commission on Civil Rights investigation in Macon County, 55, 59–60; and desegregation of trade schools and junior colleges, 174; and Doar, relationship with, 60, 61–62, 64*b*–65*b*, 68; as Eisenhower appointment, 60, 64*b;* and federal response to Wallace's obstruction of desegregation, 73–74; hearing on state tuition grants for Macon Academy (1966), 101; and *Lee*, 4–5, 59, 60–62, 64*b*, 64–65, 68–69, 81–82, 85, 115, 131, 213n40; and Macon Academy, investigation of, 98; Macon County voting rights cases heard by, 60; and NAACP lawsuit on Alabama's anti-guidelines laws, 103; order desegregating Tuskegee High School, 4; order forcing release of Alabama voting records, 5; and school desegregation in Alabama, 97–99, 133–135, 144, 145, 178; trial of plantation owner who killed Black employee, 60, 63*b;* and Wallace, 5, 51*b*, 65*b*. See also *Lee v. Macon County Board of Education*
Johnson, Lyndon B.: and Civil Rights Act of 1964, 86, 89, 90; and civil rights legislation, pressure to pass, 89; and DOJ authority to prosecute school segregation cases, 92; and Fair Housing Act, 141; record on civil rights, 27; reelection bid, dropping of, 141; and school desegregation, efforts toward, 6; and school desegregation in Alabama, preparations for violence in, 79
Johnson, Pete, 4, 76
junior colleges: segregation in, DOJ research on, 110; Wallace's expansion of, 174
junior colleges, desegregation of: appeals court weakening of, 175; delays in implementation of, 175; DOJ report on, 174; HEW plan for, 175; *Lee* court ruling requiring, 122–123, 176; Nixon administration request for increase in, 154, 174
juries in the South, as unwilling to enforce desegregation laws, 58

Kagan, Elena, 12
Katzenbach, Nicholas: and Alabama school desegregation in 1964, 95; and Civil Rights Act of 1964, 87–88; and desegregation of University of Alabama, 70; successor as attorney general, 104; and Wallace's resistance to desegregation, 63
Kennedy, John F.: African American views on, 26, 27; assassination of, 89; *Brown*, need for federal implementation of, 63–64; and Civil Rights Act of 1964, 86, 87–88; inaugural address, 27; March on

Washington, concerns about, 67; *Profiles in Courage*, 26–27; and school desegregation, 6, 30–32, 33, 34–35, 36, 49, 74; speech on Civil Rights Act of 1964, 63–64; views on Reconstruction, 26–27; visit with Wallace, 32; and Wallace's blocking of desegregation at University of Alabama, 63–64. *See also* Civil Rights Division, under Kennedy

Kennedy, Robert F.: on *Brown v. Board of Education*, 28; and Civil Rights Act of 1964, 62, 87, 89; and King's "Letter from the Birmingham Jail," 37; and Ralph Bunche speech at University of Virginia law school, 195n82; and school desegregation in Alabama, preparations for violence in, 79; as senator, 136; support for civil rights initiatives, 28; and Tuskegee High School desegregation, 73–74; and Wallace's blocking of desegregation at University of Alabama, 63

Kerner Commission, 141

King, Coretta, 26

King, Martin Luther, Jr.: arrest of (April 1963), 37; assassination of, 141; "I Have a Dream" speech, 67; "Letter from the Birmingham Jail," 37; and March on Washington, 67; on voting rights as key to civil rights, 36

Kohn, John, 74–75

Ku Klux Klan: and Sixteenth Street Church bombing, 75; and Wallace's inaugural speech, 50*b*

Landsberg, Brian (author): career of, vii–viii; on DOJ-HEW committee to review desegregation plans, 171; good relations with HEW, NAACP, and school board officials, 160; and *Green v. County School Board of New Kent County. Virginia* (1968), 139; as head of new CRD school desegregation section under Nixon, 160, 170; and hearing on state tuition grants for Macon Academy, 101, 103, 105; and *Lee*, work on, vii–viii, 111, 115; and reorganization of CRD (1967), 136; and school desegregation plan for Anniston, Alabama, 178, 179–180, 181; and *Swann* ruling, 181

Layton, George, 111, 179

Lee, Anthony: at Auburn University, 80, 133; career of, 187; and desegregation of Macon County High, 79, 80; and desegregation of Tuskegee High School, 76; letter to MaryLee Campbell, 187; on personal importance of *Lee* case, 187; views on attendance to Tuskegee High School, 71–72

Lee, Detroit, 59

Lee, Hattie, 59

Lee, and Civil Rights Division of the Department of Justice: close supervision of desegregation, 67–68; coordination with NAACP LDF in, 66; CRD shaping of relief, 68; Frank M. Johnson's request for involvement of, 60–61, 62; and statewide expansion, 82–83; training of Black students prior to transfer, 69–70

Lee, appointment of US as party to, 64–65; and CRD close supervision of desegregation, 67–68; and CRD shaping of relief, 68; and federal role as protector of law, 64–66; and statewide expansion of *Lee*, 84–85

Lee, enforcement of: addition of noncompliant schools as defendants, 126–127, 133, 134, 155; and closer inspection of individual school systems after *Green*, 173; closing of Black schools, 133, 146, 155; components of, 126; conflicts between court and HEW in, 126–133; and danger to rapid desegregation, 144; delegation to state school superintendent, 126–127; detailed court order on desegregation (1968–1968), 145; DOJ report on level of compliance (1967), 136; and expansion of case, 126–127, 133, 134, 135; freedom of choice plan in, 115, 126, 127, 131, 133, 146–147; under Nixon, 173; and school boards' requests for delay, 155, 223n38

Lee, expansion to statewide case, 111–113; DOJ support of, 81; and original plaintiffs as long gone from school, 182; plaintiffs' argument for, 81–83; Wallace's and state school board's legal missteps and, 71, 77, 78, 81, 100, 123

Lee, relief, design of, 113–116; DOJ brief on, 114–115, 213n40; DOJ discussions on, 114; DOJ supplemental brief with proposed decree, 115; freedom of choice plans and, 114; likely noncompliance as issue in, 113–114, 115

Lee, ruling ordering statewide desegregation, 121–124; appeal to Supreme Court, 125, 126; and end to HEW supervision, 162; exclusion of larger districts already under court order, 176; extension to trade schools and colleges,

Lee, ruling ordering statewide desegregation, *continued*
122–123, 176; influence of *United States v. Jefferson County Board of Education* on, 121; as precedent for future statewide relief cases, 124, 126, 156, 161; reaction of Governor Lurleen Wallace to, 125; reactions to, in Alabama, 123, 125–126; required methods of desegregation in, 122; on state officials' support of segregation, 122

Lee v. Macon County Board of Education: addition of Alabama Education Association as amicus curiae, 146; addition of Alabama School Board, Wallace, and Meadows as defendants, 78; addition of ASTA as plaintiff, 135; addition of school athletic associations as plaintiffs, 135; author's work on, vii–viii; defendants' attorney, 66; defendants' clear violations of law in, 62–63, 66; defendants' offer to prepare desegregation plan, 66–67; desegregation methods in, as pioneering, 4; and DOJ experience with civil rights cases, 32; DOJ's key role in, 7–8; events leading to, 57–59; filing of suit, 59; importance to desegregation effort, vii, 1, 2, 4, 7; influence on interpretation of Civil Rights Act of 1964, 92; initial ruling, modest relief provided by, 67; limited progress in school desegregation prior to, 49; and Meadows, replacement as defendant, 121; oral arguments in, 116, 118; plaintiff's attorneys, 66; plaintiff's motion for immediate relief, 64; repercussions for prison and mental institution conditions, vii; ruling ending freedom of choice plans, 149; ruling ordering desegregation, 4, 66–67; ruling ordering desegregation, Wallace's blocking of, 4–5; rulings enjoining interference, 72–75, 83–86; school systems affected by, as rural and small-city, 173, 176; school systems' compliance with, 126–127, 134; students applying for transfer to Tuskegee High School, 69; trial, 111–113; and Wallace, replacement as defendant, 121. *See also* Johnson, Frank M.; school desegregation in Alabama; state tuition grants for Macon Academy

Leonard, Jerris: as assistant attorney general for civil rights under Nixon, 154; background of, 154; on cities withdrawing from school systems under court desegregation order, 174; on difficulty of enforcing desegregation, 159; as Pollak's successor at CRD, 147; and school desegregation, 154, 158, 159, 160, 162, 167, 170, 172, 179, 183; on second-generation discrimination, 172; and *Swann*, 180

"A Letter to My Nephew" (Baldwin), 184, 186–187

Libassi, Peter, 129, 131

Little Rock, Arkansas. *See* school desegregation in Little Rock, Arkansas

Loper, Merle, 131, 139

lynching, Congress's resistance to passing law against, 11

Macon Academy: accreditation of, court hearing on, 82; creation of, 72, 75; federal investigation of, 98; football team of, 96; number of students in 1964, 95; state funding of, court's addressing of, 78, 82, 83; transfer of white students to, 77, 80. *See also* state tuition grants for Macon Academy

Macon County, Alabama: Black political participation after Civil War, 41; black versus white population, 41, 50; black versus white schools, disparities in quality of, 12, 50–51, 57–58; boycotting of white businesses (1957), 54; Commission on Civil Rights investigation of voting rights restrictions in, 55–56; CRD voter discrimination suit against, 37; educated African Americans in, 41; efforts to absorb into other counties to dilute Black vote, 54; first Civil Rights Division cases in, 25; number of Black registered voters (1940), 50; number of Black versus white students, 57; as part of Alabama's Black Belt, 41; school attendance rates, racial disparities in, 50; and school desegregation, refusal to comply with *Brown* order for, 48; social upheaval after Civil War, 41; white violence suppressing Black political participation, 41–42. *See also* racial caste system of Alabama (Jim Crow); Tuskegee Institute

Macon County High. *See* Notasulga, Alabama, High School

Macon County schools: freedom of choice forms distributed to students (1964), 98; School Board desegregation proposal of 1964, 97. *See also* Notasulga, Alabama, High School (Macon County High);

school desegregation in Alabama; Shorter, Alabama, High School; Tuskegee High School
Madison, Gordon, 47, 66, 68–69
Making the Unequal Metropolis (Erickson), 3
Malone, Vivian, 63, 70
Many, M. Hepburn, 24, 31
March on Washington, 67
Marshall, Burke: adversaries' admiration for, 30; as assistant attorney general for CRD, 1, 28, 29; on *Brown v. Board of Education*, force required to compel adherence to, 37–38; and Civil Rights Act of 1964, 87–88, 89; and CRD prosecution of schools receiving federal "impact aid," 34, 36; on CRD role in desegregation, 70; on DOJ's revolution by law, 1; good teamwork with Doar, 29; and *Goss v. Board of Education* (1963), 60–61; and Kennedy administration support of CRD, 28; lack of civil rights experience, 28–29; and *Lee*, request for FBI involvement in, 65; nomination hearings, 31; noteworthy cases handled by, 29; preference for behind-the-scenes work, 29; response to Wallace's obstruction of desegregation, 74; and school desegregation, 33–34, 35, 36, 38; and statewide expansion of *Lee*, 82–83; tempering of zeal with human kindness, 29–30; tour of South to encourage civil rights action (1961), 28; on voting rights as key to civil rights, 36
Marshall, Thurgood: and *Brown v. Board of Education*, 18; on difficulty of achieving school desegregation, 48; and Macon County school segregation, 57
McShane, James P., 32, 70
Meadows, Austin: background of, 78; on *Brown*, 78; and DOJ research on state role in segregation, 110; Gray and, 61*b;* and *Lee*, 78, 111–112, 121; and NAACP lawsuit on Alabama's anti-guidelines laws, 103–104; opposition to desegregation, 75; paean to segregation sent to school superintendents, 112; and segregation of trade schools and junior colleges, 174; and statewide expansion of *Lee*, 81, 82
Meredith, James, 29, 31–32, 70, 72–73
Merritt, Vernon III, 79, 207n8
Mississippi: desegregation of University of Mississippi, 29, 31–33, 72–73; school desegregation, Nixon administration support for delay in, 149, 157–159, 160
Mississippi Summer, 85
Mitchell, Clarence Jr., 15, 27
Mitchell, John: as Nixon's attorney general, 147; and school desegregation, 150, 156, 157, 167, 171, 172; and *Swann* ruling, 181
Mondale, Walter, 163, 171
Morgan, Ed, 167, 173
Moses, Robert, 36, 103

NAACP: in Alabama, equal education goals, 53; and *Brown v. Board of Education*, 18; candidate questionnaires in 1954 Alabama election, 54; Eisenhower and, 18; and *Lee*, 57; school desegregation efforts, 20; and school desegregation in Little Rock, Arkansas, 23; and "separate but equal" doctrine, disavowal of, 51; Truman's address to, 14; Tuskegee branch, 53–53, 57; on US Office of Education segregation policies, 15; views on best approach to achieving equality, 43
NAACP LDF: aggressive push for desegregation, 161; assistance with parents' desegregation lawsuits against schools, 49; and *Brown v. Board of Education*, 49; complaints about state-wide desegregation suits, 173; and desegregation, modesty of early successes, 97; and *Lee*, 59, 66, 103; and limited funding, 47–48
NAACP v. Wallace, 103–104; oral arguments, 116–118; ruling in, 122
New York Times, 30, 78, 79, 150, 159, 169, 172, 187
New York Times Co. v. Sullivan (1962), 62*b*
Nixon, Richard M.: on *Brown*, 148, 168; on busing, 148, 150, 168, 173; civil rights leaders' dislike of, 150, 153; election as president, 147; as first Republican with Southern support, 148; inability to back away from predecessors' civil rights initiatives (ratchet principle), 6–7, 149, 152; press's skepticism about motives of, 153; reelection, and replacement of some appointees, 181–182; Southern strategy of, 148–149, 153, 160, 161; and Southern vote, necessity of winning, 148–149; as vice president, support for civil rights, 148; views on school desegregation, 151–152, 154, 158. *See also* Civil Rights Division, under Nixon

Nixon, and school desegregation: advances in, as greater than any other presidency, 149, 151, 160–161, 171; advisors' conflicting advice on, 149–150; call for delay in Mississippi desegregation, 149, 157–159; concerns about position on, 148, 152; courts' role in forcing, 2; desire to quickly complete, 149, 161, 163, 171, 181; and DOJ-HEW plan to flood South with federal agents, 171; early policy missteps in, 154; effort to minimize destructive disruptions from, 167; emboldening of Southern resistance to, 152–153; Mondale committee criticisms of, 172; preference for litigation over funding termination, 156–157; range of opinions about, 150–151; ratchet principle demanding action, 149, 152; request for increased desegregation of trade schools and junior colleges, 154, 174; support for freedom of choice, 148, 150, 151, 154–155

Nixon's statement on school desegregation, 163, 164–170; content of, 168; CRD reactions to, 169–170; criticisms of, 169; on de jure versus de facto segregation, 168; focus on moderation and realism, 168; initial plan for Agnew to deliver, 164–165; input from Southerners on, 167; moderate middle ground of, 165; as muddled and disorganized, 169; policy review prior to, 167–168; reasons for, 164, 165; White House battle over content of, 165–166

Norman, David L.: and court ruling prioritizing court authority over HEW's, 132; and *Lee*, 66, 67; as mentor, 160; Nixon's removal of, 182; on requirement for desegregation or integration, 119; and school desegregation plan for Anniston, Alabama, 183; and *Swann* ruling, 181

Northern schools: barriers to pursuing desegregation of, 161; Southerners' insistence on application of desegregation to, 90, 118, 161, 172

Notasulga, Alabama, High School (Macon County High): desegregation of, 75, 79–80, 83, 98, 207n8; destruction by fire, 80; police presence to enforce, 80; transfer of white students to, 69, 77; white students' transfers from, 80

Obama, Barack, 26

Office for Civil Rights, creation of, 129

Orfield, Gary, 3, 128–129, 150–152, 173

Panetta, Leon, 152, 158–159, 169

Parker, Allan, 96

Parks, Rosa, 61*b*–62*b*

Parrish, Janice Ward, 205n62

Patterson, John, 5, 35, 47, 53, 55, 70

Peltason, J. W., 59–60

Plessy v. Ferguson (1896), 6, 11, 16, 19

Pollak, Stephen J.: background of, 136; and desegregation of trade schools and junior colleges, 174; on DOJ's awkward legal status as both plaintiff and agent of the court, 136–137; on freedom of choice plans, 144; and *Green*, 139–140, 144; and *Lee*, enforcement of, 147; and Mondale committee, 172; on Nixon administration school desegregation policies, 159; resignation from DOJ, 147; and school desegregation enforcement, 136–137, 172; as successor to Doar at CRD, 136

postsecondary education. *See* desegregation of higher education

Pottinger, J. Stanley, 171, 182, 183

Powell, Adam Clayton, 88

President's Committee on Civil Rights, 13, 14, 15, 185

Pruitt, C. A., 4, 69, 71, 73, 82

Public Health Service, Tuskegee syphilis studies, 42

pupil placement laws: court rejection of, 97; freedom of choice laws and, 138; and Macon County desegregation, 66–67, 69, 70, 97; and school desegregation in Alabama, 70; as Southern strategy to resist school desegregation, 48, 49, 96, 138; suits challenging, 60, 83, 84; Supreme Court on, 49; unsure future in desegregation environment, 77, 82

racial caste system of Alabama (Jim Crow), 39–49; in Alabama Constitution of 1901, 40, 44; as cemented into culture and tradition, 44; completeness of segregation, 40–41; consequences of ending, white concerns about, 46; economic subjugation of African Americans in, 42; indirect and explicit arguments in favor of, 45–46; as still alive

in hearts of white Alabamians, 40, 186; undermining of democracy by, 184; white politicians defending, 44–45, 47
racial caste system of the South (Jim Crow): courts' reluctance to move against, 49; Doar on, 26; economic subjugation of African Americans in, 42; ending of, Federal force and, 1; existing in present culture, 40, 186; exposure of, through television news, 17, 23–24; federal failure to address, 41–42; federal government's historical support of, 10, 12; *Plessy v. Ferguson* (1896) and, 6, 11; ratchet principle and, 185; segregated schools' role in maintaining, 2, 40, 46, 184; Supreme Court's failure to address, 42. *See also* revolution by law
racial discrimination: in education, government's responsibility to challenge, 184; as ongoing problem, 1
Rankin, J. Lee, 18, 24
ratchet principle: definition of, 6; Eisenhower and, 6, 18; and ending of racial caste system, 185; Kennedy and, 88; Nixon and, 6–7, 149, 152; as no guarantee of future progress, 186; and preservation of progress, 186; Truman's civil rights efforts and, 6, 7, 12–13, 18
Rea, James, 79–80
real estate sales, racial discrimination in, 163–164
Reconstruction: Congress's civil rights legislation during, 10; end of, and backtracking on civil rights, 10–11; Kennedy's views on, 26–27
Reconstruction Amendments: federal failure to enforce, 41–42; Supreme Court's defanging of, 11
Redstone Arsenal (Huntsville), anti-segregation lawsuit on behalf of, 58
Reeves, Frank D., 28, 103
Rehnquist, William, 166
restrictive housing covenants: as contributing factor in school segregation, 163–164; DOJ amicus curiae briefs on, 15–16; Supreme Court ruling against, 16
revolution by law: desegregation of schools as, 1; *Lee* as roadmap for future completion of, 4; moral imperative to continue, 186–187, 188; as still incomplete, 184, 186
Rilling, Paul, 127, 161, 169
Rives, Richard: and Alabama poll tax case, 99; and DOJ and HEW desegregation enforcement conflicts, 131; on *Green*, 144; and *Lee*, 60, 74, 83, 118, 121; and NAACP lawsuit on Alabama's anti-guidelines laws, 103; and *NAACP v. Wallace*, 116–118
Roosevelt, Eleanor, 78
Roosevelt, Franklin D., 10
Russell, Richard, 22, 28, 89, 90, 167

Satterfield, John, 89, 117, 119, 158
scholarship on desegregation of schools, 2–3
school desegregation in Alabama: in 1964, 95–96; African American teachers' concerns about, 135; and athletic programs, 80, 96, 98, 135–136, 175; centrality of federal role in, 184–185; closing of some Black schools, 133, 146, 155; completion of, 1–2; court orders (1969–1970), 155–156; CRD lawyers present during, 68; CRD's close supervision of, 68; and extracurricular activities, discrimination in, 135; and freedom of choice plans, 126, 127, 131, 133, 146–147; HEW monitoring of, 135–136, 137; history of, 7; level of desegregation in 1967, 134–135; level of desegregation in 1968, 146; under Nixon administration, 154; and overcoming of effects of past segregation, 175; and second-generation issues of discrimination, 135, 173, 175, 185; slight increases in 1964 and 1965, 86; and state law allowing student to choose race of teacher, 134; success of, 173, 184, 188; token desegregation in early stages, 77. *See also* faculty desegregation; *Lee v. Macon County Board of Education*
school desegregation in Alabama, resistance to: cities withdrawing from desegregating school systems, 174, 228n132; and failure to close inadequate Black schools, 146; and failure to desegregate faculty, 146; intimidation of Black parents, 121, 131, 137–138, 177; in Nixon era, 173–174; by parents, 135; reasons for, 46; refusal to comply with *Brown*, 48; by state, 133–134; by state legislature, 175; strategies to stop or delay, 45, 47–49; and support for freedom of choice plans, 143–144; weakening of, 98; and white flight, 1–2, 77–78, 184. *See also* Wallace, George
school desegregation in Huntsville, Alabama, 35

school desegregation in Knoxville, Tennessee, 35
school desegregation in Little Rock, Arkansas: Arkansas state government intervention to stop, 47; blocking of Black children's entry, 72; causes of violence in, 33; DOJ involvement in, 23; forced compliance with court order, 23; Kennedy's critique of Eisenhower's approach in, 33; local resistance to, 23; local school boards' compliance with *Brown*, 47; military sent in to enforce, 22, 23, 32; Supreme Court on, 24; violence in, 32
school desegregation in New Orleans: CRD efforts to preempt resistance to, 33, 36; federal involvement in, 24–25, 31–32
school desegregation in the South: in 1965, 116; in 1970, 171; African Americans' goals for, 96; court decisions on (1967–1968), 7; as embattled concept in current debate, 3–4; at end of Johnson's term, 152; enforcement plans (1970), 170–171; federal court orders, federal enforcement of, 21–22; and federal force, 74; further delays after 1969, as unacceptable, 164; and *Green*, disruptive nature of, 163; versus integration, as issue, 119, 138, 140; judicial leadership in, 3; under Nixon, 171; ongoing racial discrimination despite, 184; parents' lawsuits against schools, 49; President's Committee on Civil Rights report on (1947), 14; private discrimination as complicating factor in, 163–164; and resegregation in some areas, 186; as revolution by law, 1; as roadmap for future racial justice efforts, 4; scholarship on, 2–3; and second-generation discrimination, 135, 172, 173, 175; shift in focus, 96–97; Southerners' insistence on, in the North, 90, 118, 161, 172; success of, 2, 7, 160; Supreme Court's backtracking on, 4, 7. *See also Brown v. Board of Education* (1954); faculty desegregation; *Lee v. Macon County Board of Education; United States v. Jefferson County Board of Education* (1966)
school desegregation in the South, resistance to, 20; administrative decentralization of schools as strategy in, 47, 48, 71; emboldening under Nixon, 152–153; pupil placement laws and, 48, 49, 96, 138; replacement of public with private schools as strategy in, 45, 48, 72, 75; retaliation against desegregation activists, 49; Southern strategies for, 45, 47–49. *See also* school desegregation in Alabama, resistance to
Schultz, George, 150, 166, 173
Seeley, David, 121, 129–130
segregated schools: reasons for federal failure to intervene, 58–59; role in maintaining racial caste system of South, 2, 40, 46, 184; and "separate but equal" doctrine, 11
segregation, de jure versus de facto: Mondale committee on, 172; Nixon on, 168; Supreme Court on, 168–169
segregation in railroad dining cars, Supreme Court on, 16
"separate but equal" doctrine: *Brown* ruling on, 19, 44; and disparities in school quality, 12, 50–51; NAACP disavowal of, 51; and *Plessy v. Ferguson* (1896), 11; and school segregation, 11; Truman administration challenging of, 6; white defenses of, 11, 44
Shelley v. Kraemer (1948), 15–16
Sherrer, Wayman, 179–280
Shorter, Alabama, High School; desegregation of, 79, 80; transfer of white students to, 69, 77
Sixteenth Street Church bombing, 49, 75
slavery, 39
Smith, Howard, 27, 86
Smith, Maury, 105, 118, 130, 144
Smith, Stanley Hugh, 54–55
SNCC (Student Nonviolent Coordinating Committee), 85–86, 153
Sobeloff, Simon E., 19–20
Southern Manifesto, 22
Southern Regional Council, 36, 159–260
state tuition grants for Macon Academy: and DOJ research on state officials' obstruction of school desegregation, 110–112; and DOJ research on state role in segregation, 102, 106–110; hearing on (1964), 81–83; hearing on (September 1966), 100–103, 105–6; hearing on plaintiffs' motion for statewide relief (November 1966), 105–106, 106–111; passage of new version of, 134
Stone, Ernest: and *Lee*, addition as defendant, 121; Lurleen Wallace's lack of trust in, 125; meeting with Seeley, 130; and school desegregation compliance, 134, 136, 137, 145; views on desegregation, 126

Student Nonviolent Coordinating Committee (SNCC), 85–86, 153
Supreme Court: backtracking on school desegregation, 4, 7; and declared completion of school desegregation initiative, 185; denial of Nixon's request for delay in Mississippi desegregation, 149, 159; on desegregation, de jure versus de facto forms of, 168–169; on desegregation of schools in Knoxville, Tennessee, 35; and freedom of choice programs, 138; and judicial leadership in school desegregation, 3; *Lee v. Macon County Board of Education*, 126; and limits on school systems' ability to combat racial isolation, 186; on pupil placement laws, 49; and Reconstruction Amendments, defanging of, 11; on requested desegregation delays in Little Rock, Arkansas, 24; on restrictive housing covenants, 16; and school desegregation, limited guidance on, 96; on segregation in graduate public education, 16; on segregation in railroad dining cars, 16; and *Swann v. Mecklenburg County Board of Education* (1971), 180–181. *See also Brown v. Board of Education* (1954)
Sutin, Jonathan: and desegregation (1964), 95–96; and desegregation in Alabama, pace of, 97–98; and desegregation's effect on athletics, 80; and relief in school desegregation cases, 114
Swann v. Mecklenburg County Board of Education (1971), 149, 180–181
Sweet Shade of the Chinaberry Tree, The (Parrish), 205n62

TCA. *See* Tuskegee Civic Association
teachers, concerns about faculty desegregation, 135
television news and public opinion, 17, 23–24, 62*b*
Thurmond, Strom, 148
trade schools: segregation in, DOJ research on, 110; Wallace's expansion of, 174
trade schools, desegregation of: appeals court weakening of, 175; delays in implementation of, 175; DOJ report on, 174; HEW plan for, 175; *Lee* court ruling requiring, 122–123, 176; Nixon administration request for increase in, 154, 174
Truman, Harry, 12–17; and civil rights, 6, 7, 12–13, 14, 15–17, 18, 185; and President's Committee on Civil Rights, 13, 14, 15, 185
Tuskegee, Alabama: as county seat of Macon County, 41; gerrymandering to exclude Black voters, 54
Tuskegee Civic Association (TCA): civil rights activism by, 52; complaint to Commission on Civil Rights about voter suppression, 55–56; focus on education, 52; and improvement projects in Black communities, 52; and *Lee*, events leading to, 57, 58–59; praise for Black students entering Tuskegee High School, 77; thanks to white parents supporting desegregation, 206n1
Tuskegee High School, desegregation of: in 1964, 95–96; Black students applying for transfer to, 69; Black students' views on, 71–72; and closure by School Board, 78; court hearings on closing of, 82; creation of private Macon Academy to circumvent, 72, 75; effect on sports teams, 4, 76, 98; escalation to law enforcement issue, 73; federal government's expectations for peacefulness of, 36–37; federal response to Wallace's obstruction of, 73–74; issues in, 98; NAACP and CRD training of Black students prior to transfer, 69–70; and new Black students in all-Black classes, 77; new Black students' views on education received, 77; PTA debate on, 71, 76; resistance to, 4, 190n9; return of some white students to, 96; Wallace's order blocking entrance by Black students, 4–5, 72–73; Wallace's order delaying school opening, 71–72; white parents' divided opinion on, 76; and white students' departure, 69, 76, 77; white support for, 71
Tuskegee Institute: as center of Black education and economic success, 41, 42, 44; founding and mission of, 43; middle-class Black community surrounding, 44; and Tuskegee syphilis studies, 42; whites' use as example of Black success under segregation, 44
Tuskegee Institute High, 78
Tuskegee Men's Club, 52
Tuskegee News, 69

Tuskegee veterans hospital; all-black staff of, 42; and anti-segregation lawsuits, 58; as center of Black education and economic success, 41, 42

Tyler, Harold, 25, 63*b*

United States v. Jefferson County Board of Education (1966): Court of Appeals en banc review of, 118–119; and establishment of effectiveness of desegregation as criterion for its constitutionality, 116; and freedom of choice plans, 119, 149; influence on *Lee* ruling, 121; oral arguments, 119–120; relief, discussion of, 119; ruling in, 115–116, 149; and school desegregation versus integration, 119

United States v. Wallace (1963), 74–75

University of Alabama, desegregation of, 32, 36; CRD role in, 70; and first Black student, expulsion of, 78

University of Mississippi, desegregation of, 29, 31–32; CRD role in, 70; efforts to block, 72–73; violence and, 32–33

Vinson, Fred M., Jr., 16, 17, 18

voting by Blacks in Alabama: significant turnout by 1950s, 54; suppression of, 44

voting by Blacks in Macon County, after Civil War, 41

Voting Rights Act of 1965: events aiding passage of, 62*b;* Johnson's pressure to pass, 89; on poll tax, 99; stiffening of federal authority in, 113

voting rights restrictions in Alabama: Commission on Civil Rights investigation of, 55–56; and election of anti-civil rights members of Congress, 11; legal restrictions on Black registration, 53; strategies to reduce Black registration, 53–54, 55; Tuskegee's gerrymandering to exclude Black voters, 54

voting rights restrictions in South, 11–12

Wallace, George: attempted assassination of, 50*b;* and Bloody Sunday, 36, 62*b*; and Commission on Civil Rights investigation in Macon County, 5, 25, 55, 59–60; commitment to segregation, 4–5; decline in support for, 134, 219n48; and desegregation of public schools, 35, 49; and desegregation of University of Alabama, 32, 36, 49, 63; and election of 1968, 147; on federal interference, 62–63; and Frank M. Johnson, 5, 51*b*, 65*b*; and HEW's withholding of funds from segregated schools, 100, 113; influence of rhetoric, 148; and *Lee*, 51*b*, 78, 121; and NAACP lawsuit on Alabama's anti-guidelines laws, 103–104; rise to national prominence, 50*b*; and school desegregation, resistance to, 4–5, 48, 70–71, 71, 73, 77, 81, 83–86, 100, 123, 174, 176–177, 207n8; "segregation forever" speech (inaugural address), 4–5, 48, 49, 50*b*–51*b*, 62–63; and trade schools and junior colleges, 174; and Tuskegee High School desegregation, 4–5, 71–72, 72–73, 74, 75, 77, 95; wife's replacement as governor, 100

Wallace, Lurleen: death of, 142; election as governor, 100; and *Lee v. Macon County*, addition as defendant, 121; obstruction of school desegregation, 133–134; reaction to *Lee* desegregation order, 62, 125

Warren, Earl, 18, 19

Washington, Booker T.: on achieving Black equality, 43; on effects of Blacks' lack of education, 43; founding of Tuskegee Institute, 43; influence of, 52

White, Byron, 29, 33, 141

White, Lee, 87, 95

Wicker, Tom, 150, 169

Wilkerson, Isabel, 40, 186

Wilkinson, J. Harvie III, 2, 115–116, 142

Wisdom, John Minor, 116, 120

With All Deliberate Speed (Daugherty and Bolton), 2

women's suffrage (1920), 52

Wright, J. Skelly, 24–25, 31–32, 65

Wyatt, Willie, 71, 76, 79, 80